WORDS
of
PROMISE

WORDS *of* PROMISE

Daily Devotions
through the Year

Edited by

DIANNE KRENZ

CPH.
SAINT LOUIS

Cover photo by S. Lissau/H. Armstrong Roberts

Concordia Publishing House expresses its deepest appreciation to the original authors of these devotions taken from 50 years of Portals of Prayer. Their spiritual insights and ability to connect the Gospel to everyday living have been a blessing to millions of people. The church is forever in their debt. (The authors are listed by name at the back of this book.)

1 2 3 4 5 6 7 8 9 10   05 04 03 02 01 00 99 98 97 96

Introduction

He remembered His holy promise given to His servant Abraham. *Psalm 105:42*

A promise is considered a sacred thing. It has been said often and properly that the person who breaks a promise made to a child will lose the child's trust and confidence. This is also frequently true between adults: all of us expect others to keep the promises they have made to us, and by the same token, we should not make promises we don't intend to keep.

Our God has gifted us with some wonderful, comforting, and reassuring promises—promises for us to remember in all of our life circumstances, promises we can rely upon. "Surely I am with you always, to the very end of the age" (Matthew 28:20). "We know that in all things God works for the good of those who love Him, who have been called according to His purpose" (Romans 8:28). "And this is what He promised us—even eternal life" (1 John 2:25). There are so many, many others. And our God never, no, never, goes back on His promises.

What a gift! We, too, have made promises and vows to our God—to love Him, to serve Him, to glorify Him, and to follow Him all the days of our life. In receiving His many promises, we grow daily in ways we often don't realize—another gift!

Rejoicing in His faithfulness, let us perform our promises to Him and our fellow human beings, asking almighty God to give us the needed steadfastness and strength to carry them out.

The devotions in the first section of this book pair a gift from God with a way in which we grow as a result. The second section provides special devotions and prayers for those times of need. A topical index is included at the end of the book to further enhance its usefulness.

Trust in God—He never breaks a promise!

Section I

Gifts and Growth

The Power of the Word

My word … will not return to Me empty. *Isaiah 55:11*

Like rain and snow, which possess mysterious germinating power, God's Word possesses creative power, though to an infinitely higher degree. Its power, too, is seen in the unfailing results it produces.

Holy Scriptures tell us that the worlds were framed by the Word of God and that Christ upholds all things by the Word of His power. But more than this, God's Word is spoken of as seed that endures forever and has power to save and sanctify people's souls. Humankind may despise it because it is seemingly insignificant and no different from any other word. But once this almighty Word has been spoken, it produces wonderful results. Sinners heed it and are cleansed; their sorrow turns to joy, their weeping to laughter, and their death to life. Through this Word they are spiritually reborn and made children of God and heirs of heaven and eternal life.

This Word is the miracle-working seed that Christ has entrusted to His followers. Whenever we sow it by preaching or teaching or personal witnessing, we have the Lord's promise that it will bring forth fruit.

Lord, make us faithful sowers of Your Word. Amen.

The Power of God

I am not ashamed of the gospel, because it is the power of God for the salvation of everyone who believes. *Romans 1:16*

In a power-mad world, where people respect only superior force, mightier bombs, and larger sea and air armadas, we need to remember that there is tremendous energy in the Gospel of Jesus Christ. To some this Gospel is a stumbling block. To others it is foolishness. But to those who believe it, it is the power of God and the wisdom of God.

"The power of God!" When we think of power, we are apt to think of a hydrogen bomb explosion, an earthquake, a volcanic eruption, or a tremendous collision of heavenly bodies. God, however, thinks of the Gospel quietly working in human hearts and lives, changing sinners into saints. What a power! Think of humble, not-so-ordinary Christians meeting their daily problems, bearing their heavy burdens, witnessing boldly to their neighbors, conducting their simple family devotions, praying for their enemies, and winning the eternal victory over themselves and the world.

Is not that the kind of power we need to live triumphant lives? Is not that exactly what we need to be more than conquerors over life and all its problems and over death and all its fears? We need the Gospel of the cross of our Savior. Thank God we have it in our Bibles.

Lord Jesus, bless us as we hear the Word of God and keep it. Amen.

God Supplies All Our Need

"Did you lack anything?" "Nothing," they answered.
Luke 22:35

Our Lord took time to discuss the practical questions of food and clothing, money and sustenance, even in the last hours He spent in the company of His disciples. Reminding them of the early days when they were first commissioned to go out in His name, Jesus asked the disciples this question: "When I sent you out with no purse or bag or sandals, did you lack anything?"

When the disciples remembered how they had been miraculously sustained and preserved during the entire course of their discipleship, they were compelled to answer, "Nothing."

God's children are always under His gracious and providential care. While some enjoy affluence and wealth, most have to be careful with their resources, and some may continually experience serious financial concerns. But somehow, and in His own definite way, God provides for them, although His methods may be above their knowing and understanding.

Christ is our King. Therefore our Lord will rule our individual affairs, solve our personal problems, and cause all things, even adversities, sickness, sorrow, and death, to work together, under His harmonious rule, for our good. He who saved us in Christ "how will He not also, along with Him, graciously give us all things?" (Romans 8:32).

Dear Lord, provide us with all things needful. Amen.

The Life of Trust

We live by faith, not by sight. 2 *Corinthians* 5:7

The new life is a life of trust. Without trust we could not live. It is the basis of our life together in human society. We trust each other more than we may realize. We trust the bus driver to take us where she says she will. We trust the surgeon to make critical decisions about our vital organs. We trust the motorist speeding toward us to stay on his side of the road. We trust the government to fulfill its contracts with us. In all these instances we make commitments, sight unseen. To trust means to accept something as real without seeing the fulfilled reality itself.

It is in trust that the life in Christ has its beginning. God says: Trust Me. I love you. I have forgiven you in Christ. I know your needs and will supply them. I will not fail you. I will always deal with you for your good. Let Me take over your life. Be assured that it will all be right. You cannot now see what is going to happen, but put yourself into My hands. The day will come when you shall see and be convinced.

Trust includes a kind of blindness, but a healthful and blessed blindness. In the new life we live by faith, not by sight. The new life is rooted in Christ, through whom we "are justified freely by His grace through ... the redemption that came by Jesus Christ (Romans 3:24).

Lord open our eyes and hearts so that we may trust.
Amen.

Thoughts

Whatever is true ... noble ... right ... pure ... lovely ... admirable—if anything is excellent or praiseworthy— think about such things. *Philippians 4:8*

Some wise person once said that there is no unexplored territory as vast and unknown as the mind. The mind can be a wasteland that produces thoughts of no real value. It can be a place filled with the trivial things of the world that produces only thoughts of passing pleasures. It can be a place where worry and fear dominate so that no thoughts of joy or confidence in the future can survive. It can be a place where the self is so important that thoughts of love and concern for others never see the light of day.

The thoughts of your mind are only reflections of what is in your mind. Fill your mind with evil and unpleasant things, and you will think evil and unpleasant thoughts. Fill your mind with God-pleasing things, and your thoughts will be those of peace, joy, contentment, concern for others, and a host of other good things.

Study God's Word. Fill your mind with those things that are true, noble, right, pure, lovely, admirable, excellent, and praiseworthy. Dwell on God's love and forgiveness in Jesus Christ, and then expect some beautiful thoughts!

Heavenly Father, send the Holy Spirit to fill our minds with thoughts that please You. Amen.

Joy in My Heart

You have filled my heart with greater joy than when their grain and new wine abound. *Psalm 4:7*

A spiritual exercise for some Christians is to pick a word as theirs for a year. As they read their Bibles daily, they notice when that word appears, and they mark it. Such words as *love*, *joy*, *hope*, and *forgiveness* have been chosen. The passages take on new meaning as the chosen word is applied to their lives.

The word *joy* permeates the Bible. It appears in the New Testament more than 60 times. Joy comes from belonging to Christ. Joy is His forgiveness and loving care. Joy is His presence in our lives. Joy is eternal.

Happiness comes and goes. Things go wrong. We don't feel well. Our grain and wine don't abound. There's not much to be happy about. The Virgin Mary had some tough times ahead as a young mother carrying her first child, but her joy overflowed in a hymn of praise and thanksgiving. Joy doesn't depend on how we *feel*; it's there because of the great things God has done for us. Christ is in our hearts, and He is our joy. The hymn writer says: "Jesus, Joy of my desiring, Fount of life, my soul inspiring."

All day today, whether things go well or badly, we can sing:

I've got the joy, joy, joy, joy deep in my heart ... today!
I've got the love of Jesus deep in my heart ... to stay!
Amen.

The Shadow of His Hand

In the shadow of His hand He hid me. *Isaiah 49:2*

In a parched and thirsty land an oasis, with its promise of cooling shade, is a welcome sight to the weary traveler. It is no wonder, then, that writers have frequently employed the term "shade" or "shadow" as a figure of speech depicting a place of refuge and safety, rest and comfort, refreshment and revitalization.

"In the shadow of His hand He hid me." What a beautiful picture of the loving, nurturing care with which God surrounds His children. It is as though the hand of God were cupped over each of us, forming its protective shield against all danger, affording us shelter from the blazing heat of adversity.

Because we are hidden in the shadow of His hand, no foe can alarm us, no harm can befall us. Under His protecting hand we are safe from every evil that would assail us.

The shadow of His hand affords peace and rest. For Jesus' sake, the hand that casts the shadow removes from us our every burden of guilt and shame.

In the shadow of His hand we find spiritual refreshment, for there we feed on His Word, and there we are blessed by His Spirit, who restores our souls and renews our hearts.

Hide us, O Lord, in the shadow of Your hand. Protect and comfort us, and renew us by Your Spirit. In Jesus' name we pray. Amen.

14

Alone with Jesus

Come with Me by yourselves to a quiet place and get some rest. *Mark 6:31*

The disciples had just returned from their first missionary tour and excitedly had shared with Jesus all of their experiences. His reaction to their enthusiasm is most remarkable. Looking at the milling crowd by which He and the disciples were surrounded and listening to the distracting hubbub, He invited them to come to a quiet spot and to rest a while.

Notice, the verb is "come," not "go." They were not merely to "get away from it all." They were to spend their quiet time with *Him*.

How important that in our modern lives—crowded, busy, and hectic as they are—we remember this distinction. There is a difference between "getting away from it all" and being "alone with Jesus."

There are moments in each day which should be spent in quiet communion with our Savior, moments of refreshment and renewal when we speak to Him and He speaks to us—through remembered passages of His Word. Such a quiet and frequent rendezvous with our Redeemer calls for conscious discipline until it becomes a way of life. How often do we meet with Him—alone?

Lord Jesus, in the midst of my busy life, help me to never neglect those precious moments when I can speak to You—alone. Amen.

His Inheritance

I pray also that the eyes of your heart may be enlightened in order that you may know the hope to which [God] has called you, the riches of His glorious inheritance in the saints. *Ephesians 1:18*

Is this ever a surprise! Normally the father offers the inheritance, and the child receives whatever is given. But God does a great reversal here. He claims an inheritance, too!

But what can be given to God that He would consider an inheritance? Would you believe that He considers His children to be His inheritance? Yes, every person He calls a "saint" He claims as His inheritance. You and I are true saints precisely because we have been made perfect in His sight by the redeeming work of Jesus. As saints, He claims us as the precious inheritance He is waiting to receive to Himself. We are the most valuable treasure He has.

Some Christians suffer from low self-esteem. They feel that they are not truly significant or important. Perhaps you are one of them. If so, this passage should be memorized and remembered often. Surely if God looks at you as His precious inheritance, you can scarcely believe that you are of little worth. God considers Himself rich because He has you as His child. It may be quite a surprise, but it is true indeed.

Father, how can I ever thank You? You consider me so precious. Thank You, in Jesus' name. Amen.

A Child of God

But you were washed, you were sanctified, you were justified in the name of the Lord Jesus Christ and by the Spirit of our God. *1 Corinthians 6:11*

A Christian is a child of God. By calling ourselves His children we acknowledge God to be our Father who cares for, provides for, and protects His children. Of course, the greatest demonstration of such dealing is in the sending of His only-begotten Son into the world to be our Savior from sin, death, and the power of the devil.

When we were baptized, God the Holy Spirit, working through water and the Word, brought us into God's kingdom. In our Baptism we find our identity as children of the heavenly Father. In our Baptism we see demonstrated the extravagant love of God for us. He takes us, born in sin and under the wrath of God, and makes us His own. How great is His love! How powerful His ways!

What a continual comfort and encouragement it is to be baptized in Christ, to know that He cared for us so much and loved us so much that He made us His own dear children! And as children we are also heirs of the Father, heirs of the free gift of eternal life through faith in Christ Jesus. Such future hope makes life on this earth bearable as we look forward to life with God in eternity.

Holy Spirit, in Baptism You worked a great work in me. Thank You that I am a child of God. Amen.

God's Secret

**Everything is possible for him
who believes. *Mark 9:23***

Among all the promises that God makes in the Bible, this is perhaps the most astounding. The statement is so bold and positive that it is almost unbelievable. To say that "everything is possible for him who believes" sounds so foreign to our frail, imperfect human experience that we are tempted to regard it as a bad joke. "Someone has to be pulling my leg," we are apt to say.

And yet the words are there, spoken by Him who said: "I am the truth." He confirmed that statement for us by His willingness to suffer and die that we might live. We might question the statement if the One who said it had no better credentials than that He went about saying nice things to please people. But this was not the case with the Lord Jesus. Whenever He said something, He meant it; deception was not His game.

And now He places the ball squarely in our court. Do you believe? Do you trust Him enough to say with the father to whom Jesus spoke those amazing words: "I do believe; help me overcome my unbelief"? Such a prayer God will answer, for with Him nothing is impossible.

Help me, O Lord Jesus, to place no limits on Your power to do what You promise. You have already proved it on the cross. Amen.

Faith Succeeds in the "Impossible"

The righteous will live by faith. *Romans 1:17*

These six words hold the key to victory for each of us. Even weak faith, Jesus said, has power to overcome mountainous problems. Think of what much faith can accomplish!

What is the secret of faith's power? Faith claims God's promises. Saint Paul, a man of strong faith, said: "The Lord shall deliver me from evil work." We, too, should say that. By faith we are sure that nothing can touch us before it passes Him. He is "our refuge and strength, an ever-present help in trouble." No believer can go down to defeat because God, in whom he trusts, cannot go down to defeat. Even if a believer dies, he will continue to live in the Father's family.

One valiant believer, who was diagnosed as terminally ill, expressed her faith this way: "I cannot lose. God will heal me now, if that is His will, or He will heal me later, or He will heal me in heaven. I cannot lose; I am living on the doorstep of eternal health."

No pillow is so soft as a promise of God. They slumber sweetly and securely whom faith rocks to sleep—faith in the Lord Jesus Christ, in whom we find peace and rest.

Lord Jesus, keep me leaning on Your promises. Then all will be well under all circumstances of life. Amen.

All Things for Good

We know that in all things God works for the good of those who love Him. *Romans 8:28*

How all-inclusive is this assertion of Saint Paul! He does not say, "We know that in *some* things," or "in *most* things," or "in *joyous* things," but "in *all* things." God works in the minute and the momentous, from the humblest event in daily life to the greatest crisis hours. And in everything He *works* for the good of those who love Him.

It is always a present operation. God is ever active in our lives in a beautiful blending of action. Many colors are needed to complete the harmonious pattern of the tapestry. Many separate tones and notes of music, even seeming discords and dissonances, make up the anthem. Many components make the piece of machinery.

But as God completes the weaving, combines the notes, and assembles the parts, we see the result. In a thousand trials, with not one exception, God works for the good of His believing children.

Blessed divine providence! God sent His Son, Jesus Christ, to die for all our sins, so all are forgiven. Having made sure of this, He adds all the lesser things of life to complete the pattern of His total concern for us. All are essential in His plan for the good of those who love Him.

Lord, I thank and praise You for Your unceasing care, Your detailed plan, Your constant activity for my good. Amen.

Trust God for the Outcome

[God] knows the way that I take; when He has tested me, I will come forth as gold. *Job 23:10*

While Michelangelo was working on St. Peter's Basilica, he was criticized by some of the men who were working on the building. They didn't like what they saw, and they told him so. The great artist responded, "Even if I were able to make my plans and ideas clear to you—which I am not—I am not obliged to do so. I must ask you to do your best to help me, and when the work is complete, the conception will be better understood." History has confirmed that he was right. Those who found fault with his work were doing so out of ignorance. Not understanding what was in the mind of the artist, they couldn't see the whole picture and full design.

When our Savior came to this world, His disciples misunderstood various of His undertakings. But when His work of atonement for our sins was accomplished for our salvation, all became plain. Right now you may be going through the deep waters of trial or affliction and may not understand what God is doing in your life. Rest assured, however, that He knows what He is doing, and trust Him for the outcome. Someday you will rejoice in His wise plan.

Lord, assure us that in all things You ultimately work for the good of those who trust in You. Amen.

Later On, However

Later on, however, it [God's discipline] produces a harvest of righteousness and peace for those who have been trained by it. *Hebrews 12:11*

Just when we think we have found a formula to fit the facts of life, something turns up to make our neat logic look absurd. So it is with God's dealings with us that the above text calls His "discipline." For the present it seems "painful" and without "pleasure." Everyone is inclined to think that it would be well for us to be spared such suffering. But there is more to it than this. In fact, the very opposite is the case. The word "however" indicates this. It gives our thoughts a new direction. We are to expect an altogether different outcome.

"Later on, however ..." says the writer to the Hebrews. With that little phrase he reaches into the middle of our trouble and takes out a prize the likes of which an untroubled life could never give us. "Later on, however, it produces a harvest of righteousness and peace for those who have been trained by it."

That prize belongs to those who are prepared to let God in upon their daily problems so that He can set their troubles in the light of the cross. There Jesus transforms them into blessings. To such, God's discipline may be painful. But afterwards comes "a harvest of righteousness and peace."

With Your benediction, O most blessed Savior, change the hard facts of our lives. Amen.

Riding High

I will cause you to ride on the heights of the land.
Isaiah 58:14

One of the rules learned by an airline pilot is to fly against the wind when taking off or landing the aircraft, or when seeking to climb above a storm. People learned this rule from the birds. In ordinary flying the bird goes with the wind. But if it meets danger, it turns into the wind, even if it means flying directly into the sun.

Sufferings, trials, and reverses are God's winds. Sometimes they are extremely contrary and strong. But these veritable hurricanes take human life and lift it to higher levels, even toward God's own heaven, if one understands their purpose.

On many a summer day the atmosphere becomes so oppressive that even breathing is difficult. But then a cloud appears in the northwest, grows larger, and then throws out its blessing of refreshing rain. The storm that seems to threaten the landscape also charges it with new life.

Trials ought to call forth from us a song. Our redemption in Jesus Christ is proof of God's love, also in days of distress. "The Lord disciplines those He loves" (Hebrews 12:6). The wind sings best when hindered by the trees or the strings of a harp. The child of God should be at his or her best in adversity. Living in God's grace, God's child rides high, no matter what the weather.

Lord, let the disciplining of Your love fill our hearts with joyful song. Amen.

Christ Forgives Our Past

If anyone is in Christ, he is a new creation; the old has gone, the new has come! *2 Corinthians 5:17*

Our past makes up our present and influences our future. Past failures, for example, are not historical relics with no effect on our behavior today and tomorrow. They leave their mark and point us in a certain direction for current conduct. Each time we commit some wrong or indulge in some sin, each time we silence the voice of conscience, we contribute to the establishment of a habit that will affect our living. Our past misdeeds raise their voices and cast their votes whenever we are faced with present decisions.

If our past could be forgiven, then we would have the chance to be freed for new living each day. We would be able to acquire the ability to forget those things that are behind and press on to better living for each new day.

That is what Christ does for us. He stands between us and our past and absorbs all the sin and shame that come charging after us. He lays down a protecting barrier of His mercy and grace in front of all our pursuing enemies. Christ not only is our hope for an uncertain future, but He is our hope for our imperfect past. And in His strength we can live a new life each new day.

Heavenly Father, stand between us and our past failures so that we can live new lives each day. Amen.

Remembering No More

I [God] will forgive their wickedness and will remember their sins no more. *Hebrews 8:12*

Our memories can be a blessing or a curse. For men and women without God, memory can be a terrible thing. It can bring tears at dawn, ghosts in moments of seeming happiness, and the long, haunting pain of unforgiven sin.

For the heart that has been at the cross, memory holds no terror. We may remember our sins; but we remember our forgiveness even more warmly. We may think of our mistakes and failures; but by God's grace we can also think of the righteousness our Savior earned for us. In fact, all we have to do is to forget ourselves and remember Him.

This is one of the problems our Savior spoke about in His last address. The Christian, He said, always has the blessed privilege of forgetting past sorrow, just as a mother does not remember her pain after a child has been born.

All of us have known people who would give all they have to forget the past. The ghosts that walk by their side give them no rest and no peace. Only Christ can help them—because He has taken away the sin and sorrow of the past and given us faith and hope—and the joy of remembering no more.

Dear Jesus, help us to trust that You have forgiven all our sins so that we may experience the joy and peace that comes from remembering them no more. Amen.

He Knows His Sheep

I am the Good Shepherd; I know My sheep and My sheep know Me. *John 10:14*

A good shepherd knows all about his sheep. He knows that this one may be strong, while another one is weak. He realizes that some are wayward or lonely or in need of special care.

Here is the greatness of our own Good Shepherd! Nothing escapes His watching and loving eye. The smallest hurt and the deepest pain are known to Him. He always helps from His holy place as the Good Shepherd of our souls.

One of the strange things about our life in the 20th century is its deep loneliness. Even in our crowded cities, men and women are often alone, lost in the noisy, confused life of our hard, cold world.

But the Christian heart need never feel lonely. Knowing that our Savior came to redeem us from the bitter loneliness of sin, we know, too, that He stays with us as our Good Shepherd, who knows, better than anyone else, how much we need Him every day and every hour of our lives. In His own good time He gives each one of us exactly the blessing and the gift that we alone need. It is never too much and never too little—never too early and never too late—because He knows His own.

Dear Jesus, Shepherd of my soul, You know me by name and know what I need. Help me to rest secure in Your forgiving love and follow wherever You lead me, for You have prepared rich blessings for me. In Your name I pray. Amen.

Easter Hope — We Have a Shepherd

I am the Good Shepherd ... I lay down My life for the sheep. *John 10:14–15*

In Christ and His resurrection from the dead we have the ultimate and perfect hope. This is a hope that is far more than an uncertain wish for the future. Rather, it is a living hope, a sure conviction, a reliance on an unbreakable promise.

That hope operates in our hearts here and now. We know Christ as our Good Shepherd, who not only has the power fully and completely to protect us but also such perfect love for us that we can without doubting believe that He will always use that power in our behalf. He is not simply in control of this infinitely immense universe, but He guides and directs each one of us in our individual and personal lives. He knows us by name. He cares for us. He loved us enough to lay down His life for us. We have an invincible basis for our belief that He will also provide us with all that we need for our earthly welfare.

But above all, our hope for the future will blossom into a glorious reality when He returns in glory and triumph. It will be an awesome event, striking terror into the hearts of those who have had no use for Him. But for those who know Him and are known by Him as blood-bought and redeemed souls, it will be a joyous welcome home.

O Good Shepherd, keep us, Your flock, by Your almighty power. Amen.

I Will Strengthen You

Do not fear, for I am with you; do not be dismayed, for I am your God. I will strengthen you and help you; I will uphold you with My righteous right hand.
Isaiah 41:10

God does not say, "Do not fear; nothing bad will happen to you." He says, "Do not fear, for I am with you." God is with us in fair weather and on stormy days, when we are celebrating and when we are crying.

"Do not be dismayed." God's children are not to walk through life paralyzed by fear. Why not? "I am your God!" The Creator of the heavens and the earth is our Father. He protects, cares, and provides for us.

"I will strengthen you." God promises to give us strength to bear whatever burdens He lets us carry. "I will help you." God has helped us so far. He will help us in the future. He promises more: "I will uphold you with My righteous right hand." His almighty power is ours when we are weak.

Since God promises to give us strength, we can respond, "I can do everything through [Christ] who gives me strength." When life's blows strike us and challenges are set before us, we can remind ourselves: God will give me strength; I can cope with this problem; I can do this job. I can take life one day at a time.

O Lord, You delivered us from eternal destruction. We believe You can help us today and every day. Amen.

Strength for Each Day

Your strength will equal your days.
Deuteronomy 33:25

A little girl, sent on an errand, had to cross a wide but shallow stream. There were firm steppingstones all the way over. "Oh, I'm afraid," said the child to a lady who was passing by. "Why are you afraid? There are steppingstones all the way across; it's easy to cross. Just try it!" Very timidly the little girl began to cross. "Just one step at a time is all you have to take," said the kind and gentle guide. So one step followed another. The first were the hardest to take, but soon she was safe on the other side, smiling at her fears.

Applying this to life, we would say, "Just one day at a time." God promises: "Your strength will equal your days." There are steppingstones all through life. These steppingstones are the many promises that God has incorporated into His Word. And certain passages, designed especially for days of stress and strain, when double strength is required, will exercise a power truly wonderful, banishing fears and supplying the extra power necessary to carry on. There are countless Christians who can testify from personal experience that God's promise is absolutely reliable: "Your strength will equal your days."

Heavenly Father, help me to trust that for Jesus' sake You will give me the strength needed for each day. Be with me and turn weakness into strength. Amen.

Who's Greater Than God?

If God is for us, who can be against us? *Romans 8:31*

Sometime in the life of every person an attempt is made to measure God. This generally happens when adversity or difficulty comes. If the adversity or difficulty is greater than our understanding of God, then God will be abandoned. It is the only sensible thing to do. If God is to be God, He must be greater than anyone or anything. If there is something greater, then God would not be the Ruler of all things.

The Bible is the history of God's mastery over every force in life. He calmed storms, overwhelmed armies, provided plenty in the midst of bareness. Twisted limbs were straightened, blind eyes opened, and diseased bodies healed. In Christ, God showed His unique power by overpowering death, the last enemy of humankind. Paul writes: "Death has been swallowed up in victory" (1 Corinthians 15:54). Christ's resurrection showed God's rule over death and sin, which causes death. Christ earned this victory for us and now gives it to us. It can confidently be said: He "has put everything under His feet" (1 Corinthians 15:27). That means no one is greater than God—no force is greater than God, no circumstance is greater than God. He rules. He rules for us. With God for us, who or what can be against us? All things are sure to work together for our good.

We are so impressed, Lord, by humankind's little displays of power that we forget Your might. Help us remember. For Jesus' sake we pray. Amen.

Victory over Discouragement

Taste and see that the Lord is good! Blessed is the man who takes refuge in Him. *Psalm 34:8*

Discouragement is one of Satan's most used tools to hurt Christians.

If being discouraged is your problem, adopt these resolves: (1) Rather than being discouraged *by what the world has come to*, I will be encouraged *by what has come into the world* through the Lord Jesus Christ; (2) Rather than being discouraged because I *do not* know what the future holds, I will be encouraged because I *do* know who holds the future; (3) Rather than being discouraged by *all that is wrong* in the world, I will be encouraged by *all that is right*; (4) Rather than being discouraged by all the sin, I will be encouraged by all the *grace*; (5) Rather than being discouraged by all the *sickness*, I will be encouraged by all the *health*.

We have our choice. We may stand in the light of faith or in the shadows of unbelief. We may look at adverse circumstances or at Him who is above circumstances.

May we all resolve to trust our loving heavenly Father, who gave His Son for our life. He will never let us down. He will grant us victory over discouragement.

Dear Lord, help me to live on the sunny side of life. Fill me with joy beyond all telling, hope beyond all describing. Amen.

By Choice—Not by Chance

I trust in You, O Lord; I say, "You are my God." My times are in Your hands. *Psalm 31:14–15*

Many of life's decisions call for trust, for a surrender of ourselves to others. Children trust parents; plane passengers trust the pilot; patients trust doctors. Most important of all is the need for trust in God.

In His Word and Sacraments God continues to reassure us that in His Son Jesus we have forgiveness of all our sins and release from the penalty of eternal condemnation. In Jesus we are sealed into God's plan for new life in this world and the one to come.

As followers of Jesus we can confidently confess that our times are not in our own hands. No longer are we under the dominion of sin, death, and the devil. Neither are we victims of chance or prisoners of fate.

Saint Paul's experience with the promises of God is this: "We know that in all things God works together for the good of those who love Him … " (Romans 8:28). He was persuaded that nothing can "separate us from the love of God that is in Christ Jesus our Lord" (Romans 8:39).

How wonderful to live day by day with Jesus! Our times are in His hands by God's choice—not just by chance.

Take my hand and lead me, Lord, all my days. Let me never forget that my whole life is in Your hands. Amen.

Riddles Will Be Solved

Later you will understand. *John 13:7*

A *strange* scene! The Master washing the feet of His disciples! What did it mean? And His words, addressed to Peter: "You do not realize now what I am doing, but later you will understand." Do they have any significance for us? Indeed, they do!

The Lord often does strange things in our lives. Sickness, sorrow, poverty, and persecution in the lives of God's children—what do they mean? We cannot always know the answer. God's children live only in the present. They ask only for strength for the day. Tomorrow belongs to God.

Pious Joseph, languishing in prison, Elijah in his cave, Jeremiah in bonds, Daniel facing the hungry lions, Mary and Martha, their beloved brother dead, all must have wondered at God's strange dealings with His children; but not for long.

At times, we, too, are permitted to know God's purpose in this life, as these men and women knew. That illness long ago was so painful, yet it led us closer to God; we can see it now. But even though we never understand in this life, "later" we will understand. Saint Paul says: "Then I shall know fully, even as I am fully known." We may go to sleep, still in ignorance of God's ways, but we shall awake in knowledge; and every child of God can say with David: "When I awake, I will be satisfied with seeing Your likeness" (Psalm 17:15).

Lord, grant faith and patience now, that later I may understand. Amen.

"Positive Thinking" Has Its Limits

If it is possible, may this cup be taken from Me. Yet not as I will, but as You will. *Matthew 26:39*

We hear and read a lot about the power of positive thinking. While it is true that positive thinking has much to say for it, even being encouraged in the Scriptures (Philippians 4:8), it is wrong (yes, deceiving and cruel) to advertise positive thinking as the unfailing cure-all for all human ills. There are some situations in life where all the "positive thinking" in the world will get us nowhere.

We think of our Savior kneeling in Gethsemane and pleading with His Father: "If it is *possible*, may this cup be taken from Me." In the divine economy of God it was *not* possible. The bitter cup was inevitable. In one of the last conversations between Jesus and Peter, the Lord told Peter that Peter's faithful witness would bring him not to a golden throne in Rome or elsewhere but to an ignominious martyr's death.

Not positive *thinking* but positive *promises* determine the believer's destiny. Our Lord has told us that we are His sheep, that He will give us eternal life, that no one can snatch us out of His hand. These are the "positives" in which we place our ultimate trust and hope.

Lord, grant me the power of positive thinking, but may my ultimate confidence always rest in Your unchanging Word. Amen.

A Cheerful Disposition

Take heart, son; your sins are forgiven. *Matthew 9:2*

This is more than a bid to smile or to strike a cheerful pose. Here we have a message of cheer from the lips of our heavenly friend which brightens the gloomiest hours of our day.

"Take heart," said Jesus—and notice the reason He gave the crippled sufferer. It was not, "Take heart, because your paralysis will be removed." That also He intended to do. But with a swift, sure diagnosis the searcher of hearts saw the real cause of His patient's glumness: his uneasy conscience. Deep within the man's soul were miserable guilt feelings, probably linked with sad memories of misconduct. The man lacked the essential of a balanced, cheerful personality, which is ours by God's grace. "Your sins are forgiven," said Jesus.

Years ago someone advertised for a traveling companion with the notice: "Christian wanted! Cheerful, if possible." A glum Christian, he realized, would make a depressing partner.

"Take heart," Jesus says. "Your sins are forgiven!" That makes possible a cheery heart. His Gospel is more than "right views"; it is good news. For a radiant, abiding cheerfulness that weathers all storms, positive thinking is not enough. The rich daily forgiveness of the Savior is needed, and a heart that accepts it gratefully, saying:

Lord, what now can daunt my spirit, since I'm at peace with You? Amen.

The End of the Lines

In you, O Lord, I have taken refuge. *Psalm 71:1*

As a child I used to drive about in an old surrey with my father. He always allowed me to take hold of the end of the lines. In my childish fancy I believed that I was driving our big sorrel horse.

So deeply was this impressed upon my mind and attitude that the memory of it continues to bob up every so often in my mind—especially when the going is rough.

As children of God we at times make a great deal of talk about what *we* are doing, as if we had everything well under control; actually the strong and sure hands of our heavenly Father are holding the lines and guiding us.

We do well to put our trust in Him and leave the solution to our problems in His hands. For God still sits in the driver's seat. He continues to hold the lines that control the world. He will not permit His children to perish. He assures us: "Even the very hairs of your head are all numbered." He will take us safely on our way through life and one day safely to our eternal home.

Be still, my soul; your God will undertake

To guide the future as He has the past.

Heavenly Father, in Christ Jesus give us faith to trust You boldly, hope to fix our souls on You. Amen.

Trust

His peace will keep your thoughts and your hearts quiet and at rest as you trust in Christ Jesus.
Philippians 4:7 TEV

"Quiet and at rest." Does that describe your heart and your mind? If you are the same as most people, probably not. No doubt there are too many disquieting and upsetting things going on in your life and in the world around you to have a heart and mind "quiet and at rest." Yet that is what God promised to all those who put their trust in Him.

Trust is turning something over to another and believing it is being safely cared for. Trust is the absence of fear and anxiety.

Maybe all of us need to examine our trust level. Maybe we are trusting ourselves more than God. Maybe we are afraid to turn things over to Him because we are not convinced He can care for them. We may think our concerns are too big. But the almighty God surely is capable of understanding our concerns and helping us deal with them.

We may think our concerns are too small. But a concern too insignificant to be given to the Lord is too small to be made into a burden.

Trust the Lord in *all* things. He will never let you down. He gave His Son for you; He will give the smaller things, too.

Dear Lord, increase my trust in You.
My heart and my mind
need the quiet and rest that only You can give. Amen.

Is God Forgetful?

How long, O Lord? Will You forget me forever?
Psalm 13:1

The problem appears to be with God. God seems to be forgetful. Our long wait for His help is more than we can endure. God made all kinds of promises. God says He will not let us be tempted above what we are able to bear. If then the pain continues, is it not because God has turned away from the ones who prayed so fervently?

What we feel and what troubles us is real. We know God is real and His promises are real. Is not the logic of our emotions correct if we say God is hiding out on us when He does not come to our rescue when we ask Him?

Are we justified in asking with the psalmist, "How long?" It all depends on whether our sense of timing is right. If, when things go wrong, we keep our eye on the clock and calendar and set our own schedule for God's help, then it may appear that God has forgotten us. God, however, does not forget. He says, "Can a mother forget the baby at her breast and have no compassion on the child she has borne? Though she may forget, I will not forget you!" (Isaiah 49:15). God did not forget His own Son Jesus Christ in the grave but raised Him up from the dead. In that fact lies the assurance that He will not fail nor forget us. We can wait on the Lord with confidence in His promise: "Never will I leave you; never will I forsake you" (Hebrews 13:5).

Heavenly Father, help us overcome our fears that You are forgetful of us. Help us to remember Your Son. Amen.

Wait Patiently

If we hope for what we do not yet have, we wait for it patiently. *Romans 8:25*

A little girl kept tugging at her mother's dress, whining constantly. "Let's go home, Mommy. Why does it take so long? I don't want to wait anymore. Is it going to take a thousand years?" Aren't we at times just as impatient, bombarding God with impertinent questions? Saint Paul says, "Wait for it patiently."

God so orders things that, along with the good, there might come bitter cups for us to drink. God's purpose is that we learn patience under His loving and merciful hand and grow in faith. Though we do not always understand the purpose of waiting, God asks us to trust Him as the One who knows the best time and place for all things. Such exercise strengthens the muscles of our faith.

We trust God for our salvation in Christ. Look at what His Son has done! He patiently took on the ruthless, death-dealing guilt and power of our sin while on the cross. He died and was raised to make heaven a blessed certainty for all eternity. We look forward to this with anticipation and joy.

A man, pacing back and forth in his office, was asked, "What's the trouble?" He replied, "The trouble is that I'm in a hurry, and God isn't." Patience requires utmost confidence in God's timing.

Lord Jesus, we ask Your forgiveness for our impatience. Lead us to trust in You patiently. Amen.

Our Divine Healer

"Go," said Jesus, "your faith has healed you."
Mark 10:52

Doctors expected the man to live only several more days. He prayed fervently. Others prayed for him. A few years later the man testified in his church: "Doctors tell me I have gone through the valley of the shadow. Someone not knowing how sick I was would not have believed what has taken place. I stand in awe and reverence before God and thank Him."

Jesus, the Great Physician, is among us today. He is the same yesterday, today, and forever. His power to heal is as great as it was 20 centuries ago. He is just as compassionate. He did miracles long ago. He does miracles today. Sometimes the Lord heals without means. Usually He works through means—medicines and the skill of doctors and nurses. God hears when we pray for healing. Does that mean that people who remain sick have no faith or not enough faith? No. God answers every prayer we offer in the best way His love, wisdom, and power can devise.

God is against sin and every result of sin, including sickness. God desires our well-being. In sickness let us pray for healing until God grants it or makes it plain that it is not His will in this particular case and gives us peace of mind about it.

Jesus, our Lord, You healed us from the leprosy of sin.
Strengthen our souls and our bodies. Amen.

Phone 911!

**Call upon Me in the day of trouble;
I will deliver you, and
you will honor Me.** *Psalm 50:15*

Phoning 911 signifies an urgent need for emergency help. When called, medical personnel respond promptly and efficiently with a speeding ambulance and pain-killing drugs to minimize trauma. Hospitals have sophisticated equipment to provide therapy and life support. We are fortunate to have such technology available.

Jesus Himself was an "emergency physician." The gospels record numerous accounts of His healing power. He cured many who were sick, restored sight and hearing, and even raised dead people back to life. Although concerned primarily with forgiving our sins, He also responded to physical tragedies with empathy and powerful curative actions.

Praise God, Jesus still does so today! As patients we may be confused and frightened in an intensive care unit, but our fears subside when comforted by the certainty that Jesus is at our side. Prayers learned in childhood relieve us, Bible passages encourage us, and pastoral visits reassure us of God's forgiveness and mercy in Christ. These spiritual aids, when joined with care by doctors and nurses (who may be regarded as agents of God's healing power), stimulate recovery and provide us with God's gift of peace.

My God, for Jesus' sake I pray that Your peace would bless my dying day. Amen.

All the Tools You Need

Every house is built by someone, but God is the builder of everything. *Hebrews 3:4*

"Always use the right tool for the job" is sound advice often given by fathers to sons and by supervisors to workers. Nothing can be more frustrating than trying to accomplish a task with the wrong tools. The job ends up taking far more time and sometimes is impossible.

The Holy Spirit uses the tools of God's Word and Sacraments to create and sustain the gift of faith in each Christian. Children usually are baptized into the kingdom of God, and the faith of Christians is nourished by the Lord's Supper and the Bible. We are to use these tools of God so our Christian faith is sustained.

At times, though, we may try to take matters into our own hands and use our own tools to do spiritual work. But we soon realize the frustration and wasted time and energy resulting from using the wrong tools.

The psalmist writes, "Your Word is a lamp to my feet and a light for my path" (Psalm 119:105). Not our own candles or flashlights, but Scripture lights the way to God. Only God's Word makes us wise for salvation through faith in Christ Jesus. We need to mark it down: God's Word and Sacraments are the only tools for growing and sharing our faith.

Father in heaven, help us always to use Your tools to do Your work; for Jesus' sake we pray. Amen.

Remember Your Guide and Comforter

The Holy Spirit, whom the Father will send in My name, will teach you all things and remind you of everything I have said to you. *John 14:26*

In preparing His disciples for the time when He would no longer be physically present with them, Jesus tells them about the Third Person of the Trinity, the Holy Spirit.

He speaks of Him first as a faithful guide: "When He, the Spirit of truth, comes, He will guide you into all truth" (John 16:13). When left to our own devices, we are so prone to err and go the wrong way, but in the inspired Word we learn how God would have us live and be. Therefore let us search its holy pages each day, seeking the blessing of the Spirit of God, who is our Guide.

Our Lord also describes the Holy Spirit as a loving comforter. So often life has a way of dealing us large portions of discouragement, disappointment, and sorrow. We would despair except for God's gracious Comforter—who would gladly heal our wounds, mend our broken hearts, quicken our hopes, and send us on our way strengthened and renewed through the Word. Let us remember our holy Comforter; be sanctified by the Holy Spirit; and ours will be a victorious life.

O Holy Spirit, without whose grace we could not believe in our Savior, Jesus Christ, be our Guide and Comforter, for we would do Your will in Christ. Amen.

God's Infinite Care

You prepare a table before me in the presence of my enemies. *Psalm 23:5*

A religious publication many years ago printed a Syrian Christian's interpretation of the Twenty-third Psalm. Being a shepherd himself, this Syrian pointed out that much of the significance of the psalm is lost unless one knows the problems of the shepherd in Bible lands.

One of his stimulating verse-by-verse explanations ran as follows:

> Preparing a table does not mean setting a dinner table indoors, but refers to the shepherd's chief concern, that of finding a proper feeding place for his flock. He must be on the constant lookout for poisonous grasses, for his sheep do not always know the difference between healthy and death-bringing plants. His ever-watchful eye must detect wily snakes lying in ambush and drive them off. All this requires unceasing vigilance.

> After finding an adequate patch of healthy grass free from snakes, the shepherd must render it safe "in the presence of enemies." Around the feeding ground, in holes and caverns on the hillside, there are jackals, wolves, and hyenas bent upon destroying the sheep. So the shepherd builds an enclosure of rocks and, if the wild beasts nevertheless attempt to enter the enclosure, slays them with his long-bladed knife.

Does not this one verse alone of Psalm 23 indicate what infinite care God takes to protect His children night and day?

Dear Lord, continue to be my Shepherd; keep me in Your infinite care; then I shall not be in want. Amen.

Fighting Our Fight

If God is for us, who can be against us? *Romans 8:31*

Some fights in life are won because of the person doing the fighting. If a noted authority or celebrity takes a stand on a certain issue, that side may win because of his or her position and influence.

In our fight against evil forces, we might say, "They are so strong. I'm so weak. How can I possibly win?" We can win because Jesus Christ took our place on the battlefield against Satan, sin, and its consequence, death. He fought and He won. He now shows up at our fight and is standing on our side. That is what the story of David and Goliath is about. God was on David's side, so he won over the larger and stronger Goliath. God assures us that if we speak one little word against the devil, he will flee from us. That one word is *Christ*.

So who can stand against us if God is on our side? Satan may accuse us, but he is powerless—filled with hot air. Our hearts may condemn us, but God is greater than our hearts. Others might try to make us feel guilty, but we know our forgiveness in Jesus is pure. God certainly would have the right to accuse us; but it is God Himself who justifies us by His grace in Christ. He fights on our side!

Lord, when temptations and accusations come, help us remember which side You are on. Amen.

Mount Moriah

I lift up my eyes to the hills … My help comes from the Lord. *Psalm 121:1–2*

How helpless Abraham must have felt trudging up Mount Moriah. God had promised him this son, Isaac, who walked next to him. It seemed that the promise would never come true—this son, almost a hundred years younger than he was.

And now God had asked Abraham to sacrifice Isaac, the joy of his old age. How the sight of the hill must have filled Abraham with horror and anguish!

But when Abraham showed his willingness to give up even this son of promise for his Lord, the Lord was there at the mountaintop to tell Abraham to desist, that there was a ram caught in the briers for his use.

Often enough our Lord seems to be distant and silent. His demands on us seem impossible. Beyond the clouds of trouble, though, we see a forgiving and loving God whose wisdom is above ours and whose ways are past finding out. Because He first loved us, we love Him more than father, mother, son, daughter, spouse, or anyone. We find Him close, a very present help in trouble.

God of Israel and our God, cheer us with the assurance that You do not slumber or sleep but are ever watchful and near. Be our constant Helper and never leave or forsake us. For Jesus' sake we ask this. Amen.

Trust Me!

Though He slay me, yet will I hope [trust] in Him.
Job 13:15

Trust is a quiet, serene word. We picture a child with his hand in that of the parent, or a heart at peace because God is in charge.

Suddenly the scene changes. Unemployment wipes out our savings. Flood or fire or wind destroys the home we've taken a lifetime to build. Violence enters our world. Then trust becomes a challenge thrown at us. God asks us, as He did Abraham: Will you trust Me though I ask you to give up a child?

Can we really trust Him that much? When God's promise is all we have left, can we rest securely?

That kind of trust doesn't just victoriously appear when the bottom falls out of our lives. The quiet trust of peaceful days precedes and prepares us for the storms. As we daily come to God for strength, as we experience Jesus' love and forgiveness, as we grow in faith, we find Him to be reliable. In the day of calamity, God's Holy Spirit will sustain us.

Jesus asks us to trust Him today—for today's needs. No more—no less! Step by step, one day at a time! Trust that in Jesus all the promises of salvation are fulfilled!

I am trusting You, Lord Jesus, Trusting only You;
Trusting You for full salvation, Free and true. Amen.

(From *LBW* © 1978. By permission of CPH.)

He Holds My Hand

You hold me by my right hand. *Psalm 73:23*

The psalmist David had total, unyielding confidence in God. It's interesting to note that he always coupled his exhortations to trust in God with specific examples. He had good reasons for his confidence in God. Our text gives us one of the reasons.

David said that God had taken hold of him by his right hand. This is a beautiful picture—God the Father reaching down to man the creature and taking his hand to keep him from stumbling along life's rocky path. As a small boy is never afraid of anything as long as his father is holding his hand, so David could conquer all with God at his side, upholding him.

The Christian truth in the above picture is immensely comforting. God's promise to sustain us becomes personal. God the Father cares about us. As it were, He holds our right hand. Here we find the assurance of divine presence, divine support and help, divine guidance.

According to this specific Word of God we in our highly uncertain world have the immovable Rock of Ages, eternal peace. We have One who is always there, ready to help and ready to direct. This calls to mind the line from an old song: "Put your hand in the hand of the Man from Galilee."

Lord, take my hand and lead me Upon life's way;
Direct, protect, and feed me From day to day. Amen.

(From *LBW* © 1978. By permission of CPH.)

48

Holding His Hand

Do not let your hearts be troubled.
Trust in God; trust also in Me. *John 14:1*

A famous surgeon once said, "I hope that when I die, it will be quick. But if there is some delay, then I hope I'll have somebody I love with me—somebody to hold my hand."

That is the need we have, too. Not only when we face death, but whenever we encounter great difficulty, we want somebody we love near us to give us support—somebody to hold our hand.

Jesus assures us that He will do this for us. He will offer us His hand. It is no ordinary hand. It is the hand that bears the scar of a nail wound in its palm. It is a hand that gives proof of Jesus' love for us. If He loved us enough to die for us long ago, we know He loves us still and is for us a present source of comfort and strength. When we experience trouble, and we fear that Jesus is far from us, He wants us to trust in His presence and protection. He is always near.

To place our hand in His is a sign of trust. When we do that, we are reminded that we are trusting no mere human being. When we trust Him, we are trusting someone who is no less than God Himself. He has said, "Do not let your hearts be troubled. Trust in God; trust also in Me."

Be with us, Lord Jesus Christ, in life and in death to keep us strong and confident in Your love. Amen.

Without a Care in the World

Do not be anxious about anything, but in everything, by prayer and petition, with thanksgiving, present your requests to God. *Philippians 4:6*

Being carefree is sometimes associated with being foolish and frivolous. Saint Paul certainly does not approve of lack of concern or planning or effort or even struggling. He himself was very serious about many things, but he put aside care.

Jesus could not have made it any clearer that we do not improve a thing through worry. Flowers and birds are daily evidence that our heavenly Father is in charge. Anxiety simply demonstrates that we have much more to learn about trust in God. Sinful pride leads us to believe that we have to fret about our needs and to work our own way through our problems. That effort is often for nothing.

Our God has established His absolute faithfulness. He planned our redemption from eternity. He chose us as His own from eternity. In time He sent His only Son to die for our sin—sin that frustrates life and removes all hope. Christ Jesus died for us and rose again. Out of His trustworthy love, our God has forgiven us and made us His kings and priests.

Since God took care of our greatest need at so much expense to Himself, of course, He will take care of all our needs. He knows what is best. He shoulders our cares. We can be carefree.

Lord, help us to be content in knowing You and Your love. Amen.

Don't Worry!

Therefore do not worry about tomorrow, for tomorrow will worry about itself. *Matthew 6:34*

A sign along a state highway on the island of Hawaii warns: "Fault Zone! Watch for Cracks in Road." Because of the active volcanoes in the area, the earth below is constantly shifting. Although the road looks smooth, the traveler has to be ready for the unexpected.

That's the way our life is, too. Things may be going along smoothly, as planned. Yet we know that at any moment the bottom could drop out, and our future would be completely changed. We have to be prepared. But we don't have to be paralyzed by worry about the unknowns of the future. Worry solves no problems, nor does it prevent them. It robs us of peace of mind and of restful sleep. Worry only weakens us. When troubles come, we are then less able to cope with them.

When anxious thoughts bother us, we ought to remind ourselves over and over again: God is our loving Father, who is in charge of all our tomorrows. He solved our greatest problem by sending His Son to free us from the eternal consequence of our sin. Surely with His power we can face any trial this life brings. He never promised us a trouble-free life. But He assures us that He is always with us to strengthen and support us.

Lord, help us to be strong and of good courage. Amen.

God Sustains Our Struggling Faith

A bruised reed He will not break, and a smoldering wick He will not snuff out. *Isaiah 42:3*

God tells us through Isaiah that His chosen Servant, the Messiah, will deal gently with people whose faith is at the breaking point. In fulfillment of this prophecy, the Lord Jesus preserved the struggling faith of many a hard-pressed person. Peter was more like a bruised reed than a firm rock during and after his denial of Christ. His faith was but a flicker, but the Lord did not extinguish it. Instead he fanned the glimmering spark into a bright flame. He strengthened and nurtured the fragile plant of Peter's faith by forgiving him and reinstating him in his apostolate.

Sometimes we all hang on by a thread. Amid family illness we may say with an anxious father: "Lord, I believe; help my unbelief." Doubt and unbelief are never far from a believing heart. Or, we trip over life's mysteries, problems, and seeming inequities, as the psalmist says: "My feet had almost slipped; I had nearly lost my foothold" (Psalm 73:2–3).

Who helps us in our weaknesses of faith? It is the Holy Spirit, who assures us that Jesus is our Lord and that He who laid down His life for us will sustain and strengthen us. The Spirit ever bears witness in us that we are the children of God.

Lord Jesus, we believe that You are always mindful of us and will lead us from our struggles to victory. Amen.

New Life

So it is with everyone born of the Spirit. *John 3:8*

Surgeons implant organs taken from donor patients, thereby bringing new life to critically ill recipients. Gardeners plant dry seeds that later sprout into healthy growth. The cycle of death before new life is a continuing miracle of nature.

Our spiritual lives follow a similar cycle. Saint Paul writes, "You were dead in your transgressions and sins" (Ephesians 2:1). Jesus told Nicodemus that we are born again when the Holy Spirit works His miracle of faith within us. New life springs forth, often without our knowing it. Dear Christian reader, rejoice! This has happened to you.

Nevertheless, some of us worry that our faith is too weak, or that God cannot possibly let us into heaven. How precious our Baptism becomes! Through that simple action, the Holy Spirit grants and strengthens faith, giving us great spiritual blessings. Each day we are assured of the forgiveness of sins and eternal salvation through the covenant of grace. No sin is too great; no doubt is too strong. Through the Gospel our hearts are opened to the sunshine of the Spirit so that we may daily grow stronger in faith.

Come, gracious Spirit, heav'nly dove, With light and comfort from above. Come, be our Guardian and our Guide; At ev'ry thought and step preside. Amen.

Take God at His Word

He will remain faithful, for He cannot disown Himself. *2 Timothy 2:13*

One of the characteristics God has revealed to us about Himself is His faithfulness. The pages of Scripture contain numerous promises. These are the promises of God Himself, promises He must keep, since He has made them. We make promises which often we are unwilling or unable to fulfill. In our life we have not kept every promise we have made.

It is different with God. He cannot deny Himself. This we must remember. We make our life more difficult because we do not always fully trust the words and promises of God. Take any shortcoming in our life: envy, hatred, unconcern for the physical or spiritual needs of our neighbor. Whatever our failings may be, we can overcome them if we seek God's help. By presenting ourselves at the foot of the cross with our many faults, by looking to Jesus for help in living a total life for Him we can by the undeserved mercies of God present ourselves as a living sacrifice to Him.

God has fulfilled His promises in our daily life. That is why our cup runs over. Yet we doubt Him! God promises and gives us forgiveness, faith, protection, and life eternal. Yet too often we fail to take God at His word. Let God be God! He is faithful; He cannot deny Himself. He does keep all His promises.

O Lord, help us place our trust in Your Word. Amen.

Behind the Promises

I know whom I have believed. *2 Timothy 1:12*

Trust is always personal. For one thing, it is something I must do for myself. No one can do my trusting for me. But more importantly, our trust has a personal object. It is directed to someone.

As Christians we believe the Word and trust in the promises of the Gospel. But the Word and the promises are sure to us only because of Him who gave them. Always in our trust we must get back to Him in whom we place our confidence.

Behind the promises is the everlasting, sure, and faithful God. He has determined what He will do, He has declared His will for us, He has always kept His promises, and He has revealed Himself to us so that by our faith we can see Him as a God of power, as a God of wisdom, as a God of goodness.

But clearest of all we see Him as the God of love. In the person of His Son Jesus Christ He came to our world to share our human life, to take away from us our burden of sin, to turn us toward Himself again, to give us new life by His Spirit. In Jesus Christ alone we see God as He really is. And only then can we trust, for only then can we say, "I know whom I have believed." Saint Paul had come to such trust in God. With trust came certainty; thus, he was able to say: "I am sure that He is able to keep safe until that Day what He has entrusted to me" (2 Timothy 1:12 TEV).

Lord, give us a trust that rests on You alone! Amen.

Loneliness

Jesus answered: "I am the way." *John 14:6*

What do we picture in our minds when we hear the word *lonely?* Perhaps we see a homeless person sleeping on a park bench, a lover who has just been jilted, or a newcomer in a strange city. Loneliness is no respecter of persons. A person can be lonely in a crowd, among friends, in a marriage, even in a church. We are advised: If you are lonely, get busy! Get involved, make friends, change spouses, join a club, take a trip. The result is often that people run from place to place, from relationship to relationship, from people to people, and they still feel lonely.

While those suggestions may fall short, there is a sure answer for loneliness. Jesus Christ knows what loneliness is all about. He was deserted by His Father on the cross. Jesus suffered our punishment, reconciling us to the Father so that we don't have to be lonely, lost sinners anymore. Jesus assures us that He is "the way" for our lives, even in times of loneliness. As we spend time with Him in His Word, we learn His grace is sufficient for our every need. Christ gives us a purpose for life as we reach out and become involved with life in ways He directs. The result? We find we aren't so lonely!

Dear Savior, by Your all-sufficient grace take away my loneliness. Amen.

Encourage One Another

Encourage one another and build each other up, just as in fact you are doing. *1 Thessalonians 5:11*

Do you ever get discouraged? That's like asking if you ever get hungry or thirsty. Some of the best-known people of Bible times knew periods of deep discouragement. Moses, Elijah, and Jonah prayed for the Lord to take their life. Job and Jeremiah cursed the day of their birth. When in prison, John the Baptizer was troubled with doubts. He sent his followers to ask Jesus whether He was the Promised One.

In our discouragement we likewise can turn to the Lord. We may say, "O God, I'm feeling low. Lift me up." When we pray, we can expect God to answer.

God answers us through His Word: "Do not fear, for I am with you; do not be dismayed, for I am your God. I will strengthen you and help you … . Never will I leave you; never will I forsake you" (Isaiah 41:10; Hebrews 13:5). The Lord may help us through people or through an uplifting sermon or an inspiring book or article.

God wants us to encourage others. We may tell them that because of what Jesus did for us on the cross, God never stops loving us. We may relate how God answered our prayer. We can write a letter, make a phone call or visit, or invite a lonely person to our home. Love finds many ways to give others a lift.

O God of all comfort, use us to cheer and encourage others. Amen.

Blessings in Disguise

Our light and momentary troubles are achieving for us an eternal glory that far outweighs them all.
2 Corinthians 4:17

People because of their sinful nature have no time for God. They are so busy digging in the dirt for dollars that they have no eyes for the Sun of Righteousness till God puts them on their back, where they can look in only one direction—upward. Only through suffering does God seem able to break the bands of selfishness, which tie us to this world, and to turn us to Jesus, our loving Savior, thus binding us to Himself with the eternal bonds of gratitude and love. Through affliction God shapes us into vessels of beauty for eternity.

As the stars are invisible by day but shine in all their glory at night, so God's promises shine most brightly in the night of adversity.

Our affliction is comparatively light and for a brief moment. The eternal glory awaiting us is of a weight beyond all comparison. Can we not afford to be patient for a season? God is faithful, who will not suffer us to be tempted above what we are able to bear. He promises: "I am your God. I will strengthen you and help you; I will uphold you with My righteous right hand." With God in charge, our afflictions are blessings in disguise.

Almighty God, for Jesus' sake grant us patience and courage in all our afflictions. Amen.

I Grow in Understanding

Yet Many Things

I have much more to say to you, more than you can now bear. *John 16:12*

This passage is one of the most wonderful statements in our Savior's farewell address. Sometimes we feel that He should have told us more about our days and years. We are puzzled by the times.

One truth should be perfectly clear to every believing heart. In His holy Word our Savior has told us everything we need to know for our salvation, life, and the time He has ordained between creation and judgment. His revelation is complete and final.

But it is also true that there are some things we do not know. Especially in hours of darkness and sorrow, our hearts cry out for more light. At such times it is warmly comforting to hear our Savior's gentle and loving voice. He knows, far better than we, just how much we should know about His thoughts and plans. He knows our breaking point—"more than you can now bear."

This is the last answer to the question that often rings in our hearts: Why? Why does God permit pain and sorrow and death? And His answer falls warm on our bewildered minds and crying hearts: "I have much more to say to you." In His own time and hour He will tell us those things, too.

Dear Jesus, be near me when I suffer pain and loss, and struggle with the "whys" of life. Do not leave me comfortless but assure me of Your constant love and care for me. Amen.

The Healer of Israel

Jesus went ... preaching the good news of the kingdom and healing every disease and sickness among the people. *Matthew 4:23*

We must always keep in mind that Jesus Christ came into the world to save sinners from their guilt and condemnation. He taught the people the true meaning of the Law and preached the Gospel of forgiveness and eternal life through faith in Him. But He also healed all manner of sickness and disease among the people. He did this because He loved them and had compassion on them. He also did this to prove that He is truly the Son of God and the Messiah of Israel, who had come to deliver all people from their sins and from eternal death.

For a time the multitudes followed Him in ever-increasing numbers. They came to Him with their diseased, the sick, the tormented, the insane, and the devil-possessed. He healed them all. Unhappily they were often more interested in His physical cures than in His spiritual redemption and His heavenly, eternal blessings.

We realize that Jesus comes to us to heal us from the spiritual disease of sin. Yet every earthly blessing, too, comes only from Him. Physicians, hospitals, institutions, clinics, and all medical science and discoveries are His gift to the world. Whenever we need medical attention, let us first ask Jesus to bless it. He will hear us.

Dear Lord, our Great Physician, bless all hospitals, institutions, and medical personnel. Help them to ease the pain of both body and mind. Amen.

I Lift Up My Eyes

I lift up my eyes to the hills—where does my help come from? *Psalm 121:1*

The more advanced a civilization becomes, the farther it draws away from God, because it inserts more and more apparatus between humankind and God. For instance, nowadays a person thinks he is in a position to say when he is sick: "I lift up my eyes to medical science—where does my help come from"; when she is grown old: "I lift up my eyes to Social Security"; when his country is threatened: "I lift up my eyes to the military."

All this apparatus has been inserted between ourselves and God, and God seems very far away. The tragedy is not that we have all these things, but that we have come to believe that because we have them we can dispense with God. God's gifts come between ourselves and Him.

This is the mark of a deeply religious man: he knows from where his help comes, and he lifts his eyes beyond the gifts to the Giver. This is the mark of a deeply religious woman: she never receives the gift without thanks and praise to the Giver. And this, too, marks her: she knows that because of Jesus Christ—because of His suffering, death, and resurrection—she belongs to God.

Open our eyes, Lord, that in the gifts we may never fail to see the Giver and never fail to give thanks for both.
Amen.

Renewable Power Source

Those who hope in the Lord will renew their strength. *Isaiah 40:31*

Centuries ago the Greeks began a competition we have come to celebrate as the Olympic Games. Every four years, spectators marvel at the agility, strength, and endurance of the participants. New records routinely replace those once thought impossible to break, as competitors push themselves to their limits.

Each of us, like even the fittest Olympic athlete, may become tired. Sometimes it is the ache of overworked muscles, and a nap or good night's sleep is all we need. Weariness can also result from the boredom of daily tasks, the stress of worry, or the concern of strained relationships. At those times, God tells us to look to Him for hope, renewal, and strength. Whenever our sins weaken us, the everlasting God is beside us to refresh us with His forgiveness for Christ's sake. He lifts the burden of guilt and gives us the power to get through the day.

Like rechargeable batteries, our Christian faith is recharged from the source of strength, God's Word. It renews our trust in God's promises and our hope in Him. Batteries run down and energy sources eventually are depleted, but God's eternal power and love will lift and strengthen us.

When we are tired or burdened with sin, Lord Jesus, refresh us with renewed hope in You. Amen.

Strength through Christ

**For Christ's sake, I delight in weaknesses … .
For when I am weak, then I am strong.**
2 Corinthians 12:10

What a strange statement! The apostle is using a form of speech known as a paradox, that is, a statement that seems to be absurd and contradictory but which is nevertheless true. Strength and weakness are indeed opposites; yet Saint Paul had frequently experienced in his own life that the consciousness of his own weakness had led to the accomplishment of great things in the kingdom of God. He declares, "I can do everything through Him who gives me strength" (Philippians 4:13).

When we are weak and realize it, we are prepared to come into possession of greater wisdom and strength than we have ever known before. Then God can step in and accomplish great things through us by His love and almighty power. When a vessel has been emptied, it is ready to be filled again, this time ready for something far more precious than what it contained before.

If our weakness leads us, who believe in Christ, to renew our strength by turning to the powerful Word of God, then the paradox of Saint Paul will manifest itself in our life. Then we too will say, "When I am weak, then I am strong."

Lord, by Your power prepare our hearts, and when we are weak give us Your strength. Amen.

Our Shield

He is my loving God and my fortress … my shield, in whom I take refuge. *Psalm 144:2*

From most ancient times the shield has been a weapon of defense among all nations. But how many have come to grief despite their shields! Ordinarily those who were stronger gained the mastery. But "those who trust in the Lord are like Mount Zion, which cannot be shaken but endures forever" (Psalm 125:1). Why? "For the Lord God is a sun and shield" (Psalm 84:11). The Lord is the protector and defender of His people against all evil in the seen and unseen world.

And this Lord is Jesus Christ, our incarnate Savior, unto whom the Father has given all power in heaven and in earth to rule all things in the interest of the church which He has purchased with His own blood. Lo, between the devil and the Christians, between the Christians and the Christless world, between the judgment of hell and the Christians, stands Jesus, our Lord, the almighty and immovable shield. He is the absolute protection, defense, refuge, fortress, shield, and buckler of His servants.

And so pleased is He with our Christian confidence in Him that He promises to let no evil befall us. He commands His angels to wait on us and to keep us in all situations of life. If we put our trust in Him, He will deliver us. He will answer our prayers. He will prolong our days on earth. He will show us His everlasting salvation.

O Lord Jesus, You are most high and almighty. Let us ever dwell under Your shadow and trust under Your wings. Amen.

Our Sun and Shield

The Lord God is a sun and shield; the Lord bestows favor and honor; no good thing does He withhold from those whose walk is blameless. *Psalm 84:11*

Scripture uses a variety of pictures to describe how God in His goodness provides for us. In Psalm 84 God is called a sun and a shield.

Think of how all of life is dependent on the sun. Without its warming rays nothing would grow. No food would be available to us or any other creatures. Plants reach out for the sun's light since it is their source of life.

God is like the sun to us since He both gives life and preserves it. Without the warmth of His grace to sustain us during life's hardships, we would eventually wither and die. His light guides our steps, illuminating the path to eternal life.

A shield protects the vital organs from arrows and the sword. With it, a soldier is able to ward off the attacks of the enemy.

God is like a shield in that He protects us from the flaming arrows of the Evil One—the devil—who seeks to destroy us. In many ways, God answers the petition of the Lord's Prayer, "Deliver us from evil." We may have no way of knowing how many times God has shielded us from the devil's attacks while we rested secure, unaware of the battle going on around us. Through faith in Christ, we are guarded by God's almighty power.

Lord God continue to warm us with Your love in Christ and protect us against all harm. Amen.

About Forgetting

I ... will remember their sins no more. *Jeremiah 31:34*

God doesn't remember. There is a thought to chill the soul. Does God forget His universe? Some think so, believing that He has gone off and left His creation to its own devices. But no! "Even the very hairs of your head are all numbered," said Jesus. Does God forget His children? We may forget Him, but He will not forget us. Even if a nursing mother would forget her child—a most unlikely event—God will not forget us. God remembers every kind and tender word you ever uttered, every genuine prayer you ever prayed. He remembers every unselfish gift you gave, every call you made on the sick, every glass of water you offered to the thirsting soul.

But God does not remember your sins. That's the good news. That really does take care of the year just past. God, who remembers when we all forget, has forgotten all our mistakes and errors, our false starts and wrong turns, the gloomy, negative things that we have said, and the foolish, childish things that we have done. He doesn't just ignore our sins, doesn't just wink an eye at them. He forgets them, because in Jesus, who took away our sins, there is nothing to remember.

He will remember our sin no more, and neither will we. That makes us free for new beginnings.

Thank You, God, for our forgiveness in Christ. Amen.

One Day at a Time

Each day has enough trouble of its own. *Matthew 6:34*

"Do not worry about tomorrow," says Jesus, "for tomorrow will worry about itself." Before we can live tomorrow, we must finish today. We need today because it prepares us for tomorrow. Limited as we are, we can handle only one day at a time because each day has its own assignment. If we borrow tomorrow's assignment, we will not have enough time to complete today's business.

"One day at a time" is all we can handle. When Jesus says, "Do not worry about tomorrow," He does not mean that we should not think about the future or that we should be careless in our approach to it. He simply tells us to concentrate on today and to leave tomorrow in His hands until He is ready to turn it over to us.

In following this procedure, God assures us that before He hands tomorrow over to us, He will wipe clean the slate of today's sins. We do not have to carry today's sins over into tomorrow. God loves us. His Son died for us. He would never handicap us with unforgiven sins.

"Each day has enough trouble of its own." We take care of today; God takes care of tomorrow.

Lord, make me realize that my burdens are not heavier than You know I can handle. Amen.

The Cure for Worry

You will keep in perfect peace him whose mind is steadfast, because he trusts in You. *Isaiah 26:3*

Our age is an age of anxiety. Many are engulfed in worry, depression, and despair. This brings on a lot of problems, both physical and spiritual. According to Dr. Charles Mayo, "Worry affects the circulation, the heart, the glands, the whole nervous system, and profoundly affects health." We can actually worry ourselves sick.

From a spiritual viewpoint, worry results from insufficient trust in our heavenly Father, who promises to care for us and provide for all our needs.

Now, we must distinguish between useless worry and loving concern. Sometimes what we call worry is really a healthy concern for someone. That type of concern can lead to prayer and deeds of kindness toward others.

May each of us resolve, "I will not spend a single minute in the fruitless fretting of worry. I will accept God's cure for anxious care." God's cure is this: "Rejoice in the Lord always. ... Do not be anxious about anything, but in everything, by prayer and petition, with thanksgiving, present your requests to God. And the peace of God, which transcends all understanding, will guard your hearts and your minds in Christ Jesus" (Philippians 4:4, 6–7).

Heavenly Father, so fill my heart with faith and trust in Your Son, Jesus Christ, that there is no room for worry. Amen.

Worry

Do not worry about your life, what you will eat or drink … . But seek first His kingdom and His righteousness. *Matthew 6:25, 33*

"Do not be anxious about anything," says Saint Paul. Yet what do we see? Why all this running, chasing, rushing, and hurrying? Worry is behind most of it.

What causes worry? Mostly meat and drink, clothing, shoes, etc., things that all come under the term "bread," for which we pray in the Lord's Prayer. What a Christian says in the Lord's Prayer is the conviction of his heart. To worry would be a contradiction. Worry, says Christ, is pagan; it means to doubt God's Word.

Worry is common to all. It is a universal evil. Worry needs no invitation. Worry has the key to every door.

Christians give wise attention to, and thoroughly plan, the trivialities as well as the important things in life. Having done so, they leave the rest to God. They are not to worry about it. God has not promised a tearless life nor exemption from duties and trials, but He has promised His children, young or old, weak or strong, grace enough to carry on each day. He has promised them forgiveness and does forgive their sins. That is enough.

The way to get rid of worry is to be loaded down with prayer. Fretting and restlessness will cease, and instead, peace will come into our troubled heart, a peace that no worry can bring us and no world can give us—the peace of Christ.

Dear Father, help us to cast all our anxiety on You and always remember that You care for us. Amen.

We Never Saw It This Way

This amazed everyone and they praised God, saying, "We have never seen anything like this!" *Mark 2:12*

These words occurred after Jesus had healed a paralyzed man. Jesus said to him: "Son, your sins are forgiven. … I tell you, get up, take your mat and go home."

This is one of 19 miracles recorded in Mark's gospel. Eight of these miracles show Jesus' power over disease, five show His power over nature, four His authority over demons, and two His conquest over death.

Jesus was always interested in the total person. His healing power was spiritual and physical. He knew that a person's needs could not be separated.

Always the purpose was the same: that God might be glorified.

Certainly the people who witnessed the miracles of Jesus were amazed. They declared: "We have never seen anything like this!"

We should say the same. No one has ever seen works like the works of Jesus. He continues to show forth His power and His love also today.

Through His Holy Word and the holy Sacraments He continues to call people to faith and keeps them in the faith. This is a special blessing of Sunday.

We are really amazed at God's continuing love and mercy as we worship Him.

O Lord Jesus Christ, bless our hearing of Your Word this day for the strengthening of our faith. Amen.

Merciful Father, Merciful Children

Be merciful, just as your Father is merciful. *Luke 6:36*

Perhaps no other attribute of God, besides His love, attracts us to Him as does His mercy. This quality distinguishes Him from all false gods. From the beginning to the end of the Bible, the endless procession of saints extols His mercy, repeating the refrain: "His mercy endures forever!"

His mercy caused Him to devise a plan of redemption that would reach every human being, moved Him to give His only Son as a ransom for all sinners, established His kingdom and His church, inspired the Scriptures, provided the sacraments, forgives all our transgressions and heals our diseases, and gives us peace, joy, and hope and time for repentance. Great is His mercy!

That indescribable, overflowing, and undeserved mercy melts away all our pride and arrogance, fills us with gratitude, and gives us a new birth, a new life, a new will, and a new viewpoint. Now we look at our fellow inhabitants of the earth with the eyes of our merciful Father.

And so the chain reaction goes on from God to us to others. As His mercy endures forever, so may our mercifulness—as that of His children—be likewise enduring.

Oh, give thanks to the Lord, for He is good! For His mercy endures forever. Amen.

Help for Doubt

When they saw Him, they worshiped Him; but some doubted. *Matthew 28:17*

"Why are you downcast, O my soul? Why so disturbed within me?" says the psalmist (42:5). Who has not experienced the pangs of doubt and depression? Sometimes these moods assail us when it makes no sense at all that we feel this way. Everything is fine, and we should be exuberant. But doubt creeps in, and we wonder why.

It is astounding that some should doubt after Jesus rose from the dead and showed Himself to the disciples. It makes no sense. But that is the way we are. These uncertain moods and doubts come over us; we know there is no good reason, but how do we fight them off? The psalmist helps us: "Put your hope in God, for I will yet praise Him, my Savior and my God" (42:5–6).

It is a comfort to know that Jesus had much experience with weak and doubting followers. And always He was kind and warm and receptive. He fulfilled the prophecy of Isaiah: "A bruised reed He will not break, and a smoldering wick He will not snuff out" (Isaiah 42:3). Jesus sought to sustain weak faith. Listen to the psalmist: "Put your hope in God, for I will yet praise Him, my Savior and my God." There is help for doubt.

Dear Lord Jesus, I am sorry for my doubts and fears. Please forgive me and hold me tight. Amen.

Portrait of a Doubter

[Thomas said to them,] "Unless I see the nail marks in His hands and put my finger where the nails were, ... I will not believe." *John 20:25*

Our name is Thomas, for we too have had our moments of doubt. We too have refused to believe the testimony of others, preferring sight to faith. We too have placed limits on God's ability to perform. We too have prescribed to God the exact conditions under which we'd accept His truths.

And because we have been where Thomas was, it is good to see Christ's sensitivity toward doubters. Jesus came to deal especially with the doubter. He did not reject him. Christ faced Thomas with love and forgiveness. He followed minutely the prescription that Thomas had laid down as absolute: "Unless ... I will not." Christ does not cast off even the most arrogant doubter with his or her unreasonable demands.

When tormenting and disquieting doubts besiege and assail us, we can with joy recall the understanding and completely forgiving attitude of our Lord in dealing with "doubting Thomas." We remember how He led him, step by step, to the glorious confession: "My Lord and my God," and then assured him that his doubts had been overcome and replaced by genuine faith. Oh, the blessed patience of Him who died for us and rose again!

Gracious and patient Savior,
we thank You for removing our
doubts and renewing us in our faith in You. Amen.

73

The Promise of Joy

I will see you again and you will rejoice, and no one will take away your joy. *John 16:22*

We have more to enjoy and more time for enjoyment than any generation before us. In fact, one of our inalienable rights, we have been told, is the pursuit of happiness—the opportunity to seek enjoyment. How can we miss? The truth is that happiness can be very elusive. Not enjoyment itself but the pursuit of it is very real—the constant struggle, the pulling, the straining. And the reward is often disillusionment.

In the Bible *joy* means something far more than wht we usually understand under *enjoyment* and *happiness*. The joy of which Jesus speaks has in it the note of victory over hardship, of conquest over defeat. He does not fool us into thinking that joy is the absence of sorrow, or that joy happens without sorrow. God is able to create joy out of sorrow. So Jesus tells His disciples that He will die and they will be sorrowful. But He also tells them that He will return to turn their sorrow into joy.

Jesus' resurrection victory means that God can lift up our sagging spirits and sinking bodies; that He can carry us through broken dreams and bitter experiences to a joy that no one can take from us. His promise of joy is sure.

Precious Savior, turn our sorrow into joy eternal. Amen.

74

Don't Waste Your Sorrows

Consider it pure joy, my brothers, whenever you face trials of many kinds. *James 1:2*

This Word of God is addressed to burden-bearers. Isn't it asking too much to extend a hand of welcome to trials and afflictions? Usually we do the opposite. We complain bitterly. We think that we are being treated unfairly.

There is a right way and a wrong way to respond to trials. The right way brings benefits and blessings. The wrong way means that our sorrows are wasted and the potential of great blessings is forfeited.

Even when God allows sorrows and tears, His love for us is sure and strong. "Though He brings grief, He will show compassion, so great is His unfailing love. For He does not willingly bring affliction or grief to the children of men" (Lamentations 3:32–33).

David put it this way: "Though You have made me see troubles, many and bitter, You will restore my life again; from the depths of the earth You will again bring me up" (Psalm 71:20). "Those who sow in tears will reap with songs of joy" (126:5). Tears are liquid anguish. They speak a language God understands. Jesus said, "Your grief will turn to joy" (John 16:20). By His atonement He made this possible.

Dear Lord, even when the burdens are heavy, You are saying, "I love you." Amen.

Faith Grasps God's Presence

He saw the disciples straining at the oars, because the wind was against them. About the fourth watch of the night He went out to them, walking on the lake.
Mark 6:48

"Go in the boat to the other side of the lake," Jesus instructed His disciples. "I'll meet you later." Don't you wonder if *they* wondered: "How will *He* get to the other side?"

Jesus saw that His disciples were struggling in the turbulent seas, so He walked out onto the water toward them. They cried out in fear at the sight of Him, thinking He was a ghost. But Jesus spoke: "Take courage! It is I. Don't be afraid."

The circumstances of life may frighten us. We may have to face someone with the truth after we've lied. We may be awaiting the results of a biopsy, or the outcome of a crucial decision. You name it.

Jesus is there for those who believe in Him. He sees our distress and comes walking toward us with His divine power. He comes to calm the storm. He Himself walks on the waters, conquering the dangers that terrify us. The forces of nature, the circumstances that cause our anxiety, even the very heavens and earth are under His command. He tells us to have no fear, for it is He; "I am with you," He says.

Lord Jesus, comfort me by Your presence and still the storms in my life. Amen.

Don't Be Afraid!

It is I; don't be afraid. *John 6:20*

Fear is a universal human emotion. We live in constant exposure to fear. Young children often fear darkness. Many children today also fear their parents will be divorced. Teenagers worry about what others think about them. Adults live in fear of the unknown, of bad memories, of physical pain, of aging, of finances, of broken relationships, of their inabilities, of death.

The struggle to combat fear is something we all must face, because we all sin and we all fear. But there is One who came to do battle with fear: the Lord Jesus Christ. He who takes away sin through His death and resurrection also alleviates our fears.

Jesus often said to people, "Don't be afraid!" In the midst of troubling times in our lives, He comes to us with His calming peace. He forgives our sins and brings us comfort and compassion. He feeds us in His Holy Supper. By faith in Him and through the Spirit's power we conquer fear when it starts to get a grip on our lives. The psalmist writes, "I will fear no evil." Why not? "You are with me!" Jesus Christ is with us. We need not be afraid, for we place our trust in Him.

Dear Jesus, my Savior, thank You for being with me. With You I never need be afraid. Amen.

The Wise Master Builder

You are ... God's building. *1 Corinthians 3:9*

To erect a building, we must use a hammer and a saw, we must trim and cut. If we would not trim a single stone or saw a single board, we could not build a house.

We are God's building. God builds us for a godly life in this world and for eternal life in the world to come. To do this, God must cut and saw and trim. We do not always think of it in this way. We call it misfortune, hard luck, trouble; yet God is building us for time and eternity through pain and suffering, through sorrow and loss. God is the wise master builder, who never makes mistakes.

Though God builds through pain and loss, He is very near to us, to strengthen us and to encourage us through His Word when the going is hard. Are we worried? He takes us into His Word and invites us to cast all our care upon Him "because He cares for you" (1 Peter 5:7). Are we sick? He says: "I am the Lord, who heals you" (Exodus 15:26). Are we troubled in conscience? He promises: "The blood of Jesus, His Son, purifies us from all sin" (1 John 1:7). Are we facing death? He promises: "I am the resurrection and the life" (John 11:25).

Heavenly Father, build us as You will, and grant us grace to understand and to praise You. Amen.

The Hand of the Lord

Which of all these does not know that the hand of the Lord has done this? *Job 12:9*

Some years ago the most exquisite diamond in the history of the world was found in Africa. Soon it was presented to the king of England to adorn the crown of state. The monarch sent it to Amsterdam to be cut by an expert stonecutter. The latter took the precious gem, cut a notch in it, and struck a hard blow with his instrument. Now the superb jewel lay in his hand, split in two pieces. What recklessness! What waste! What carelessness!

Not at all! For weeks that blow had been planned. Models and drawings were made of the stone. Its quality, its defects, its cleavage lines had been studied with care. The blow was but the climax of the lapidary's skill. By it he brought the stone to its most perfect radiance and splendor. From the two halves came the two magnificent gems that the skilled eye of the cutter saw hidden in the stone.

Redeemed through Christ, we are God's precious possession. Yet sometimes He lets a stinging blow fall upon our lives. We cry out in agony: it all seems an appalling error. But no, for to God we are the most precious jewel in the world. Some day we shall emblazon the diadem of our King. By His grace, the blow that falls only fits us better for the splendor of the crown of His glory.

Lord Jesus Christ, discipline us in love and truly fit us for the crown of life. Amen.

Casting All Our Cares upon God

**Humble yourselves … under God's mighty hand … .
Cast all your anxiety on Him because
He cares for you.** *1 Peter 5:6–7*

Life has its cares and concerns. Illness, loneliness, grief, financial woes, family problems, and national and international problems.

Saint Peter, writing under the inspiration of the Holy Spirit, has a good word for us today as we struggle with life in the middle of a busy week: "Cast all your anxiety on Him." We are not alone. God sent Jesus, who gives us courage, for He cared enough to go to the cross for us and die for all of our sins. This same Jesus can give us strength as we struggle with life. We can't often control whether or not we lose our job, but in Christ we can decide on other options for our life. We can't control whether or not we get seriously ill, but in Christ we can make a heroic adjustment to our illness. We can be weak, yet—in Christ—strong.

Christ is on our side. He gives us power. In moments of doubt and desperation, in moments filled with fear, we can cast all our anxiety upon Jesus. We can thank our great and good God for all of His bountiful blessings, both physical and spiritual. We can look to the mighty hand of God, which holds a multitude of divine gifts for us.

*Dear Lord Jesus, we thank You that we can cast all our anxiety upon You, for You bore all our sins and griefs.
Amen.*

Courage from Christ

Immediately [Jesus] spoke to them and said, "Take courage! It is I. Don't be afraid." *Mark 6:50*

Medals are given to courageous heroes who rescue people from burning buildings, icy lakes, or wrecked cars. There are other forms of courage that may not be noticed by the news media.

This may be the case with Christ's disciples. The heroes of faith have greater strength because they have Jesus with them, supplying the confidence and bravery they need.

We know that Jesus promised courage to those who were afraid. "Take courage! It is I!" He said to His terrified disciples as He walked towards them on the water.

Jesus also supplies courage to a father going from place to place to apply for a job so that he can feed his family, to a mother who continues to care for her children after the death of her husband, to a boy defending his small brother from a bully every day on the way to school, or to a girl who day after day is shunned by others at school because of the reputation of her family.

These unsung heroes remember Jesus' courage when He let unbelievers nail Him to the cross. It is Jesus' death and resurrection that gives us the courage to live as He expects. When He appeared to His mourning disciples, He gave them courage to spread His message. So it is with us.

Help us, Lord, to tell Your message of
love and forgiveness.
Amen.

The Little Things

Catch for us the foxes, the little foxes that ruin the vineyards, our vineyards that are in bloom.
Song of Solomon 2:15

Little things have the ability to destroy the big things. Little foxes spoil the grape vines; little germs ruin health; a little hole in the bottom of a dam causes floods; little snowflakes stopped Napoleon from conquering Russia.

Little things also have the ability of becoming big things. Everything is made of tiny atoms which cannot even be seen. Many moments make a total day, many days make a year, and many years make a lifetime. A small acorn becomes a mighty oak tree. A little faith will move mountains. A grain of mustard seed becomes the kingdom of God, and a little flock becomes the Christian church. This is the miracle of little things. And who will despise the day of small things?

The greatest miracle of all is that a little child should be born in Bethlehem as the Savior of all humankind. He is the mighty God, the everlasting Father, the Prince of Peace, our great Savior. God indeed works wonders with little things.

Lord God, make us great enough to appreciate the little things entrusted to us every day. Above all, may we appreciate and accept Your great love in our little lives, through Christ. Amen.

How Much Faith?

I do believe; help me overcome my unbelief!
Mark 9:24

Here was a poor, distracted father, around whom a great crowd had gathered. On the ground lay his son, rolling about, foaming at the mouth, possessed by an evil spirit that had tormented him for many years. Then Jesus drew near, and they brought the boy to Him. The father cried: "If You can do anything, take pity on us and help us."

Our Lord's reply put the father's real need where it belongs: "Everything is possible for him who believes." The father saw it: "I do believe"—but not as I should. Of how many of us is this still true! Perfect faith is wonderful, but who among us has it?

Yet this is not to lead us into despair. Let us begin with what we *are* and use what faith we have. This was what the father did. He could not fail to see his shortcomings and His need. He did not fail to do what he should do—seek from his Lord a stronger faith.

As we meet with Him in His Word, we see anew the wonder of our Lord's power and love. Let us begin with where we are and meet with Him often even though our days may seem untroubled and calm with no cloud to darken them. We still need the Savior every hour.

Lord, save us from the blunder of believing that the faith we have need not be strengthened through the Gospel. Amen.

God Has His Purpose

Our God is in heaven; He does whatever pleases Him.
Psalm 115:3

There are plenty of things going on nowadays that seem to be the devil's handiwork—things that make our times look like "the hour and the power of the dark." Yet even in the hour of darkness God has His purpose.

Often it is precisely in the hour and the power of darkness that God has His moment. It was so at Calvary. In the very moment when Satan was making his most powerful impact up there on that awful hill, God was fulfilling His most glorious purpose and plan for our salvation. God took hold of Satan's finest hour and used it to crush him forever.

What this means is that our desperate moments, when terribly crushing things keep happening to us, are not out of control but are being turned by the all-powerful One Himself into the great benedictions of our lives.

Maybe we can't see that at the moment. Maybe we can't see it in our lives. But surely we can see it in the life of Christ, and that is quite enough. God has His purpose. He had His purpose in what happened to Christ. He has His purpose in what happens to us.

God of Abraham, Isaac, and Jacob, even in the hour and the power of darkness, with our hand firmly in Yours, we will walk with confidence. Amen.

The Control of Unavoidable Issues

[For He] has put everything under His feet.
1 Corinthians 15:27

These are royal words written about a kingly conqueror, our risen Lord. God has put all things under His feet, the blessed feet that walked the dark redemption road for us. Especially when the circumstances of our lives seem so far beyond our puny power to control, it is good to know this.

For there are so many things in our life in which our choice is never asked, from our cradle to our last bed. Testings, heartache and loss, puzzling and distressing times all come to us. And they will come again. Yet to try to hide one's face from these inevitable issues is not the way to peace.

Rather we are to remember that He who died for us now has all things under those feet of His which were pierced for us. We may not be able to alter what comes to us without our desire, perhaps. But in the faith that God has put all things under the feet of Christ, we can trust in His unfailing power and His unwavering purpose to transform from curse to blessing those great issues that we *cannot* remove and that He *will not* remove. We may say with the psalmist: "The Lord is close to the brokenhearted and saves those who are crushed in spirit" (34:18). So we can hide daily in the Rock of Ages and feel safe.

O Christ, Ruler over all things, rule my life in love and power. Amen.

Burned Out?

We do not know what we ought to pray for, but the Spirit Himself intercedes for us with groans that words cannot express. *Romans 8:26*

In our society people are expected to be achievers. Sometimes the pressure and competition become too great. A person reaches the breaking point, and he or she can't function effectively anymore. We call that burnout.

It's happened before. Moses, the patient leader of Israel, had more than he could take. He said, "I am not able to carry this people alone; the burden is too heavy for me."

Even the great apostle Paul became mentally and physically exhausted. He was so worn out that he could not even pray properly. When he reached the point of utter weariness, Paul knew that God would not forsake him. It was at that moment that the Spirit of God stepped in to pray for him.

Have we reached our breaking point? Do we feel like we can't take it anymore? Like we want to run away from our cares and responsibilities? Like we can't see God through our pain? That's when God's Spirit takes over. The Lord does not abandon us. He will say for us the prayers we can't utter ourselves.

That we can believe. That we can hold on to. That precious promise is ours!

Lord, I spread out my hands to You. When You hide your face, when I have no strength and my soul is full of troubles, I cry to You. Amen.

Waiting for the Lord

Those who hope in the Lord will renew their strength. They will soar on wings like eagles; they will run and not grow weary, they will walk and not be faint. *Isaiah 40:31*

Isaiah reminds us in chapter 40 that "the Lord is the everlasting God, the Creator of the ends of the earth. He will not grow tired or weary, and His understanding no one can fathom."

With His own almighty power He strengthens those who are faint. We often grow weary on our journey through life, both physically and spiritually. We get tired of telling people the good news of our salvation without seeming success. We grow weary when we plead for what we think is the right thing for us along life's path, and apparently there is no answer from God.

But let's look at the Lord's promise in this word of the prophet. When we patiently wait for the Lord, He will renew our strength even as our tired bodies are renewed through a good night's sleep. Just as an eagle flaps its big wings as it mounts high up in the air, so the Lord gives us the strength to rise above our wearisome attitudes and serve Him with renewed love and zeal.

Let us rejoice anew in our redemption in Christ and share this joy with the people around us. Our sufferings cannot compare with the joy of our salvation.

Lord, renew our strength when we become weak and faint, and uphold us with Your Spirit. Amen.

Hands of Blessing

**Joshua son of Nun was filled with the spirit of wisdom
because Moses had laid his hands on him.**
Deuteronomy 34:9

"What happened to Your hand?" a little girl asks Jesus
in a present-day picture of Christ with children. Her question gives the picture its title. She is looking at the imprint
of the nail by which Jesus was fixed to the cross.

The scars in Jesus' hands were marks of His sacrificial
act of love. He had given Himself into the death of the
cross to be "the Lamb of God, who takes away the sin of
the world!"

Our Savior had often used these same hands to serve
men. He had laid them on men to heal them in their sickness. These same hands had lifted up the daughter of Jairus
from her sleep of death. These same hands had been raised
in blessing over little children whom Jesus loved.

God's hands of blessing rest on us when we trust Him
to forgive us all our sins through the atoning death of
Christ.

Moses used his hands to bless Joshua, and God
bestowed the blessing in the gift of the spirit of wisdom.

We may use our hands for evil or for good. They may
become tools of violence or instruments of charity. They
may destroy or they may build. Do our hands bear the
marks of service and love as did our Lord's?

*Take my hands and let them do
Works that show my love for You. Amen.*

Sympathy

For we do not have a high priest who is unable to sympathize with our weaknesses. *Hebrews 4:15*

The word *sympathy* comes from two Greek words that mean "to share suffering." To sympathize with another person means to understand the pain the other person is feeling and to actually experience the suffering.

Jesus demonstrated sympathy so often while He was here on earth. His compassion was overwhelming when Lazarus died. He so completely shared in the suffering of the sisters Mary and Martha that He wept with them. And those who saw Him said, "See how He loved him!"

We, too, are loved—loved so much that Jesus is willing to share in our suffering. No matter what our problems or trials or pains, Jesus understands them. We do not have to experience them alone. What a great comfort!

Having known His sympathy, we also know how important it is to sympathize with others. The pain we have felt equips us to share in the sufferings of others. It is said that the kindest hearts are the ones that have known sorrow. How true! With Jesus as your example—and as your Redeemer giving you strength—may you give to others the great and kind gift of sympathy.

Lord, as You share in our suffering, so may we share in the suffering of others. Amen.

Messages from God

I have a message from God for you. *Judges 3:20*

This is what Ehud, the Benjamite, said to Eglon, king of Moab. Have we had any message from God? We have had not only one, but many. Every Bible in our homes says to us: "I have a message from God for you." The Bible has a message for us on the most important subject of all, the way back to God, which all sinners must travel. It tells us that Jesus said: "I am the way and the truth and the life. No one comes to the Father except through Me" (John 14:6). If we have been careless, the Bible has a word of warning; if we have been troubled, it has a message of comfort; if we have been worried, it tells us what to do with our cares. The Bible has a message from God for us for every condition of life.

God sometimes sends us messages in other ways. He speaks to us through the providential manner in which He orders our lives. Have we been especially prosperous in our affairs, in our business, in our family? Have there been long seasons of joy and gladness? God is speaking to us. Or the messengers may have been draped in black. There may have been losses and reverses, sickness and death. They, too, say to us: "We have a message from God for you." Then, like Samuel of old, let us always say: "Speak, for Your servant is listening."

By Your Spirit, O Lord, bless our reading and hearing of Your Word and whatever other means You use to speak to us so we may always learn to know and do Your will. In Jesus' name we pray. Amen.

Knowing Hereafter

Jesus replied, "You do not realize now what I am doing, but later you will understand." *John 13:7*

There is a Hebrew legend that tells of a rabbi journeying on a mule through a wild country. His only companion was a rooster whose shrill crowing at sunrise awoke him to his devotions. He came to a small town at nightfall and sought shelter, but the inhabitants turned him away. Outside the village he found a cave in which to sleep. He lit his lamp before retiring, but a gust of wind blew out the light. During the night a wolf killed his rooster and a lion devoured his mule. Early in the morning he went to the town to see if he could buy some food. To his surprise he found no one alive. A band of robbers during the night had plundered the settlement and killed all the inhabitants.

"Now I understand my troubles," said the rabbi. "If the townspeople had received me, I would now be dead. Had not my rooster and mule been killed, their noise or the light of my lamp would have revealed my hiding place. God has been good to me." In similar manner, the troubles and reverses of life are intended to direct you and me to put full faith and trust in the Savior, whose redemptive work secured our eternal good.

All-knowing Lord, help us to trust You in all circumstances of life, even in those we do not now understand. Amen.

Our Hiding Place

Each man will be like a shelter from the wind and a refuge from the storm. *Isaiah 32:2*

Some, who lived in the "dust bowl" of our country years ago remember the relentless wind and the heavens dark with dust; until in helplessness and despair they packed what they could in their cars and fled from their homes.

In the days of Isaiah the prophet the people lived where the desert was not far off. And so his words were clear: some shelter, some hiding place, some great ledge of rock to give men its quiet shelter when the whistling blasts of sand blew was their only hope.

The winds beat about our lives, too—the winds of sorrow in deep bereavement; the winds of fear in time of peril; the winds of affliction when we suffer in mind or body. But most of all the blast of sin beats hard to drive us to the death of our souls and the destruction of our hopes.

God through Isaiah encourages His people with a picture of the Messianic kingdom where "each man will be like a shelter from the wind and a refuge from the storm." In God's kingdom His redeemed will reflect the Messiah, who is the true source of blessing and protection. Isaiah believed in the Messiah to come. Seven hundred years later this man was born, and then He died as the blast of our sins beat upon Him. But He became our perpetual hiding place from the wind. Who was He? Jesus, the Rock of Ages.

O Savior, Rock of Ages, let me hide myself in You. Amen.

Jesus Means Peace

I have told you these things, so that in Me you may have peace. In this world you will have trouble. But take heart! *John 16:33*

Two artists each produced a painting to depict the idea of peace. One painted a picture of a quiet lake beside a mountain. Not a breeze was stirring. Not a ripple disturbed the quiet waters. All was silent.

The second artist painted a roaring waterfall with a mighty oak hanging over it. On a limb bending over the turbulent waters, nearly in reach of the rising spray, was a tiny bird sitting unperturbed on her nest. In the midst of the mighty roar, surrounded by frightful danger, the bird was secure.

Both artists agreed the second picture depicted a higher conception of peace. It also is an excellent portrayal of the peace found in Jesus.

In this world we are surrounded by manifold dangers and evils that threaten our security and deprive us of joy. We see broken hearts and graves watered with tears. Yet Jesus bestows on us a peace that transcends and overcomes this world. His words of forgiving mercy comfort us, even in the face of death. His peace passes all understanding and will sustain us for all eternity.

Heavenly Father, reassure us and all Your people with Your surpassing peace in Christ Jesus. Amen.

When God Says Nothing

**Do not turn a deaf ear to me. For if You remain silent,
I will be like those who have gone down to the pit.**
Psalm 28:1

Does it bother you that God never seems to say anything? There is plenty for Him just now to talk about. If only He'd come out and prove by some word that He is there and with that word resolve the things that are so wrong about His world. But God says nothing. Why?

There is a silence on the part of God that condemns us. We cannot pass off lightly what we have done to break His heart. But listen, you can always take whatever it is that you have done and lay it before your God and ask Him for forgiveness. And if you do, God will tell you, "Your sins are all forgiven." If God is silent with you, you can break that silence by asking Him to forgive your sins.

Do not interpret God's silence as a sign that He has ceased to care. Remember He is the One who left His throne in heaven and exchanged it for a bed of straw at Christmas time because He cares; He is the One who let the soldiers mock and beat and crucify Him because He cares; He is the One who bore our griefs and carried our sorrows because He cares. We mustn't believe He doesn't care. Oh, yes, He cares, even when it seems He says nothing!

*Give us faith, O blessed Savior, to look up and see that
You are there. Amen.*

Discipline Brings Blessings

No discipline seems pleasant at the time, but painful. Later on, however, it produces a harvest of righteousness and peace. *Hebrews 12:11*

Discipline is not a pleasant word, raising thoughts of discomfort, often of punishment. As God's dear children we cannot miss its meaning. "The Lord disciplines those He loves," says the holy writer, pointing even to God's redeeming love in Jesus. Discipline is training. Often it tests our submission to the divine will, tries our patience and piety, even our faith in the Savior, who has promised to sustain us.

We remember how God's servant Job was chastened—and Saint Paul (2 Corinthians 12: 1–10) and the Christians at Smyrna (Revelation 2:8–11). From them we learn that if we do not feel the discomfort of discipline, we can derive no profit from it. If it were not painful at the moment, it could not result in blessings later.

But there is a "later." Discipline is like a tree. It requires time and cultivation to produce the ripened fruit of peace and righteousness. It always contains the fruitful seed of future joys. It is the spring pruning of our vines that, in God's judgment, is needed to make us fruitful. May we wait patiently in discipline for the later blessings! They will surely come.

Lord, discipline me in Your love, but enable me always to see its purpose so that I may draw closer to my Savior. Amen.

Into All Truth

When He, the Spirit of truth, comes, He will guide you into all truth. *John 16:13*

The work of the Holy Spirit in the world is to lead us into all truth. This is what our Lord said the Comforter would do for all believers. As long as the world lasts, we never have to be uncertain about anything belonging to our salvation. He will lead us into the truth.

Our Savior kept His promise. Yesterday, today, and tomorrow the Holy Spirit speaks to us constantly in the Word of God. When we hear the Word during worship or read it in our devotion time, the Comforter reaches through the words, takes us by the hand, and leads us into all truth.

And this truth will never die. Changing circumstances of life and history cannot touch it. It is proof against every storm. It is sure in the day of life and unbroken in the hour of death. It is the one great, unchanging fact in a world of change and decay.

It is always a dark hour for humanity when they forget the truth of God. That has happened in our time. We who believe have the responsibility to know the truth, to speak it whenever and wherever we can, and to bring it, with everything in our power, to the dark and lonely hearts of all people.

Preserve Your Word and preaching,
The truth that makes us whole,
The mirror of Your glory,
The pow'r that saves the soul. Amen.

Hold Me, Please!

Your right hand sustains me; You stoop down to make me great. *Psalm 18:35*

At two o'clock in the morning a little child is awakened by the discomfort of a high temperature and pleads: "Mommy, please hold me!" How comforting such holding is! The child is still ill, but wrapped in Mother's arms, healing, rest, and sleep come more easily.

All of us find ourselves at times in a night of pain and suffering, which leaves us feeling crushed and overwhelmed. Then we reach for the precious Word of our Lord and receive its assurances into our hearts. There comes the realization that we may join David in exclaiming: "Your right hand sustains me; you stoop down to make me great."

Each time the Holy Spirit revives our faith, we realize that we are being held, sustained by the mighty hand of our God. Each time, through Word and Sacrament, we are impressed with the glorious truth of the forgiveness of our sins for the sake of the sacrifice of the Lord Jesus Christ. We know that our Lord is stooping down to make us great. We have good reason for pleading with our Lord: "Please hold me!" As we are held in the forgiving arms of our Lord, we are encouraged to hold others by giving them the great word of forgiveness.

Dear Lord Jesus, You are strong in grace and forgiveness. Please hold us in Your strength. Amen.

Don't Worry

Therefore do not worry about tomorrow, for tomorrow will worry about itself. *Matthew 6:34*

It requires only a little reflection to convince ourselves that worry is entirely useless. Worry changes nothing. It cannot solve our problems, correct our mistakes, add to our income, alleviate our pain, improve our health, or prolong our life. On the contrary, worry is harmful. It robs us of our energy and generates fear and frustration, despondency and despair. Besides harming us, it aggravates those who live with us and makes life unpleasant for them.

Above all, worry is sinful because it ignores God's help. It assumes that we are the helpless and hopeless victims of circumstance and that our lives are controlled by blind fate.

Worry is caused by insecurity. As such it should have no place in our lives as Christians. For if our heavenly Father so loved us that He gave His own dear Son to die for our sins, will He not with Him also freely give us the lesser things we need?

Christ's prescription for the cure of worry is to behold the birds of the air, to consider the lilies of the field, and to learn of them how carefree and joyous life can be when we cast all our anxiety on Him who cares for us.

The Lord is my Shepherd, I shall not be in want. Amen.

A Divided Mind

No one can serve two masters. Either he will hate the one and love the other, or he will be devoted to the one and despise the other. *Matthew 6:24*

Worry fragments the mind. A divided mind keeps a person from doing anything wholeheartedly. It causes inefficiency.

None of us needs to be taught to worry. It comes naturally. But it is helpful to know what causes worry. Worry is often the result of a divided mind. And indecision squanders our energies.

Someone drew a cartoon of a donkey standing between two haystacks. The aroma of the hay tantalized the hungry donkey. He would look toward one haystack and start in that direction; then he would think of the other haystack, look back, and start toward it. The outcome suggested by the cartoon was that the poor donkey, standing between the two fragrant haystacks, starved to death simply because he could never make up his mind.

A divided mind may eventually destroy us. That is why we need to have our mind fixed on the Lord. God fills our minds with serenity because He has made it possible to be at peace with Him, with ourselves, and with others. He has removed the guilt of sin. Through Christ He has provided forgiveness for all our sins. The God of peace helps us to overcome a divided mind.

Lord, unite our minds with Your love through Christ.
Amen.

The Faithfulness of God

God is faithful. *1 Corinthians 10:13*

These are tremendous words. They are like bedrock. They are like the thick rocky layers builders look for when they seek to erect a skyscraper.

No one can read the Bible's story of humankind intelligently without realizing that God is faithful. We may not be able to understand how this faithfulness can be. We look back over the long history of humankind, or even over the history of those nations who have called themselves God's people, and see how often they have been faithful only to their own sinful selves. One would think that God would have long since called it all off and turned from them.

But we need not look this far abroad to find examples. We need only look back upon our own lives. We have loved, indeed, and been loyal, so often only to our own selves; yet God has never broken faith with us.

One thing He has allowed: He has allowed His people to know the testing of trials. But there is another thing He has not permitted: that we be tried beyond our power. He is faithful; He lets us know our weaknesses. He tests us, but He does not break us. He tries us, but He does not leave us or forsake us. He leaves us always stronger than we were. Through all these trials God wants to lead us to the cross to give perfect healing.

Dear Father, hear us when we cry to You and cause our troubles to produce in us blessings; we ask this for the sake of Your dear Son. Amen.

In the Shadow

In the shadow of His hand He hid me. *Isaiah 49:2*

Sometimes the glare of a sunny summer day is too brilliant for our eyes. Instinctively we move into the shadows, lest we lose the ability to discern the delicate shades of color or to appreciate natural tints.

In the exercise of His infinite wisdom our God reminds us that it is not good for our spiritual vision to remain constantly in the sunlight of prosperity. There we are often blinded to the full measure of life, losing both our understanding of divine mercy and the need to have sympathy for others. God's grace is often best viewed in the shadows—the shadowed chamber of sickness, the shadowed house of mourning, the shadowed life from which the sunlight of earthly joy is gone.

It is God who leads us into the shadow. But it is "the shadow of His hand." There are lessons He teaches us there. The light of His loving and glorious face is clearly seen in the dark chamber. In life's shadows we grow in Him. There are beautiful flowers that bloom in the shade—flowers that could not grow in the sun. In the shadows of life the Savior reaches us best with the glory of His forgiving love. There He says: "I have redeemed you; you are Mine."

Lord, let us dwell in the shadow of Your grace so that we may see Your glory. Amen.

The Rock That Is Higher Than I

I call as my heart grows faint; lead me to the rock that is higher than I. *Psalm 61:2*

To what does a drowning man cling when he feels that death is only a moment away? To his watersoaked briefcase which he is hugging to his breast? To his wet clothing which can finally only drag him down to a watery grave? No! He reaches out and away from himself to something solid and immovable—something to which he can hold fast despite the undertow of the swirling water.

It was such a crisis moment that made David cry out: "Lead me to the rock that is higher than I." It is significant how often David refers to the Lord as his rock. He says: "The Lord is my rock, my fortress and my deliverer" (Psalm 18:2). Again, "He alone is my rock and my salvation" (Psalm 62:2).

David knew that his own heart was not reliable in moments of crisis. When the storms of life were upon him, he dared not look in (there was only doubt, uncertainty, guilt, and despair); but he could always look out and up to the rock that was higher than he. That rock was the changeless Lord and His changeless Word. In that rock is safety, in that rock is salvation not only for David, but also for you and for me. That is why we pray:

Rock of Ages, cleft for me,
Let me hide myself in Thee. Amen.

Too Low!

I lift up my eyes to the hills—where does my help come from? My help comes from the Lord, the Maker of heaven and earth. *Psalm 121:1–2*

Some people do not look high enough. This is tragic. Think what happens when we look too low. If we look only at our troubles, our difficulties, our problems, our sicknesses, our trials, we shall finally throw up our hands in despair. The troubles of life will loom so large that we shall lose courage and say, "What's the use?"

The secret of the Christian life is to look up. "I lift up my eyes to the hills—where does my help come from? My help comes from the Lord, the Maker of heaven and earth." When we lift our gaze above the troubles of life and look up to the Lord, we find new strength and courage. As we lift up our eyes, we see the almighty God, who is also our loving heavenly Father. We lift up our eyes "to the hills," particularly the hill of Calvary, and see the great love of God as He gave His only Son to die for our sins and to accomplish our eternal salvation. We lift up our eyes and see the Good Shepherd leading us every step of the way through life until we reach heaven.

Let us not look too low! Rather hour after hour and day after day let us lift up our eyes to the Lord. So shall we find the burdens of life lighter and the strength inside us greater!

Lord, we lift up our eyes always to see You, our Father, through Jesus, our Savior. Amen.

What Lies Beyond

Thomas said to him, "Lord, we don't know where you are going, so how can we know the way?" *John 14:5*

For travelers, a map is as basic and vital as the alphabet. Explorers have relied on maps to open up new worlds. The maker of an early map of America wrote across unknown and unexplored regions such frightful comments as, "Here there are fiery scorpions," "Here there are dangerous giants," and "Here there are dragons." A brave explorer, who was also a Christian, crossed out all these warnings and wrote in large letters, "Here is God!"

Times come when God seems far away. Troubles and worries overwhelm our lives. Our sin has created a vast chasm between us and God. We may feel like we are lost without a map.

Yet through Jesus, God comes near to us and shows us the way. "God was reconciling the world to Himself in Christ, not counting men's sins against them" (2 Corinthians 5:19). Jesus assures us, "I am the way." Take a map, place your finger on the place where you are, and write, "God is here!" Take your calendar, with future scheduled events that worry you, and write, "God is here!" For He says, "I will never leave you nor forsake you" (Joshua 1:5). The way to God is Jesus Christ. He has gone ahead to prepare a place for us, and has come back to lead us there.

Be with me, Lord Jesus, every minute of each day, and every place I may go. Amen.

The Meaning of Trust

Commit your way to the Lord; trust in Him, and He will do this. *Psalm 37:5*

When traveling in the Far East, one sees many interesting sights, especially toward evening. It is interesting to observe the people as they return home from a day at the market. Some return with heavy packs on their backs. Others drive half-filled, three-wheel put-puts. Still others lumber along with a beast of burden pulling a near-empty wagon.

Sometimes one will even see a cart without a driver. At first it appears as if the cart and the animal are all alone. A closer look, however, reveals the driver sound asleep in the cart. If we would ask one of the villagers why the driver is asleep, he would answer, "Why not? The animal knows the way home. And he'll take the driver right to his house."

If only we could relax like that and have more trust and confidence! And why shouldn't we? We know the answer and have the solution—Jesus Christ. He traveled our way before. He knows the way. In fact, He is the way. He leads. None of us can reach the Father's home but by faith in Him.

Men often trust animals but not one another. Should we not have more trust in God than what the farmer has in his animal?

Lord, we commit our way to You and trust in You, for You are the way to our Father's heavenly home. Amen.

Listen As the Good Shepherd Speaks!

My sheep listen to My voice. *John 10:27*

A young boy who had been blind from birth underwent surgery which the doctors were confident would give him vision for the first time in his life. You can imagine the excitement of his mother as she waited for the bandages to be removed. How would her son react the first time he saw her? The bandages came off, and the boy could indeed see. But when he looked at the woman at the side of his bed, there was no smile, no sign of recognition. It was only when his mother spoke that he smiled, and the tears of joy flowed.

You see, he had never seen his mother. But he had learned to love and trust her voice. That's the way it is with Jesus and His sheep. We have not seen, but we believe. We live by faith, not by sight. We, too, love and trust the voice of our Good Shepherd.

"My sheep listen to My voice," Jesus says. And we know that's a voice we can trust. The voice that says, "Come to Me" and "Believe in Me" does not hold out an empty promise. Heaven and earth will pass away, but not His Word. What He says is based on what He did on the cross and at the empty tomb. As His sheep, let us hear and follow that voice. It will never fail us.

Lord, open now my heart to hear,
And through Your Word to me draw near. Amen.

(From *LW* © 1982 CPH.)

Real Security

My sheep listen to My voice … . I give them eternal life, and they shall never perish; no one can snatch them out of My hand. *John 10:27–28*

Security is important to us. Many people today have security systems to protect their homes. Businesses hire security guards. People in our nation are hoping Social Security will be there for them.

While we all need and want physical security, it is even more important in our spiritual lives. We need to be secure in knowing that God loves us and has good plans for our lives. We want the security that when we fall or fail, our God is there to forgive us and pick us up. We desire the confidence that God has an eternal home waiting for us when we pass through the gate called death.

Sin makes us doubt or question God's security for our lives. But Jesus is our Good Shepherd. He laid down His life for us, His sheep, then rose again in triumph so that we never need doubt His care and compassion. He reminds us that we are secure in Him and that no one will ever be able to snatch us out of His hand. Our faith is made secure as we listen to the voice of the Good Shepherd, Jesus Christ, who knows us, who died and rose for us. His Word assures us of His security.

Dear Good Shepherd, thank You for being my security in this life and forever. Amen.

The Work of Healing

He went around doing good and healing all who were under the power of the devil, because God was with Him. *Acts 10:38*

These words are a summary of Jesus' ministry. The four gospels overflow with accounts of those healed by His loving hand. Some were upset that Jesus claimed the authority to forgive sin. But Jesus answered, "Which is easier: to say, 'Your sins are forgiven,' or to say, 'Get up and walk?' But that you may know that the Son of Man has authority on earth to forgive sins… ." He said to the paralyzed man, "Get up, take your mat and go home" (Luke 5:23–24).

We, too, look for healing for our various aches and pains, for arthritis or cancer, for limbs paralyzed or senses dulled. Often healing is beyond *our* reach, but not beyond the reach of our Lord who went about "doing good and healing all who were under the power of the devil." In our Baptism we received healing: the forgiveness of our disease of sin. With the forgiveness of sin, we are made whole and holy and given the promise of incorruptible resurrection bodies in heaven which will be free of every ailment.

Though physical ills and disabilities may remain for now, we have been healed of oppression from the devil and the fear of death. Thank God, our Great Physician has healed us!

O Lord, thank You for forgiving all our sins and remind us that You love us and will work all things for our good. Take away the gloom of sadness and worry that we often feel, and heal us of our diseases according to Your will. Amen.

Cure of the Soul

May your whole spirit, soul and body be kept blameless at the coming of our Lord Jesus Christ.
1 Thessalonians 5:23

Body and soul are inseparable in God's eyes. The soul receives spiritual power to live out in the body what it means to be sanctified "through and through." Yet when bodily illness strikes, we tend to pray more for healing of the body than of the soul. It is healing of the soul that enables us to bear illness. What we need more than anything at the moment of illness is the strength to bear it while we await bodily healing from God.

Yet we may find that bodily illness remains and is not cured. Then more than ever we realize the great gift God gives in the offer of the healing of the soul. Since much of life is an accumulation of bodily problems that will not go away, cure of the soul becomes essential in life.

Cure of the soul—and strength to bear bodily illness—takes place when we begin to appreciate the sufferings of Jesus Christ on the cross. Then we come to experience all of life as lived in faithfulness to God, whether in sickness or in health. In the "cure of the soul" we will find spiritual medicine to bear all things. "May God Himself, the God of peace, sanctify you through and through" (1 Thessalonians 5:23).

Father, in Jesus heal our souls daily so that we may bear the physical distress of life also. Amen.

A Bruised Reed

A bruised reed He will not break, and a smoldering wick He will not snuff out. *Isaiah 42:3*

The suffering Savior, Jesus, is gentle with those who suffer. He wants to see that truth and righteousness will prevail in the earth.

The fact that our Lord will not break the bruised reed nor quench a dimly burning wick shows His great love for fallen sinners, a love that prompted Him to go into death for them and that continues to move Him to receive sinners.

A reed or stick that has been bruised is in danger of total breakage. The least little snap could break it. Persons who have been bruised by their sins are especially vulnerable to the attacks of Satan, but the Savior will not let that weak faith be broken. Through His call to repentance and faith, extended in the Gospel, He allows the reed to stay intact, that is, the person does not succumb to despair or to Satan's lures.

A wick that burns dimly could easily be quenched, but our Lord does not let the lamp of faith go out. He sustains us, even as He calls and pleads, "O sinner, come home to Me." Our sometimes small faith is replenished through Word and Sacraments. We praise our patient, pardoning God for making His strength perfect in our weakness.

Lord, strengthen our weak faith and keep us with You.
Amen.

God Will Finish His Work

I always pray ... confident of this, that He who began a good work in you will carry it on to completion until the day of Christ Jesus. *Philippians 1:6*

In six days God completed His creation. On the seventh day He rested, for "the heavens and the earth were completed." In Christians God has begun another work—that of creating them anew in Christ. Will He finish also this work?

We have often witnessed an infant Baptism. Through the Sacrament God created faith in the child and received it into the kingdom of His dear Son. He began His good work. Will faith survive during the lifetime lying ahead for this child?

The same question occurs as we look at ourselves. Much of our Christianity seems to be at loose ends. Our faith is plagued by doubts. Our life is far from perfect, for the struggle with sin continues as long as we live. We may wonder: Will God uphold us until the end?

Saint Paul states it as his conviction that God will sustain us and bring us to perfection in heaven. He will not leave our faith an unfinished symphony; He will bring it to a grand climax. On the target date—the day of Jesus Christ—He will have put the final touches on each Christian. That will be a day when we give all glory to God—to the Father who created us, to the Son who redeemed us, and to the Holy Spirit who kept us in the faith.

God of all grace, keep us by Your power through faith in Jesus Christ unto salvation. Amen.

Everlasting Joy

Instead of their shame My people will receive a double portion, and instead of disgrace they will rejoice … everlasting joy will be theirs. *Isaiah 61:7*

Do you have everlasting joy? Now before you start feeling guilty about a lack of joy, you should remember this: Happiness is a surface emotion, dependent upon circumstances. Joy is a deep sense of serenity that endures, whatever the circumstances.

Through the extremes of our mood swings, and regardless of circumstances in life, God remains the same. His saving love toward us in Christ Jesus is constant. His promises hold true. His assurance of victory through our Savior, risen from the dead, always stands.

Our degree of feeling close to God can vary a great deal, but our moods and emotions may have little to do with God's truth. Satan tries to undermine the reality of our faith by planting doubts. But our hope is fixed firmly in the accomplished reality of Jesus' life, death for our sins, and resurrection. Nothing can change that fact. The joy we have as His redeemed people is a lasting reality; it is for eternity!

Thank You, Lord, for never changing, despite our unstable feelings and despite the changing circumstances in our life. Thank You for providing us with a double portion of Your blessings and everlasting joy—a joy that cannot be taken from us. Amen.

This Is the Day!

This is the day the Lord has made; let us rejoice and be glad in it. *Psalm 118:24*

The Christian religion has often been criticized for being too otherworldly—for putting too much emphasis on the life that lies beyond the grave, and too little emphasis on the life that is here and now. The Christian religion, it is claimed, offers the believer only "pie in the sky," while providing little joy in the work-a-day world in which we live. What shall we say to this?

It is true that our Lord expects us to keep the eyes of our faith fixed on the glories that lie at our journey's end. But He does *not* want us to forfeit all the legitimate joys, heart-lifting gladness, and soul-refreshing beauty that grace our path from here to there.

That is why He has David exclaim: "This is the day the Lord has made; let us rejoice and be glad in it." *Today* is ours to enjoy. We need not keep our "hallelujahs" in moth balls; we can live the "hallelujah" life today. No matter how hard the road, no matter how steep the path, we are walking arm in arm with the God of all goodness, whose Son has claimed us as His own. With each new morning we can say:

Lord, this is the day which You have made; we will rejoice and be glad in it. Amen.

Feeding His Flock

He tends His flock like a shepherd: He gathers the lambs in His arms. *Isaiah 40:11*

These words portray one of the most beautiful pictures of our Lord, namely, that of a faithful shepherd who tenderly and patiently cares for His own, the sheep of His pasture.

The little ones, the lambs, receive special attention from their shepherd. They are not able to keep up the pace of the grown-ups; so the shepherd lovingly carries them in his arms. The mothers and those who will soon give birth are also given special concern, and they are led gently, tenderly.

What a lovely picture of our Lord's love and concern for each of us, His sheep and His lambs! He knows each of us by name; He knows our needs, our weaknesses, and our cares.

As our Good Shepherd, Jesus Christ has given His life for us. He continues to provide for our spiritual needs through Word and Sacrament. None of us escapes His all-embracing care. Faithfully He leads and guides us past all the dangers and pitfalls of life to our eternal fold with Him in heaven. Truly we say with King David in the Twenty-third Psalm, "The Lord is my shepherd, I shall not be in want. He makes me lie down in green pastures, He leads me beside quiet waters."

Savior, like a shepherd lead us, for we need Your tender care. Amen.

Trust in the Lord

Commit your way to the Lord; trust in Him, and He will do this. *Psalm 37:5*

The Lord invites us to place our confidence in Him and in His power to act. We can put all our problems, concerns, and burdens upon Him to bear them for us.

But that often does not satisfy us. We still want to manage everything by ourselves. Instead of peace and security, we experience anxiety, and our human heart is filled with unrest and fear. When cares and troubles multiply and weigh heavy upon us, or afflictions of one kind or another strike and bother us, we become alarmed and insecure about the future and wonder how we shall manage.

How precious the invitation then becomes to go to the Lord with our problems and to commit our way to Him! We can place ourselves into His hands and rest assured that He will take care of us, for we are His children whom Christ has redeemed.

The reassuring appeal, "Fear not," occurs about 300 times in the Bible. Over and over God bids us to confidently place our hand in His and walk with Him in full trust of safety and care. When we stay close to the Lord, our fears will vanish and our heart and soul will be strengthened on our way.

Our faithful Lord, thank You for the gracious invitation to walk with You in safety and companionship on our way. Amen.

Never Down and Out

We are more than conquerors through Him who loved us. *Romans 8:37*

Time and time again we hear the refrain, "We shall overcome." If anyone can say these words with the greatest of confidence, it is the Christian. His confidence does not rest in himself but in the power that God supplies.

True, the Christian daily battles his own sinful nature. Fears, temptations, envy, hatred, pride, loneliness, sorrow, failures, and frustrations cause him at times to cry out, "Nobody knows all the trouble I've seen." Clinging to God's promises, the Christian experiences in his own life God's promise: "We are more than conquerors through Him who loved us."

A Christian whose life seemed to be filled with more than her share of trouble said one day: "I have changed my disappointments to His appointments." She knew that God knew what was happening. In the end, the trying things that came her way always worked out for her own good. She received a stronger faith, a deeper understanding of God's way with His children, a clearer insight into the things that really count, and new strength to face her tomorrows. She had learned to "sing in the rain"—even when it poured. What has been our experience?

Lord, give us faith to believe that whatever we may experience we shall be more than conquerors through Christ. Amen.

Use Trouble for Good

God is our refuge and strength, an ever-present help in trouble. *Psalm 46:1*

Trouble is the most democratic thing in the world. It snubs no one. It's everyone's shadow. Job said people are "born to trouble as surely as sparks fly upward" (5:7). Every person born to this world experiences a bundle of trouble.

Trouble can send us into emotional wheel-spinning through worry. This makes things worse. Worry never robs tomorrow of its sorrow; it always saps today of its strength. Brooding over troubles means hatching despair.

God wants us to believe that some good can result from trouble. Troubles never come alone; God, although not the author of evil, always comes with them. We ask God to help us live with the trouble until we have learned the intended lesson and He takes it away.

God wants to help us in our trouble—of that we can be sure. We know His love for us in Christ Jesus. He knows how to help us in our troubles, through our troubles, and out of our troubles. In this way our troubles turn into triumph. Instead of getting us down, they lift us up, for whatever drives us to God in prayer, in trust, and in confidence always brings victory in due time.

O Holy Spirit, help me to convert every care into prayer so that I may become better, not bitter, for Jesus' sake. Amen.

Help at the Right Time

At just the right time, when we were still powerless, Christ died for the ungodly. *Romans 5:6*

When a fireman rescues an aged man from the ledge of his old burning hotel; when a lifeguard pulls a drowning youth from the swimming pool and gives mouth-to-mouth resuscitation, restoring breath to the unconscious lad; or when a lumberjack pushes a man out of the way of a falling log, we join in thoughts of thanksgiving for the rescued ones. We hope someone will be around to help us in similar situations.

Our Lord Jesus Christ did not wait for us to get ourselves into a safe or comfortable position before He came to an easy rescue. He saw us as we were—utterly helpless in sin. He came to give us a new life. That's mercy! That's courage! That's the undeserved grace of God!

Our Lord does not forsake us in the problems and messes we create or others impose on us. As in love He once gave Himself to restore us to unity with our heavenly Father through the forgiveness of sins, so He will be with us in love today and tomorrow. We rejoice in God, who shows His love for us, even when we fail to recognize His hand at work behind the scenes of life. He gives help to the weak and helpless.

Lord, give me grace to change the things I can, strength to accept the unchangeable, and wisdom to know the difference. Amen.

Who's in Charge Here?

The earth is the Lord's. *Psalm 24:1*

A cartoon showed a keeper in a cage full of monkeys. The mischievous creatures had taken the keeper's cap, keys, broom, and pail of food, then left him standing in stunned silence. Outside the cage an onlooker asked, "Who's in charge here?"

Perhaps that scene is the way our daily life sometimes appears to us. Things have gotten out of control. We have set out to control life, and it has turned on us. We feel threatened, anxious, inadequate to cope with even the simplest events. We have been tricked, and we resent it.

Sense will return to life when we learn that "the earth is the Lord's." Jesus' mission was to teach us what that means. He inverted our entire relation to life and the world around us. He freed us to trust our heavenly Father and to live under His order. Suddenly the world opens up to us when we discover that God really is in charge here and His good will is going to prevail. Life is not a cruel trick. Our Lord has overcome the great deceiver, Satan. Jesus said that we might have peace of heart and mind: "In this world you will have trouble. But take heart! I have overcome the world" (John 16:33).

Purpose and order return when we recognize God's will in Jesus and let His will be done through us.

Forgive us, Lord, for ever doubting Your good will. Amen.

Courage

Be on your guard; stand firm in the faith; be men of courage; be strong. Do everything in love.
1 Corinthians 16:13–14

It takes a great deal of courage to live as a Christian in our modern world. There are so many powers at war against the life with Christ that all of us daily need His wisdom, His power, and His guidance. We need the quiet, steady courage that He alone can give through the assurance of the forgiveness of our sins.

Our Savior knew that very clearly. For that reason the entire Bible is a book of love and sympathy and courage. Its pages are full of cheer for those who are weary in heart. It brings new hope to the disappointed, the defeated, to those who have failed, to those who have crushed and broken lives. The voice of our Savior in His Word, "Take heart! I have overcome the world," will fall over the world as the sound of courage from heaven—a courage we can never have of ourselves.

And the greatest thing of all is that this courage always comes to those who need it most. When Saint Paul was discouraged, our Savior said to him: "My power is made perfect in weakness" (2 Corinthians 12:9). Before He can put His strength into us, we must know that we have no strength of our own. But when we confess that, humbly and penitently, then His courage comes to us, full and brave, and the treasures of His grace make us strong and unafraid.

Dear Lord, help me to remain confident in Your love and care for me at all times. Amen.

Pressed but Not Crushed

We are hard pressed on every side, but not crushed; perplexed, but not in despair. *2 Corinthians 4:8*

Often the little irritations of daily living get us down. The hum-drum, ho-hum routine of life gets to us. There are the little irritations of daily life due to leaky faucets, bumper-to-bumper traffic and dented fenders, and long lines at the supermarket or at the bank.

There are big problems also: illness, loss of a job, and the death of a loved one. But we have hope. God's golden Gospel can give our life a lift. God's love lifts us up when we are down and out. We are pressed, but not crushed. Listen to what Saint Paul says in the above text: "We are pressed on every side by troubles, but not crushed and broken. We are perplexed because we don't know why things happen as they do, but we don't give up and quit. We are hunted down, but God never abandons us. We get knocked down, but we get up again and keep going" (2 Corinthians 4:8–9 TLB).

We have a God who loves us in Christ Jesus. Jesus, crushed and broken on the cross, spilled His blood to earn for us the gift of forgiveness and the assurance of eternal salvation. The Gospel is power packed. By God's power we are kept safe and are strengthened for every encounter.

Dear Lord Jesus, give us the courage and the comfort to face the irritations of daily life. Amen.

Prescription for Worries

Do not be anxious about anything, but in everything ... present your requests to God. And the peace of God ... will guard your hearts and your minds in Christ Jesus. *Philippians 4:6–7*

What the apostle is doing here in effect is writing a prescription for one of our commonest ailments: worry. It's a remedy God recommends in Scripture in dozens of places. It's really effective, but so often we just don't use it—we don't even try.

"In everything, by prayer and petition, with thanksgiving, present your requests to God," this prescription of the apostle reads. Now notice how it goes on—words that many of us have heard again and again—"And the peace of God, which transcends all understanding, will guard your hearts and your minds in Christ Jesus."

What a promise! The peace of God, which Jesus gained when He took our place under God's justice and reconciled us with His Father, will keep (the word really means to stand guard like a sentinel or bodyguard) our heart and mind safe and serene.

That promise still stands. It has never been revoked. The power of prayer has not been diminished. It is still the key that unlocks God's omnipotence and brings it to bear on the burdened, anxious hearts of His praying children.

Grant, mighty Lord, an increasing measure of the peace and strength that is ours when we through implicit trust and confident prayer cast all our anxieties on You. For Jesus' sake we pray. Amen.

The Sentinel at the Door

And the peace of God ... will guard your hearts and your minds in Christ Jesus. *Philippians 4:7*

Unfortunately, much of the talk about peace today has nothing to do with the peace of which Paul speaks. He is not referring to the spurious peace that makes daily headlines, nor was he even speaking about the peace that should exist between brothers.

He is speaking, rather, about the peace that exists between God and the forgiven sinner—the peace of reconciliation, the peace of which the angels spoke above the fields of Bethlehem, the peace about which we sing: "Peace on earth and mercy mild, God and sinners reconciled." It is a peace that Paul admits cannot be described: it "transcends all understanding."

What does Paul say about that peace? Literally, he says that "the peace of God shall stand guard over our hearts and minds through Christ Jesus." It will not permit the troubles of this world to overcome us. Like an armed sentinel, God's peace will guard our hearts through faith in Christ. Fear, anxiety, and distress may seek to overwhelm us, but the peace of God, standing guard over our heart, will prevail. The peace of which the hymn writer wrote will always reassure us: "This child of God shall meet no harm."

Lord God, heavenly Father, let Your peace forever guard my heart. I ask this in Jesus' name. Amen.

We Have a Lord Who Cares for Us

When Jesus saw her weeping ... He was deeply moved in spirit and troubled. ... Jesus wept. *John 11:33, 35*

Many Scripture passages describe God as a majestic ruler and all-powerful judge. We may wonder who can stand in His presence when at the end of time we find ourselves before His glorious throne and see Him as our judge. Before His glory, brighter than a million suns, and before His majesty, more magnificent than all the combined kingdoms of this world, who indeed can stand? And yet, we know that we have a Lord who cares for us.

We know this because Christ, the eternal Son of the eternal Father, is the same Jesus of Nazareth who walked our dreary planet, full of mercy and compassion. He saw the misery and the agony of our world, and His heart was moved to pity. He cared.

His heart is filled with pity still, and His pity is real. Into our lives may come pain and anguish, heartbreak and despair. Our world has a tendency quickly to pass us by should we wish to pause and weep. Our world's mercy and compassion is often a shallow and fleeting mist, and we are left alone.

But we have a Lord who cares. He has a heart that is touched and moved by our tears. And He acts in His mercy. He invites our cares and our troubles. He was able, fully and victoriously, to bear our sins. Just as fully, just as victoriously He can and will bear our griefs.

Jesus, our Lord, fill our lives with Your healing power and loving concern. Amen.

Someone Who Understands

We do not have a high priest who is unable to sympathize with our weaknesses. *Hebrews 4:15*

Have you ever tried to explain your troubles to someone who just could not understand? Perhaps you tried to describe a pain to your doctor and felt that he or she did not begin to realize how bad it really was. It is disheartening to think that no one is sympathetic.

How wonderful to know that there is someone who understands fully just what our needs and troubles are! Jesus, our High Priest, is able to sympathize with us because He has experienced our weaknesses. Since He had human flesh and blood, Jesus felt the needs of the body just as we do. He was hungry after He had been in the desert 40 days without food. He felt loneliness when His disciples deserted Him. He felt the hatred and envy of His enemies. He knew poverty and had no home of His own. He knew horrible pain of the type inflicted on Him during the time of His trial and crucifixion. He knew what it was to face death.

It is good to know that this Lord Jesus, who was in every respect tempted as we are, invites us to bring our needs to the throne of His grace. We are urged to come "with confidence, so that we may receive mercy and find grace to help us in our time of need" (Hebrews 4:16). Jesus is a sympathetic friend who always understands.

Dear understanding Lord Jesus, be at my side in every difficulty. Amen.

Victory

See, the Lord is coming with thousands upon thousands of His holy ones. *Jude 14*

You may not think that there are many genuine saints in this world, but there are many of them in heaven who also once lived in this world. What is more, they form so great "a multitude that no one could count" them. "Thousands upon thousands" is just a symbolic way of saying "a very great many." They are all the saints.

These, says John in Revelation, have come "out of the great tribulation" (Revelation 7:14). Nobody need tell us that. There is much trouble in the world, and some of us have had more than our share. The most vicious part of it is that it tends to make us bitter and causes us to lose our faith so that we "curse God and die." Therefore the book of Revelation keeps telling about those who have "overcome." Overcome what? Clearly they have overcome the temptation to let injustice, cruelty, and suffering turn one against God. If you can hang on to the great fact of God's love in Christ in view of that, you are an overcomer.

Almost unbelievable glories are promised to the faithful, but they all come down to this: We shall participate in Christ's victory over death and have eternal life.

So order our lives, gracious Lord, that we with all Your saints may come to the joys promised to all who love You in Christ Jesus. Amen.

Hard Things

You have shown Your people desperate times; You have given us wine that makes us stagger. *Psalm 60:3*

The psalmist is frank in his approach to God. Like the patriarch Job, he lets his feelings be known. He affirms that God has shown His people hard things. The pious wish of many, namely, that those who have found in Jesus and His atoning sacrifice the happy solution to the problem of sin may expect life to be an undisturbed journey, has no foundation in God's revealed Word.

There are, indeed, hard things in life. In the lives of God's children they are often more easily identified. Christians may feel that as God's people they are entitled to preferential treatment. But for reasons rooted in His wisdom and goodness God does not follow that course. Faith does not thrive on ease but on "hard things." They teach us that, instead of removing difficulty, God draws us to Himself by assuring us that He is an "ever-present help in trouble" (Psalm 46:1).

The tests of life are to make, not break, us. Hard things may demolish a business or deprive one of material security, but in Christ they build up reliance on God. If God designs or permits hard things, close at hand are His counsel and His sustaining hand of love.

Lord Jesus, help me to accept the hard things of life as Your gracious invitation to lay hold of Your sustaining love. Amen.

God Picks Up the Broken Pieces

I said, "O Lord, have mercy on me; heal me, for I have sinned against You." *Psalm 41:4*

During World War II a bomb scored an indirect hit and shattered the beautiful stained-glass rose window in the Rheims Cathedral. The members of the congregation got down on their hands and knees and picked up all the small glass fragments of the window.

After the war, they hired some of the most skilled workmen available to rebuild the window, fragment by fragment, from the pieces they had saved. Today, the rose window in the Rheims Cathedral is more beautiful than ever before.

God can take our broken hearts and our shattered dreams and reshape them into a life that is holy and beautiful.

Does God, who loved us enough to send His Son to die for us, not also care for us in the daily things of our lives? It is precisely Christ's death and resurrection that, like a magnet, draw all the sin-smashed pieces of our lives into a whole new way of living. Jesus promised us: "I, when I am lifted up from the earth, will draw all men to Myself" (John 12:32). In drawing us to Himself, He heals us and makes us whole.

Thou, O Christ, art all I want; More than all in Thee I find. Raise the fallen, cheer the faint, Heal the sick, and lead the blind. Amen.

A Broken Heart

The sacrifices of God are a broken spirit; a broken and a contrite heart, O God, You will not despise.
Psalm 51:17

What is it that pleases God the most? Burnt offerings and sacrifices? Weekly visits to His house of worship? Regular contributions? The performance of religious duties? Deeds of service?

The psalmist declared, "You do not delight in sacrifice, or I would bring it; You do not take pleasure in burnt offerings. The sacrifices of God are a broken spirit; a broken and contrite heart, O God, You will not despise."

It is our heart that God wants. And the heart that is pleasing to Him is one that is broken and contrite. Its pride is shattered: the walls of shame that have surrounded it are broken down. It is filled with sorrow for its many sins. It is a faith-filled heart, one that trusts solely in the merits of Jesus Christ for full forgiveness. It is a loving heart, one that loves God and people and seeks to serve both.

Certainly God delighted in the sacrifices of His Old Covenant people, so long as they were offered from penitent, loving hearts. And God is pleased with our sacrifices—our worship, our gifts, our service—so long as such tributes flow from hearts that have been changed by His power, melted by His love, and filled with His Spirit.

Break our hearts by Your law, O God, and mend them again by the healing power of Your Gospel; in Jesus' name we pray. Amen.

Hands Lifted in Blessing

He lifted up His hands and blessed them. *Luke 24:50*

The last glimpse the disciples had of Jesus was at His ascension as He was lifting His hands over them in blessing. This last look left a deep impression on their hearts and minds all their life. So they were to remember their Lord.

Jesus still holds His hands of blessing over all of His disciples. The hands raised in blessing bear the marks of the price He paid to bless His own. The nailprints tell the story of His great love.

Jesus blesses His own in every circumstance of life, when they walk in the valley of affliction or rejoice on the hilltops of prosperity. They know He not only wishes them every good but with His blessing gives them every good.

Oh, the glory of it all! He blesses us, our homes, our children, our labors, our rest, our pleasures, our years, our trials, our sorrows, our dying. He blesses us, but not because we deserve it. The very essence of all that is contained in the word *blessing* is love, mercy, and grace. We know that without His blessing life is not really living. With it, goodness and mercy must follow us all the days of our life.

Bless us, dear Lord Jesus, throughout our earthly life, and bring us at last to Your eternal glory. Amen.

The Blessing of Mercy

Blessed are the merciful, for they will be shown mercy. *Matthew 5:7*

"It is more blessed to give than to receive" (Acts 20:35). Jesus lived and died by that truth. He "gave Himself for our sins to rescue us from the present evil age" (Galatians 1:4). "In His great mercy He has given us new birth into a living hope" (1 Peter 1:3).

Mercy is love expressed. When Christians practice mercy, they place the needs of others above their own, in much the same way that Jesus placed our need for forgiveness and salvation first, allowing Himself to be insulted, abused, and finally crucified in order to procure that salvation for us. God so loved that He gave. Calvary is the proof of God's mercy.

To be merciful is to act out of love and compassion for others, to try to see with their eyes, think with their minds, and feel with their hearts. God's Son did just that when He took on human flesh and blood to experience life's struggles just as we do, though without sin. He offered His life in our place as the substitutionary sacrifice for our sins.

As we display mercy in Christ's name, we become more like our Lord. By His grace we will obtain the ultimate mercy: entrance into God's heavenly sanctuary, to abide with Him forever.

O God, be merciful to me, a sinner. Let me show mercy daily in the name of Jesus Christ, the merciful. Amen.

The Great Promise

[Jesus] gave them this command: "Do not leave Jerusalem, but wait for the gift My Father promised."
Acts 1:4

Before He ascended into heaven Jesus told His disciples to wait for "the gift My Father promised." The promise is from the Father, given through the Son. But the promise itself is the Holy Spirit.

The initial act of the Holy Spirit is to lead us to accept our total loss in sin and our complete redemption in Christ.

But there is more. As executor of Christ's estate, the Holy Spirit wants us to have and hold the magnificent riches of that estate. Jesus said, "The Spirit will take from what is Mine and make it known to you" (John 16:15).

The Holy Spirit gives us power to live in faith, in love, in joy, in peace, in hope, in triumph over sin and death and hell.

He gives us power to stand firm, to remain in conversation with Christ, to hold our ground against Satan, to put up a good fight, to endure hardship, to be faithful unto death, to march joyfully toward the splendid glory.

Through the Holy Spirit we are God's special agents, fit to be used by Him as instruments of His love and grace. In this way we glorify God and serve one another.

Holy Spirit, give us power to be true to Christ and to proclaim His Gospel of redemption everywhere in the world. Amen.

Our Adoption

In love He predestined us to be adopted as His sons through Jesus Christ, in accordance with His pleasure and will. *Ephesians 1:4–5*

Webster says that *predestine* means "to appoint or ordain beforehand by an unchangeable purpose." And this is exactly what our text for today is talking about. God, in His grace and out of love for us, ordained beforehand that we should be His adopted children. Are you doing cartwheels for joy? We all should!

What have we ever done to deserve to be called the children of God? We are by nature prone to lie and cheat. We are a rebellious, arrogant lot. We often think we have all the answers and are very proud of our accomplishments … until our world begins to collapse, leaving us beaten, destitute, and very insecure.

And yet, undeserving as we are, God's love for us has prevented Him from abandoning us to our fate. Even before the creation of the world, it pleased Him to decide to adopt us in Christ as His sons and daughters, so that we would live in His kingdom and enjoy all the blessings He grants those He loves. And all this God did out of pure grace, calling us out of the darkness of our selfish natures into the light of a life lived for Him and with Him through the atoning work of His Son.

Lord God, thank You for making me Your child. Amen.

Help in Time of Need

Approach the throne of grace with confidence.
Hebrews 4:16

Sooner or later, perhaps sooner than we realize, we come face to face with moments of desperation. We like to boast of our accomplishments, our successes, our personal triumphs, and the like. Then suddenly and unexpectedly the Lord lays us low on a bed of sickness, permits some unexplainable calamity to happen to us, sends some heavy cross to bear, or confronts us with dire need.

The immediate impulse of human nature is to murmur and complain, to fault God, to accuse Him of being unfaithful to His promises. But also in such moments of weak faith we have a great High Priest who has passed into the heavens, Jesus, the Son of God. He is "at the right hand of God and is also interceding for us" (Romans 8:34).

How important that we daily rethink our lives and the purpose God has for us in His divine plan! When we experience hardships and distress, let us remember that only God can help. Christ, our High Priest, who "took up our infirmities and carried our diseases" and who took away our sins on Calvary's cross, invites us to come boldly to the throne of grace with all concerns. God assures us that "before they call I will answer; while they are still speaking I will hear" (Isaiah 65:24).

O Jesus, grant that we accept Your will in all our needs.
Amen.

A Cross Just for You

If anyone would come after Me, he must deny himself and take up his cross and follow Me. *Mark 8:34*

There is a lovely legend which says that Jesus and His father had a sign in front of their carpenter shop with this inscription: "Our yokes fit." To avoid being rubbed sore, it was important that the neck of the ox and the yoke be perfectly fitted to each other.

There is a lesson here for us. God perfectly fits our crosses to us. The cross of a Christian is spoken of as his or her cross. No one can bear our cross for us. Parents cannot carry the crosses of their children, nor should they want to. In His wisdom and love God has prepared a cross for His children in keeping with their need. Without that cross life would never be near to God.

There is sweet comfort in knowing this, especially when our cross becomes heavy. God never expects us to bear a strange cross. He will give us a cross neither too heavy nor too light. It will be so perfectly fitted to our need that it can belong to us only.

Now we can be sure that crosses that burden us will become wings that lift us. There will be no unnecessary tears. The love that delivered us from death will discipline us unto life. That's God's way, and it's the best way.

Heavenly Father, help us to know that our crosses are for our good. Help us bear them in faith, through Jesus Christ. Amen.

My Plan Will Work

[Sarai] said to Abram, "The Lord has kept me from having children. Go, sleep with my maidservant; perhaps I can build a family through her." *Genesis 16:2*

A form of conceit is an exaggerated opinion of one's own ability to solve problems. People often come up with ideas that are supposed to bring about a solution when God does not at once answer their prayers or show them a clear direction in life. At such times we, too, are inclined to offer our own plans. Sometimes we are very positive and proudly affirm, "My plan will work." What a sad mistake! What tragic pride!

Sarai made this mistake. God had promised Abram a son, the heir to whom the blessed promise was given. The years passed, and still there was no son. Sarai finally decided the Lord had forgotten, or worse, was not going to keep His promise. Therefore she determined to take things into her own hands. She gave her maid to Abram to be his wife. This was going to solve the whole matter. Instead it caused nothing but misery.

This is a warning to us not to take things into our own hands. God has a plan. It will not fail. That was evident in the gift of Isaac, and later in his descendant, the "unspeakable gift," Christ Jesus. The coming of Jesus should convince us that God always keeps His promises.

Heavenly Father, teach us humility so that in dependence on Your promises we may learn patiently to wait for the fulfillment of Your wonderful plans for us. Help us in Jesus' name. Amen.

God's Good and Gracious Will

Your kingdom come, your will be done on earth as it is in heaven. *Matthew 6:10*

A seminarian, when asked where he'd like to serve his first parish, answered: "Anywhere the Lord leads me—in Texas." Sometimes we fail to understand the nature of God's will.

Jesus expressed the will of God as the sovereign justice, goodness, and wisdom by which He governs all things. Some people have reduced the will of God to cold, cruel fate or even to "luck." Many speak of the will of God only in connection with tragedy. Actually God's good and gracious will is active in every event of our lives, if only we will seek to become aware of it.

Too often we try to impose our own will on the will of God, and that isn't good. Isaiah says: "We all, like sheep, have gone astray, each of us has turned to his own way [will]; and the Lord has laid on Him the iniquity of us all" (53:6). Praise God! Sinless Himself, Jesus has paid for the sins of our stubborn will. We stand forgiven before God.

So we pray that God's divine will may become the regulator of our attitudes and ambitions, as well as the divine blueprint for all our actions. Even as the angels in heaven know and joyfully do God's will, so may we come to understand it and do it gladly.

Lord Jesus, You have set the perfect example for doing the Father's will. Lead us in the way we should go. Amen.

Worry

Do not worry about your life, what you will eat; or about your body, what you will wear. *Luke 12:22*

A wise person once observed, "Do you know why Jesus was always saying to His disciples, 'Don't worry'? It was because they were always so worried!" We might find ourselves chuckling over this, thinking that it does not apply to us.

But after our little laugh, we come back to serious business. Worry is a destructive thing. Obviously worry can hurt our physical health. Eventually it can kill a person. To top it off, there is another destructive dimension to worry that is even worse than the loss of physical life. Worry can destroy a person's spiritual life. Worry is one of Satan's favorite weapons. He encourages us to believe that worry isn't all that serious. Meanwhile he uses worry to separate us from our heavenly Father. Before we know it, we can find ourselves worrying about virtually everything. When we get to that point, worrying has actually become idolatry. Worry has become our god. This need not be true for us.

Having acknowledged what worry is—a temptation of Satan—we can take our worries to God in prayer. God gave us the greatest gift, His Son. He will also give us the gifts we need for the lesser needs of life.

Lord, give us a deeper awareness of Your love. Amen.

Stop Worrying

Do not be anxious about anything, but in everything, by prayer and petition, with thanksgiving, present your requests to God. *Philippians 4:6*

Worry is so common. It is experienced by everyone but does no one any good. It only wounds the mind and kills the spirit. In Matthew 6:27 Jesus indicates how foolish and useless it is to worry: "Who of you by worrying can add a single hour to his life?"

On the other hand, worry can do a lot of harm. It's like getting sand into the wheel bearings of one's car. In a short time the bearings become damaged beyond repair. Worry is the sand that hastens the wrecking of our human machinery.

In overcoming our anxieties we must do more than recognize that a cure is possible. We need to recognize that Jesus Christ is the cure. He is the Savior who takes away the cause of worry. He forgives sins.

Therefore, Paul writes, "Do not be anxious about anything, but in everything, by prayer and petition, with thanksgiving, present your requests to God. And the peace of God, which transcends all understanding, will guard your hearts and your minds in Christ Jesus" (Philippians 4:6–7).

Lord God, we cast all our anxieties and worries on You, for You care about us. Amen.

God's Compass

By faith Abraham ... went, even though he did not know where he was going. *Hebrews 11:8*

As you travel life's road, do you often feel insecure because of the unknowns? A husband and wife were traveling in unfamiliar territory when he finally admitted, "We're lost." As he chided himself for not bringing a map, the wife calmly pointed to the compass above the dashboard and said, "The compass shows we're going in the right direction. We'll get there."

Abraham probably would have appreciated a map as he headed for the unknown Promised Land. We too may wish for maps detailing and explaining the roads we will travel on our life's journey. We may long to know where the "side roads" of pain and discouragement intersect the overall route. Are we possibly lost? Has God abandoned us?

God's compass points us in the right direction—heavenward—through faith in His Son, who has redeemed us from sin, death, and hell by His atoning sacrifice for our sins. With the compass of His Word in hand, we need not be bewildered by the specific trails we travel. We need not demand an explanation of every turn our life takes. Like Abraham, we trust our loving Savior to bring us to the Promised Land.

Gracious God, strengthen our trust that You are guiding us through our life here toward life with You forever in heaven. Amen.

A Great Deep

Oh, the depth of the riches of the wisdom and knowledge of God! How unsearchable His judgments, and His paths beyond tracing out! *Romans 11:33*

Scientists have gone down to the bottom of inland waters and even of oceans near the shore. But the great depths of the oceans remain relatively unexplored. They still contain many mysteries.

It is thus with the judgments of God. There are times when God's ways are clear and understandable to us. We realize His wisdom and His goodness. We can say with confidence: "He guides me in paths of righteousness for His name's sake" (Psalm 23:3). There may be whole periods in our lives when our hearts can sing the song of the psalmist: "The boundary lines have fallen for me in pleasant places; surely I have a delightful inheritance" (Psalm 16:6).

Then—sometimes very unexpectedly—conditions change. There may be prolonged sickness, unemployment, reverses in business, financial losses, other types of care and sorrow. Prayers seem to go unanswered. "Has God forgotten to be merciful?" we ask with the psalmist (77:9). In such dark nights we must remember how God dealt with Mary and Joseph and with His own Son: no room in the inn; the flight into Egypt; the agony in the Garden; the torturesome death on the cross. "God spared not His own Son!" With the apostle Paul we exclaim: "Oh, the depth of the riches of the wisdom and knowledge of God! How unsearchable His judgments and His paths beyond tracing out!" (Romans 11:33).

Lord, give us grace to trust when we cannot understand. Amen.

Alone—Yet Not Alone

Be content with what you have, because God has said, "Never will I leave you; never will I forsake you." So we say with confidence, "The Lord is my helper; I will not be afraid." *Hebrews 13:5–6*

All of us have experienced the aching pain of loneliness—days when the world seems to have passed us by and left us to our single, solitary selves. If only we had someone, preferably a friend, to talk to, to share our inmost thoughts, our hopes, our dreams, our fears!

As believers in Christ, we have such a friend. Again and again we are assured of His presence in our lives. The verse above and the Matthew reading are only two such assurances. The Lord has told us: "Never will I leave you; never will I forsake you." And Jesus assures us: "I am with you always, to the very end of the age" (Matthew 28:20). We may be sure: He will never go back on these promises.

We may well ask ourselves: Have we cultivated this sense of nearness to our Lord? Do we "walk with Him and talk with Him"? Do we share our thoughts with Him—not only in our formal prayers but also in those frequent quiet moments that occur throughout the day?

There may indeed be moments in our life when we feel lonely. In those moments may we always remember: we are never left alone.

What a friend we have in Jesus, all our sins and griefs to bear! Lord, we thank You for Your presence. Amen.

God's Willingness to Listen

When I called, You answered me; You made me bold and stouthearted. *Psalm 138:3*

We need not worry about the problems we face daily, for Jesus, out of love, will gladly carry them for us. God's Word for today assures us that we have a ready listener—One who does not get bored with our constant pleading, but who listens and answers our prayers in the best possible way for us.

Quite often, one of our biggest frustrations results when people are so involved with their own concerns and affairs that they do not have time to listen when we are hurting or despairing. Sometimes even our loved ones may turn a deaf ear to our words. This only makes us hurt more and wonder if anyone cares.

At such times, we do well to remember that our Lord Jesus has promised to hear us and to answer our prayers. He is always close by and never too busy—never too tired to offer us His word of comfort. He makes our hearts bold and strengthens us so we can face the difficulties and heartaches that life sends our way. He is always by our side, ready to support and defend us as we struggle with our flesh, the world, and the devil. He is our gracious Savior.

Thank You, Lord Jesus, for listening and for helping me face those things that would rob me of faith and joy.
Amen.

Disciplined by Grace

Blessed is the man You discipline, O Lord, the man You teach from Your law; … For the Lord will not reject His people. *Psalm 94:12, 14*

Webster's dictionary defines the verb *discipline* as "to punish and to teach." It is interesting that a word that has as its root the idea of molding a person through instruction should, over the years, acquire the idea of punishment as its primary definition.

In our text, the psalmist tells us that we are blessed when we are disciplined by God. Does he mean that we are punished by God? Hardly! As children dearly loved by Him, He may chastise us—and we certainly may need it! But God does not punish us Christians in anger. He has already vented His wrath on His own Son, our Lord Jesus, who willingly went to the cross so that we would be spared the punishment our sins deserve. This is divine grace at its best!

And now, having been reconciled to our heavenly Father, we can truly enjoy the blessings He has in store for us and live secure in the fact that we are loved by Him—loved so much that He will never reject or forsake us, so much that He will be by our side constantly to watch over us and keep us safe.

Thank You, Lord, for being gracious to us in Christ and for watching over us. Amen.

I Grow in Understanding

The Use of Adversity

I know, O Lord, that Your laws are righteous, and in faithfulness You have afflicted me. *Psalm 119:75*

There are lessons we cannot learn in the light but which become obvious in the darkness. Adversity is a form of that darkness. It is the means our loving God employs to open our eyes to the reality of His goodness to us.

Afflictions are to our moral and spiritual life what periods of rest are to our bodily life. They stop the rush; they affirm that there is something more important than self-interest; they give opportunity for reviewing and rethinking. God tells us that His work of grace can be carried on through trials. To train children, parents use discipline involving correction, even pain. Faithful fathers and mothers must be chasteners.

God is committed even more than earthly parents to nurture in us a high moral and spiritual character through adversity. The psalmist shows great understanding of his God when he declares that in God's afflictive measures he sees His faithfulness. He notes that God's purposes are always for our good.

Our Savior Jesus Christ lived under the Father's deep chastening of suffering and death on our behalf. As His redeemed children we mature spiritually, using adversity for God's intended purpose in us.

Gracious God, help me to see Your purpose in my adversity. Amen.

145

The Secret of Contentment

I have learned to be content whatever the circumstances. *Philippians 4:11*

No matter what life threw at him, the apostle Paul was content. He had to learn the secret, but he did learn it. The secret was total trust in the Lord's love and wisdom. This made him quite independent of circumstances.

In times of trouble God's trusting child may say: (1) God brought me here; it is by His will that I am in this trouble; (2) God will give me strength to behave as His child, trusting in His love and wisdom; (3) God will make the trial a blessing, teaching me the lessons I need for my growth; (4) In his good time He can bring me out again; how and when, He knows.

So, child of God, when your turn comes to "face the arrows of outrageous fortune," make up your mind to say, "I am here (1) by God's appointment; (2) in His keeping; (3) under His training; (4) for His time."

To be content under His care, we must believe God's promise to make all things, even the most grievous losses and painful trials, work together for the final good of His beloved, believing children. That is His promise to all who are reconciled through Christ.

Lord, I cannot understand how You can make life's bitter experiences work out for good, but I believe You will do so.
Amen.

Life on Hold

Wait for the Lord; be strong and take heart and wait for the Lord. *Psalm 27:14*

After our new office phone system was installed, a representative from the company instructed us on the operation of the phones. In describing the "hold" button, she mentioned that when you are on hold, it sometimes seems like an eternity. And she is right!

When we are put on "hold," we fidget, we doodle, and we may pace—but mostly we wait.

Sometimes in life it seems that somebody pushes the "hold" button. We want to move ahead, but life is saying wait! We want all our questions answered, but life is saying not yet. We want our dreams fulfilled, our hopes realized, but for some reason they are not.

The question is: What shall we do when life puts us on "hold"? The answer is: "Hold on!" When we come to one of life's holding times, we shouldn't hang up; we should hang on. And we can hang on because of Jesus, who hung on the cross to enable us to know that even in the holding times of life, God is for us and not against us. Therefore, sooner or later the lines will click open, and life will go on. So, "hold on!" "Wait for the Lord; be strong and take heart and wait for the Lord."

Lord God, You whose love will not let us go, help us to hold on until help comes. For Jesus' sake we pray. Amen.

Who Can Do the Impossible?

His disciples answered, "Where could we get enough bread in this remote place to feed such a crowd?"
Matthew 15:33

There can be no question about it. No one can feed 4,000 people with only seven loaves of bread and a few small fish! It's absurd to even consider the possibility! Unless—unless the one who determines to do so is the ruler of heaven and earth. Then every protesting tongue must fall silent.

The disciples were sincerely logical in their protest. Jesus was dynamic and immediate in His response. The 4,000 were fed. Seven loaves of bread and a few fish filled every stomach, with food to spare, because He willed it so. "With God all things are possible" (Matthew 19:26).

But why does the human mind find this miracle impossible to believe? There is no other reason than pride. We can't do it, and pride insists that what we can't do no one can—God or man. Yet the history of God's work in the lives of humankind is a recitation of the impossible accomplished. Where humanity stands overwhelmed, God easily succeeds. God's dynamic "Let there be!" mystifies human insistence on creation painfully progressing for eons. God's intrusion into history with the sacrifice of His Son makes humankind's struggle to become acceptable to God unnecessary. Humanity's "impossible" is God's signal to act. And He acts powerfully.

Lord Jesus, how often we try to limit Your power! Show us again and again that with You all things are possible.
Amen.

Do You Feel Let Down?

She [Rahab] let them down by a rope through the window. *Joshua 2:15*

Have you ever had your back to the wall? Look at the Israelites: desert to the left and to the right. Behind them were the armies of Egypt coming to capture them. God spoke to Moses: "Tell the Israelites to move on." They went forward into the Red Sea. The waters parted. Their backs had been to the wall, and God saved them.

Joshua's spies also had their backs to the wall. Soldiers were searching for them and came near the rooms in Jericho's wall where the men were hiding. Rahab lowered them by a rope down the outside wall. In Matthew 1:5 Rahab is listed as an ancestor of the Savior.

David's wife Michal helped him escape through a window when her father, King Saul, wanted to kill him. Paul was let down in a basket over the wall of Damascus when enemies sought to get him.

When our backs are to the wall, God can provide unusual ways out. So just trust the Lord! He may not save us by a rope or a basket, but He tells us that He will never send us more than we can bear. He will always provide a means of escape. If we feel "let down," He can pick us up. If our backs are to the wall, He will save us. As sinners we were in dire distress, but God sent Jesus Christ to save us.

Lord, deliver us from evil. Amen.

If God Be for Us

If God is for us, who can be against us? *Romans 8:31*

The apostle's question comes after a recital of all God has done to bring us to Himself. In eternity He foreknew us and chose us in Christ to be His children. In time He called us to faith, through the Gospel. Having brought us to faith, He declared us just and righteous in His sight. He also glorified us, the full state of glory awaiting us in heaven.

How do we know that God will carry out His purpose to the end? May not our enemies intervene to set aside God's good and gracious will? Saint Paul answers with a counterquestion: "If God is for us, who can be against us?"

This is not to say that we don't have opposition, for we do. Tribulation, distress, persecution, famine, nakedness, peril, and the sword may try to separate us from the love of Christ, but to no avail. God is for us, and so this opposition fails.

With God for us, even we ourselves—everything we are or have done to defy Him—all our sins, our evil, our unbelief cannot keep Him from coming to us. In Jesus Christ, His Son, God takes our sins, needs, and weaknesses into and upon Himself, that we might be forgiven and reconciled with Him. In Christ God has found us—found us when we sought Him not. Now no one can be effectively against us.

Thank You, Lord, for finding us. Amen.

Hold On to Christ

Let us fix our eyes on Jesus, the author and perfecter of our faith. *Hebrews 12:2*

According to Old Testament law a man who had unintentionally killed someone could flee for safety to the temple in Jerusalem and hang on to the horns of the altar of burnt offering. These horns were actually projections resembling horns that were placed at the corners of the altar.

The horns of the altar, as well as the altar itself, were considered places of absolute safety. The person who grabbed the horns was appealing to the pardoning power and grace of God.

For New Testament Christians, the cross of Jesus Christ is our refuge. Because God sacrificed His Son on the altar of the cross, we are assured that all our sins are forgiven.

As we cling to Jesus in childlike faith, looking to Him as the beginner and fulfiller, the author and perfecter of our faith, no one can harm us. We are in absolute safety.

With Saint Paul we can confidently declare that "neither death nor life, neither angels nor demons, neither the present nor the future, nor any powers, neither height nor depth, nor anything else in all creation, will be able to separate us from the love of God that is in Christ Jesus our Lord" (Romans 8:38–39). Our hold on Christ is firm.

Lord, help me to trust in You above everything and everybody else. Amen.

Always the Same

He who watches over you will not slumber; indeed, He who watches over Israel will neither slumber nor sleep. *Psalm 121:3–4*

One of the things that all of us have in common is our inconsistency. We have our ups and downs, our good days and bad days. And because we continue to be both saint and sinner, we are not consistent in our response to God's grace. Sometimes we feel strong, sometimes weak. Too often we need to admit with Saint Paul that "what I do is not the good I want to do; no, the evil I do not want to do—this I keep on doing" (Romans 7:19).

Only God is perfectly consistent. He does not have ups and downs. Jesus Christ is the same yesterday, today, and forever. The psalmist reminds us that God's steadfast love endures forever. In the giving of His Son, God made a commitment that will never change. He has sealed His promise with the blood of Jesus.

We fall asleep on the job at times. Love cools and commitment wavers. Not so with God! He does not vary between strong times and weak times. Nor does He ever fall asleep on the job. There is no moment or situation when we are beyond His care—not because we are so strong in holding on to Him, but because He is strong in holding us. He who keeps us will neither slumber nor sleep.

Change and decay in all around I see;
O Thou who changest not, abide with me. Amen.

Dealing with Doubt

Immediately the boy's father exclaimed, "I do believe; help me overcome my unbelief!" *Mark 9:24*

Many believers have experienced moments when they were not quite sure of their faith. With all their accumulated knowledge, all their broadening "education," and with the "tune of the times" dictating much of their thinking, they have wondered if they can still sing with the children of their Sunday school class: "Jesus loves me, this I know; for the Bible tells me so."

Yes, you and I can still sing that hymn and mean it—if we maintain the attitude of the man quoted in the above Scripture passage. He had asked the Lord to cure his son, who was suffering from a severe mental disorder. In response the Savior asked: "Do you believe I can?" To which the man replied: "Yes, Lord, I believe; please help me deal with my doubts and disbelief." And the Lord healed the man's son!

It was not the father's faith, weak or strong, that saved the boy. It was the strong Lord. And we may be sure that in the process the faith of the father was mightily strengthened. Let us always remember: we are not saved by the strength of our faith; we are saved by the redeeming love of our Lord Jesus Christ. In Him we trust whatever the circumstance of life may be.

O Lord, I do believe. When doubts assail me, please be at my side to strengthen me. Amen.

We Have a Lord Who Knows Us

He calls His own sheep by name and leads them out.
John 10:3

We have a Lord, a Lord who owns us body and soul. We have a Lord who holds our lives in His hands. Were we His impersonal, unknown subjects, we would have cause to fear. Were He a proud and imperious ruler, well could we tremble.

But we have a Lord who knows us. His wisdom is past our understanding. He knows all things. Most important for us, He knows us. He knows us far better than we know ourselves. He knows each one of us by name.

He knows us as people. Though we are but dust, He knows us as priceless, immortal souls. Though the star-filled universe makes us like a grain of sand, He knows us as the crown of all creation. Though our sins present us as enemies, rebels filled with the ugly fruits of Satan, yet He knows us as sheep for whom He was willing to die.

He knows who we are and what we are. But most important, He knows us for what we can be in and through His power and love. He knows us for what we will be, by His grace, in the endless reaches of God's eternity. He knows us as children of our heavenly King. He had each one of us personally in mind when He came to redeem us and to make us His very own, when He went to Calvary to purchase us with His own blood.

Jesus, our Lord, keep us ever in Your sight, and lead us to know You better, even as we are known by You. Amen.

Written in Heaven

Do not rejoice that the spirits submit to you, but rejoice that your names are written in heaven.
Luke 10:20

We all look for reasons to rejoice and celebrate. It may be getting an A on a test, receiving an honor or award, winning a game, recovering from an illness, or moving into a new home. These and many more can be reasons for rejoicing and praising God.

At the top of each day's list of reasons for rejoicing is the precious knowledge our Savior gives us that our names are written in heaven. It does not matter how many or few reasons we may have for joy in our lives this day. We have something to celebrate. God knows our names. He has reserved a place for us with Him in heaven. Our names are listed among those who through faith in Christ will receive all the joys and blessings of eternal life.

May this truth be what always gives us the greatest joy in life! May the joy and the hope of knowing that our names are written in heaven sustain and help us through days when sadness or difficulty leave us no other reason for rejoicing! To have our names written in heaven is reason enough to rejoice, even in time of trouble.

Lord Jesus, our dearest Savior, thank You for the joy it gives us to know our names are written in heaven. Amen.

Doing the Impossible

Our enemies ... were afraid and lost their self-confidence, because they realized that this work had been done with the help of our God. *Nehemiah 6:16*

Walt Disney once said, "The most fun is seeing the impossible done." The Bible is the continuing story of the impossible being done—by God's action.

Imagine the fun—and triumph—of Nehemiah and his workers, who returned from exile in Babylon to a seemingly impossible task. They rebuilt the walls of Jerusalem in 52 days—walls which had lain in destruction for 150 years. Seeing the impossible done had a great impact on the enemies of God's people—they were forced to acknowledge that this work had been done only with the help of the Lord.

There are no impossible situations that can keep God from fulfilling His promises. What could be more impossible than to rescue humanity from the clutches of Satan and death? God did so when Jesus lived, died, and rose for us.

When God chooses to act in our lives, no enemy can stand in His way. He has promised to be with us in all situations, even the seemingly impossible ones. We too must acknowledge that any good which we accomplish is done only with the help of the Lord.

Lord, we celebrate Your victory over the impossible—Your triumph over sin and death—in Christ Jesus. Amen.

Nothing Too Hard for God

Is anything too hard for the Lord? I will return to you at the appointed time next year and Sarah will have a son. *Genesis 18:14*

Like her spouse, the faithful Abraham, Sarah passed through times of doubt and disbelief. There was the laughter of doubt in her heart that God could or would keep His promise.

But here is God's loving challenge for us as we, too, are given to wonder about the ability of God. We hear and accept the assertion of capable people: "The difficult we do immediately, the impossible takes a little longer." But the ability of the Almighty still creates problems. So He puts the above question to our hearts. In doing so He reminds us that nothing is demanded of faith which is not justified by His actions of the past. He has opened the gate of life to us; is it too hard for Him to lead us through it?

The "impossible child" promised to Sarah was born at the appointed time. The "impossible Child" promised to the Old Testament people was born in Bethlehem's stable to redeem the world.

Is anything too hard for God? Not when we believe in Him enough to let Him do the "impossible" for us. Nothing is ever too hard for Him to do for those who place their trust in Him. God's love for us is backed up by His might.

Lord, You did the "impossible" in bringing me to faith in Jesus. Help me to believe that nothing is ever too hard for You. Amen.

God Cares!

He cares for you. *1 Peter 5:7*

Peter wrote these words to the suffering and sorrowing Christians of Asia Minor, scattered by persecution. This message was to give them comfort and hope and to assure them that God cared for them.

They needed this assurance. "If God cares, why are we in trouble? If God cares, why did we lose our homes, our possessions? Why were our families torn apart by persecution?"

What a familiar ring! Have you asked why in this way? "If God cares for me, why does He allow so many difficulties? Why does He let me become ill? Why does He permit tornadoes and floods to wreak havoc? Why does God permit suffering?"

God knows us well. God knows we have a way of straying from Him. He knows the world is mined with booby traps. When we stray away from God, we fall into these traps designed for our destruction. If we are not to be destroyed, our faith must be strong. We must remain sturdy, loyal, and true.

It is for this reason He allows us to endure certain trials and fiery tests. Though they are not pleasant, though they are difficult to bear, they are still intended for our good. God loves us. God cares for us. So He purifies us, as gold is purified in fire, by making us pass through the hot fires of adversity. Our way of trouble may not be easy, but it leads to glory in heaven.

O Lord, make me strong through adversity. Amen.

Why Bad Things Happen

Dear friends, do not be surprised at the painful trial you are suffering, as though something strange were happening to you. *1 Peter 4:12*

Bad things do happen to good people. We often ask: Why, when we love and serve God, do so many bad things happen to us?

It bothers us, but Peter suggests that we should not regard this as strange. It is going to happen. The cross of adversity dominates our lives. It is our reality. Christ had to suffer; we shall have to suffer. But we shall not only share His suffering; we are assured that we shall also share in His glory.

Saint Peter tells us that through the resurrection of Jesus from the dead, God has given us an inheritance, safe in heaven for us. Our trials can have the helpful purpose of refining our faith, as gold is refined, so that we cling all the more strongly to our Savior and thus gain what God wishes to give us: eternal life with Him in heaven.

There is evil, and we should resist it. But when bad things happen to us, with God's help we can move toward acceptance and the useful purpose He would make of them in our lives. Above all, God's desire is that we may enjoy good things with Him in all eternity.

Father, let me trust You completely with my life, even to the extent of accepting—and using for good—the bad things that happen to me. Amen.

When Weak Is Strong

My grace is sufficient for you, for My power is made perfect in weakness. *2 Corinthians 12:9*

The apostle Paul had a physical infirmity, the exact nature of which has never been determined. Whatever it was, it was a source of pain and embarrassment to him as he carried out the duties of his apostleship. He called it his "thorn in the flesh." Repeatedly he asked the Lord to rid him of this painful "thorn," but repeatedly the Lord replied, "My grace is sufficient for you, for My power is made perfect in [your] weakness."

In God's unsearchable wisdom He knew that Paul would be a more effective witness to the Gospel with his thorn than without it. In a sense the "thorn" became a part of Paul's witness; not only did it keep him truly humble, but it also enabled him to give an eloquent firsthand testimonial to God's grace.

How about you and me? Do we have our thorns in the flesh, our limitations, our weaknesses? Even these can become open doors for the spreading of His Gospel. To each of us He says: "Give Me your weaknesses, and I will make them My strength." The important thing is that we recognize our weakness and dedicate it to His service. He can do wonders, even with our weakness.

Lord, I am weak but You are mighty. Use me as I am, dear Lord. In Jesus' name I ask it. Amen.

Able to Do All Things

I can do everything through Him who gives me strength. *Philippians 4:13*

The story is told of a great violinist who was giving a concert—when the A string on his violin broke. Without stopping, he adjusted to the situation and finished the piece on three strings. A lesser violinist might have stopped and complained about his bad luck. But it takes a really great artist to do what he did. He was able to work with what was available to him.

So it is with life. None of us has all that we would like to have. We struggle through life with our problems: illness, financial difficulties, an impossible boss, or loneliness.

Saint Paul, that great soldier of the cross, had his problems. He suffered from pain, persecution, perils, and many other adversities as he proclaimed the good news of God's saving Gospel. Paul did not complain. He looked to the cross for help and hope. He exclaimed, "I can do everything through Him who gives me strength." That's a great word for our age. In Christ we have a marvelous friend. Our confidence is built on the Lord Jesus Christ, the Rock of Ages. Someone has said, "Christ did not come to make life easy. But, Christ did come to make life strong."

Dear Lord Jesus, thank You for Your saving strength. Your grace is made perfect in my weakness. Amen.

Thanks for Nothing

No harm will befall you. *Psalm 91:10*

When someone is not much help, people might say sarcastically, "Well, thanks for nothing!" The comment draws attention to the failures of another.

In a positive way, however, we *can* thank God for nothing. When we think of all the troubles that exist in the world, as we contemplate all the diseases and afflictions that face humanity, while we hear of all the persecutions against religious faiths around the globe, we should pray to God and say, "Thank You, Lord, for keeping me safe."

God has three ways to keep us safe from all harm and danger in life. First, He pushes many troubles and dangers away from us so that we don't even come into contact with them. Second, He turns evil into good. We can in all truth affirm that God uses everything for some good. Third, Christ promises to lift us out of this vale of tears into heaven. This assurance comes through faith in Jesus Christ, who died to take away our sin. He rose from the dead on the third day and ascended to heaven to prepare a place for us. Therefore we pray with trusting hearts, "Lord, thanks for everything!"

God, thank You for keeping us from all harm and danger and for guarding us against evil. Amen.

Be Happy

Rejoice in the Lord always. I will say it again: Rejoice!
Philippians 4:4

"Religion takes the joy out of life." That may be true of religions that require people to attempt to achieve perfection on their own. But the one religion for which that statement is completely false is Christianity. The Christian faith gives us constant reason to be joyous.

There is reason for joy when God lets us wake up in the morning. With the psalmist we say, "This is the day the Lord has made; let us rejoice and be glad in it" (118:24). With God's love and mercy in Christ, we go about our activities relaxed and at peace.

Paul experienced many hardships and disappointments in life. At the time he wrote the words of our text, he was under arrest for proclaiming Jesus as the Christ. And yet, even in chains, he encouraged the Philippians to be joyous.

Knowing that all things work together to good for those who love God, we can face challenges, hardships, and suffering with joy. God will give us courage and strength to deal with whatever confronts us. Even in disappointment and failure, God is still with us to comfort us and help us with our problems and sorrows.

No, the Christian faith does not take joy out of life. Rather, it alone assures us that God is at our side.

Thank You, Lord, for the many reasons for joy each day of our life. Help us to rejoice in You today and always.
Amen.

The Good Shepherd

As a shepherd looks after his scattered flock … .
Ezekiel 34:12

One of the most comforting Old Testament pictures of the Messiah was that of the shepherd. Jesus claimed the title *Messiah* for Himself when He said: "I am the Good Shepherd." He based His claim not on His teachings and miracles alone, but rather on His Saviorhood, as the One who laid down His life for His people. Christ laid down His life as a ransom to purchase His sheep.

Why did He have to die? Because "we all, like sheep, have gone astray, each of us has turned to his own way" (Isaiah 53:6). Willfully we left the fold. We became lost in the night, in the storms of a troubled world. We became lost in our own pet theories and the blinding fog of our doubts, our sins.

For such lost sheep as we are, the Good Shepherd came and freely, willingly, lovingly laid down His life that we might once again be led back into the fold. What a wonderful shepherd is ours!

No wonder we love this picture of Christ! No wonder we love to sing:

The King of love my shepherd is, Whose goodness faileth never; I nothing lack if I am his And he is mine forever.
In death's dark vale I fear no ill
With thee, dear Lord, beside me,
Thy rod and staff my comfort still,
Thy cross before to guide me. Amen.

Encore!

Though the doors were locked, Jesus came and stood among them and said, "Peace be with you!"
John 20:26

Jesus is the Good Shepherd. When He died, His sheep scattered, but as soon as He rose from the dead, He set about gathering them together into the one flock, His church. Individually and in groups He rounded them up. But Thomas was not with them on the first Easter as they huddled in fear behind closed doors.

Jesus, however, heard every word spoken by doubting Thomas. Our Savior knows all. He is also patient and forgiving. Jesus had refused to perform a miracle for the entertainment of King Herod. Yet for the sake of restoring an obstinate apostle, Jesus made a repeat appearance so that Thomas would believe. Overwhelmed by the proof of the resurrection, Thomas made that great confession every Christian makes: "My Lord and my God!"

How comforting to know our Lord will not let us go! He understands our frailty and knows the doubts within us. Through the Scriptures He reveals to us that He is risen and alive. In His mercy He offers us a second chance, and restores us when our faith flickers. He calls us not to be faithless, but to believe. He wants us to come out from behind closed doors and gather with the rest of the church in His name.

Jesus, though we have not yet seen or touched You, grant us to confess with the whole church, "My Lord and my God!" Amen.

Help in Trouble

God is our refuge and strength, an ever-present help in trouble. *Psalm 46:1*

The shaking of the earth and the trembling of the mountains are not such strange sights to us who live in an age when media coverage frequently brings us news of volcanic eruptions and earthquakes around the world. However, even beyond this, the little world in which each of us lives is often shaken by some personal crisis or tragedy, and life caves in on us. We may be able to find short moments of relative peace, but most of the time we are in the midst of trouble.

Above the roaring of the storm God's own promise speaks clearly in this psalm. Not only is He the refuge to which we may flee, but He stands with us in the midst of the torrents that rage around us. His loving presence grants inner stillness to the heart.

Dare we hope that the Lord of all is eager to be with us? Yes! In Christ God is with us. He is the Word made flesh dwelling among us. He pledges His presence with those who rightly bear His name, and He keeps that promise.

He is by our side in battle with His good gifts and Spirit. Though we lose our fame and goods, our spouse and child, the victory is still there. "The Kingdom ours remaineth!"

O God, our Refuge and Strength, give us the courage to seek You and to find forgiveness and peace through Christ's cross. Amen.

Tribulation—Peace

I have told you these things, so that in Me you may have peace. In this world you will have trouble. But take heart! I have overcome the world. *John 16:33*

None of us faces a trouble-free life. All types of hardship crowd in upon us. We are not responsible for much of it, but we are victims of the age in which we live and the world that surrounds us. Disease threatens our vigor, if not our vitality. Threats of war rob us of security. Automation crowds us out of a job. Easy immorality sneaks up to destroy our virtue—sometimes our very life. Into this ugly picture steps our Lord Jesus Christ, who says, "Peace. You have trouble in the world. But take heart! I have overcome the world."

He understands the tribulation that is heaped upon us, for it was heaped on Him as well. The assault of humankind, the wiles of Satan, the forces of nature all conspired to bring trouble into His life. He did not complain under its burden, but He carried it victoriously. In a triumphant speech He tells us that when trouble comes, we may face it with good cheer, for He will turn it into our victory. Peace will permeate our lives again, for He has reconciled all things to Himself and orders them for our good. As Jesus went to the cross with our sins upon His shoulders and atoned for them with the shedding of His blood, He has brought to us that perfect peace that gives us eternal life.

Give me peace, O Lord, by trusting Your Word that You have overcome the world. Amen.

The Heavenly Father in Control

We know that in all things God works for the good of those who love Him. *Romans 8:28*

"In all things God works for the good" is a staggering promise. Note "in all things"—whether they seem good, bad, or indifferent—"God works for the good." We usually make these distinctions. Some things we consider to be always of benefit to us. Other things we call misfortunes, believing them to be contrary to our best interests. Then there are things that we ordinarily regard as of no consequence one way or another.

In all things "*God works* for the good." The storms of adversity, the fires of affliction, the showers of God's blessing, the sunshine of happiness—in all these experiences God works to fashion one harmonious design and purpose.

Not in themselves, of course, are all things working for good. All the various things that make up life's experiences work together for good to bring us closer to Christ and, by faith in Him, to the gracious Father in heaven.

That is precisely what all of God's dealings with His own are designed to bring about. For the best interest of His people "days of sadness, days of gladness, in strange alternation braid."

Heavenly Father, strengthen our faith and trust in Your providential guidance and direction. In Jesus' name we pray. Amen.

The Use of Decaying Trees

We know that in all things God works for the good of those who love Him. *Romans 8:28*

Scattered in the forest along mountain trails lie the decaying hulks of downed trees. The passing hiker notices them but doesn't always realize their value. Small animals and birds use them for shelter. Delicate plants grow on and around them. Gradually these trees enrich the ground for other vegetation. Even decaying trees have their use.

As we follow life's trail, we hardly notice some incidents that happen. Other experiences are painful, forcing us to be aware of them but not always of any good purpose they serve. Much in life seems rather pointless.

But God reveals that "in all things" He is working for our good when we love Him because of Jesus, who died and rose as our Savior.

That promise can be very comforting when painful things happen. But if He works "in all things," we can look for good even in what might at first seem insignificant. We won't always understand the why or realize the good He intends. But if we try, we often will find unexpected meaning or blessing in what otherwise we might have taken for granted.

Lord, help us to appreciate more fully today Your work in everything and make it occur for our good. Amen.

A Little While

I will be with you only a little longer. *John 13:33*

On different occasions Christ told His disciples that He would be with them only a little while longer. During that little while that was still left, He instructed them in His Word, in the purpose of His ministry, and in the method of their testimony about Him. At the very end of His ministry Christ told them that He was now leaving them for a little while and that they would see Him no more. He was going to the Father by way of the cross.

Life is full of "little whiles." Sometimes they seem very short because their moments are filled with joy and contentment. We have our friends and our loved ones around us for a little while, and we enjoy their companionship. But they are taken away, and we see them no more.

On the other hand, there are the "little whiles" that seem like eternities. There is discomfort and pain, disappointment and tension. We think these moments are eternities. The night of pain is endlessly long, and the morning never seems to dawn. We toss and we turn, but there is no relief.

But it is only a little while. "For a brief moment I abandoned you … . In a surge of anger I hid my face from you for a moment." The promise is added, "But with deep compassion I will bring you back. … with everlasting kindness I will have compassion on you," says the Lord your Redeemer (Isaiah 54:7–8).

Dear Jesus,
Take my moments and my days;
Let them sing Your ceaseless praise. Amen.

Pain

O Lord, heal me, for my bones are in agony. *Psalm 6:2*

The pain strikes suddenly. The lower back aches. The pain spreads up the spine. Movement increases the discomfort. Lying down helps, but even sleep becomes difficult. Day after day the pain continues. Why is this happening? Who can help? When pain leaves, we often forget, but when symptoms persist, we wilt and lie helpless.

The psalmist struggles under affliction and cries out, "O Lord, heal me!" He adds, "I am worn out from groaning; all night long I flood my bed with weeping" (v. 6). No pat answers to the problem of pain. No help from philosophical speculation about the inevitability of pain or its maturing benefits. Like the psalmist, we turn to God in our despair. We ask for healing, for relief, for strength.

But most of all, we focus on God's Son, who took on flesh and experienced pain for us. He hurt when roughly handled and scourged. The nails in His hands and feet sent pain stabbing through His system. And the hours of tortured breathing on the cross took their toll. In the process, He conquered sin and death. Pain continues now, but God heals, soothes, and strengthens. Risen and ascended, Jesus will come again to take us to eternal life with Him, where there will be no more pain.

But the pains which He endured, Alleluia!
Our salvation have procured; Alleluia!

171

Our Help Comes from the Lord

I lift up my eyes to the hills—where does my help come from? My help comes from the Lord, the Maker of heaven and earth. *Psalm 121:1–2*

Most Christians have experienced times when they seemed without help or hope. Health, family problems, financial distress—whatever the trouble—there seemed to be no one to turn to.

Yet we know where to seek help. We can confidently approach the throne of Christ, who sympathizes with our weaknesses. His throne is a throne of grace. Our Savior knows our sins. He covers our weaknesses, even our weak faith, with His love and forgiveness. From Him we receive mercy and grace in our time of need. It is to Him we turn in distress.

So the psalmist says confidently, "My help comes from the Lord, the Maker of heaven and earth." Again: "The Lord will keep you from all harm—He will watch over your life; the Lord will watch over your coming and going both now and forevermore."

God may not always give us what we want. We may not always understand God's ways, but we can trust Him. He has our earthly welfare and our eternal salvation at heart.

Lead us, Lord, as You will. If it is through sorrow or want, make us content to go Your way patiently, and bring us safely home to heaven. For Jesus' sake we pray. Amen.

His Will, Not Ours

My Father, if it is possible, may this cup be taken from Me. Yet not as I will, but as You will. … My Father, if it is not possible for this cup to be taken away unless I drink it, may Your will be done. *Matthew 26:39, 42*

Many of us are acquainted with Heinrich Hofmann's inspiring painting entitled "Christ in Gethsemane." In this painting Christ is shown kneeling on the ground, with His forearms resting on a large stone, His hands folded, and His eyes directed toward heaven. As we look at the scene, we can almost hear Jesus pleading: "My Father … not as I will, but as You will. … Your will be done."

At that moment, of course, Christ was more than an example for us to follow. He was our Savior, suffering for the sins of all people. But in a secondary sense, He was on that sorrowful night also an example for us to follow.

How many of us have had to live through our own "Gethsemanes"—a painful illness, a broken marriage, a friend lost, a wayward child, days of doubt and dark despair? Whatever the tragedy, it was our own "Gethsemane."

In moments like that, may we be given the childlike faith to say: "My Father, You have redeemed me through Your Son. You are my anchor and my stay. Into Your fatherly hands I place my life. Not my will, but Yours be done."

Lord, I place my life—with every burden—into Your hands. I trust Your good and gracious will. In Jesus' name I pray. Amen.

Don't Leave Home without It

I have hidden Your word in my heart. Psalm 119:11

When life gets tough, we need something more solid to cling to than feelings and emotions. "In time of trial we should rest not on our feelings but on the Word of God" (Luther). God's Word is like the Rock of Gibraltar. In it there is help for every need.

The best we can do is to cling to the promises of God. God will always meet us there—and effectively so. When it comes to power, nothing can match the power of God's Word. It replaces negative attitudes. It gives attitudes that have altitude.

Here are some words to take with you wherever you go. Hold them and they will hold you. "By this I will know that God is for me" (Psalm 56:9). "If God is for us, who can be against us?" (Romans 8:31). "My grace is sufficient for you" (2 Corinthians 12:9). "Cast all your anxiety on Him because He cares for you" (1 Peter 5:7). "Never will I leave you; never will I forsake you" (Hebrews 13:5).

The Word is powerful, eternal, imperishable. "Heaven and earth will pass away, but My words will never pass away" (Luke 21:33). Nothing on earth can do more for you than the Word that testifies of Christ, our Savior.

Lord, I want to love Your Word more and more. It holds, it helps, it builds me up. Amen.

Focusing on Jesus

Let us fix our eyes on Jesus, the author and perfecter of our faith. *Hebrews 12:2*

After picking up her photographs at the developer one day, a young traveler was disappointed to discover that many of her vacation pictures were blurry images of unrecognizable objects. She had failed to focus her camera.

The apostle Peter learned about the necessity of proper focusing when Jesus called him to walk on water. When he kept his eyes on Jesus, he was fine. But when he looked around at the wind, fear engulfed him, and he began to sink. He had the wrong focus.

Such is our experience at times. We don't focus on Jesus, but rather on our circumstances. Then we begin to doubt God's care of us. Confusion and fear may drown us.

The writer to the Hebrews counsels us to "fix our eyes on Jesus." We are to look to Him, meditate on Him, and consider the sufferings and shame He underwent to redeem us. Such a focus will assure us of His immeasurable love for us and give us confidence that He will keep us and perfect the faith He has begun in us. God supplies our needs, guides us through our perplexities, and comforts us always. What an encouraging picture!

Help me, dear Lord Jesus, to focus not on my circumstances, but on You, my Life and my Salvation. Amen.

He'll Hold Our Hand— Today and Tomorrow

I am with you always, to the very end of the age.
Matthew 28:20

A little girl was walking with her father through the downtown streets of the city to which they had recently moved. They turned corner after corner, taking in one new sight of the unfamiliar city after another.

After some time the little one looked up and asked: "Daddy, are you lost?" Instead of answering her directly, he tightened his grip on her little hand and, smiling warmly, asked: "Why, are you lost?" "Oh, no!" she said brightly, "I'm with you, Daddy! How could I be lost?"

We are dealing here with a parable. How can you and I be "lost" as long as we know that our loving Lord is with us—and that we are walking hand in hand with Him? One of our Savior's last words to us was: "Remember, I am with you always." The timeless Christ was speaking, the great "I AM" of John 8:58, with whom there is no present, past, or future. It is He who assures us: I am with you always—today, tomorrow, and forever.

With our hand in His, we can walk courageously through each today and all of our tomorrows.

Lord, keep my hand in Yours until I reach my journey's end. Amen.

One Step at a Time

Not that I have already obtained all this, or have already been made perfect; but I press on to take hold of that for which Christ Jesus took hold of me.
Philippians 3:12

Pursued by chariots and horses (the fastest mode of travel in that day), the children of Israel walked across the Red Sea. Forty years later, after a circuitous and tedious journey, they walked into the Promised Land.

That's the way our journey through life usually is—a daily walk, one step at a time. Occasionally we "fly with the eagles," but more often we just plod along, day by day, and the perfection we dream of seems far away.

Like the apostle Paul, through faith in Jesus Christ we look ahead and see perfection, the kind of Christian God wants us to be, the promised land of heaven. Looking at today, however, we see slow progress, slipping and falling, rocks along the way, a step backward for every one forward.

But looking backward, we can echo the old man's dialog with his Maker quoted by Dr. Martin Luther King: "Lord, I ain't what I ought to be; I ain't what I want to be; I ain't what I'm gonna be; but thank God, I ain't what I was!" Day by day, as in faith we come to God for guidance, we press on in our upward journey, one step at a time.

Take my hand, Lord, and lead me. Make a wide place for my steps so that my feet will not slip. Amen.

The Lost Is Found

And when he finds it, he joyfully puts it on his shoulders and goes home. *Luke 15:5*

The shepherd's search for his lost sheep is begun at the moment the sheep becomes lost; it is carried on with great vigor and urgency; and it continues until the sheep is found. Such was the concern of a shepherd in our Lord's day for his sheep. When at last the great moment of discovery comes and the lost sheep is found, this is an occasion for nothing but pure joy over the fact that the lost is no more lost but found; the missing one is safe and sound. As a spontaneous expression of joy and relief, the shepherd tenderly picks the sheep up, examines it for cuts and bruises, and gently lays it on his shoulders as he heads back to the fold.

By this simple illustration our Lord reassures us and all His sheep that each one is very precious in His sight. For each one who strays or wanders from the fold of faith He has an all-consuming concern. Our Good Shepherd goes forth, seeking the lost one and hoping to restore him or her. He does this each time a sheep strays.

What a comfort to all of us wandering sheep! We experience not only our Lord's loving concern and persevering search but also His forgiveness that takes away our lostness. With rejoicing He restores us to the fold of the faithful.

Gracious and Good Shepherd, may we stray no longer but remain found by You forever. Amen.

178

Straying—Returning

**You were like sheep going astray, but now you have
returned to the Shepherd and Overseer of your souls.**
1 Peter 2:25

To be called sheep is not exactly a compliment. Sheep
are weak and helpless, stupid and fearful. Take your eyes off
them, and they wander away. Scripture always talks about
them getting lost or being in danger. We are often called
sheep, sheep who stray. And we do, do we not? Not that
many of us get into major trouble very often, but we skirt
the edges of law and morality enough to be reminded that
we are full of sin and that we need a shepherd to rescue us.

And what a shepherd we have! He calls His sheep by
name; He leaves the major portion of the flock to attend
one who has strayed; He lays down His life for all; He rises
again to feed and nourish His flock.

To be returned to such a shepherd is sheer joy, and we
are not embarrassed to be called sheep. On the contrary, we
recognize our need and are grateful that God has not abandoned us in our lost condition but has sent the Good Shepherd to guard, feed, and lead us. With the sheep of Psalm
23 we are able to say, "Surely goodness and love will follow
me all the days of my life, and I will dwell in the house of
the Lord forever."

Savior, like a shepherd lead us! Amen.

Heading for Home

Take My yoke upon you and learn from Me, for I am gentle and humble in heart, and you will find rest for your souls. For My yoke is easy and My burden is light. *Matthew 11:29–30*

Who can lighten our burdens—the pains and problems of life that inevitably plague us all?

When a team of horses used to pull a hay wagon out to the fields, they plodded along with little enthusiasm. But when the wagon was stacked high with hay and they were heading for home where there was food and water and rest, the heavy load seemed to be no load at all!

On the road to our heavenly home with Jesus, our burdens become light. Granted, we do wear His yoke. We are His servants. But our Master is the loving Lord Jesus, who gave His life on the cross to redeem us. It is when we lose sight of Jesus and the glory that awaits us that our burdens seem unbearable. Caught up in the cares and worries of this earthly life, we easily chafe even under the light loads.

Do we envy those Christians who bear up so well under their burdens? Jesus' invitation is for us, too: "My yoke is easy." He does not promise to remove every burden. His promise is to guide us safely to the heavenly home.

Lord Jesus, we thank You for Your promise of heavenly glory, which makes Your yoke easy and our burdens light. Amen.

Unevenly Yoked

Take My yoke upon you, and learn from Me.
Matthew 11:29

Strange, isn't it, that God would consider a sinner to be just as innocent as the Sinless One; that for a condemned person, Jesus would dare to die; and that a wayward son would be welcomed home by a forgiving father as if nothing had happened!

Yet here we are, people who have trouble keeping God's will uppermost in our minds and hearts. Like King David of Old Testament days, we are surrounded by problems and troubles on every side. Some of our difficulties are of our own making; some come as a result of the actions of others. All are burdens to carry, and quite often no one seems willing to help.

Yet the Savior's invitation comes to burdened souls with rich assurance. "Come to Me," says the Sinless One. "Take My yoke upon you." Finally, the message sinks in. Someone cares! God sees us in our need. He sent His Son, Jesus Christ, who was willing to bear our burdens of sin and sorrow, and even to die for us!

Talk about being "unevenly yoked"—we who are weak with the One who is strong! Christ carries us with His tender love. He takes on our burdens and shares with us His Holy Spirit so that we have the needed strength to endure whatever befalls us.

O Lord Jesus Christ, accept our praise for taking away our burdens and making them Your own. Amen.

Cast All Your Anxiety on God

Cast all your anxiety on Him, because He cares for you. *1 Peter 5:7*

There is no question but that illness of any kind brings with it a degree of anxiety. Normal life is halted; other members of the family are inconvenienced; one's work or activity schedule is interrupted; an operation may be in the offing; the time of the full restoration to health is unknown. Whatever our worries, fears, and doubts, the apostle urges us to gather them together and cast them all on God, our heavenly Father.

Saint Peter cites the reason for placing our burdens on the Lord: "He cares for you." God cared about each one of us before we were born. He continued to be concerned after our birth, keeping and preserving us from harm. In answer to prayer He freely gave us the blessings we needed. Surpassing all these benefits is the greatest gift: Jesus Christ. A greeting card company urges people who care enough to give the very best. God cared enough that He gave the very best: His own Son to be our Savior and Helper.

Keeping this in mind, we can confidently come to our Lord with all our cares and prayers in time of sickness. He will take care of us. He will be with us when we need Him the most.

Lord Jesus, I am privileged to have You as my friend, for You bore all my sins and griefs. Amen.

Divine Physician

[Jesus] … healed all the sick. This was to fulfill what was spoken through the prophet Isaiah: "He took up our infirmities and carried our diseases."
Matthew 8:16–17

We usually think of the Lord Jesus as teacher or preacher or redeemer from sin. As He is pictured in the gospel accounts, however, it would be just as true to look upon Him as medical doctor. The record of His early ministry, at least, indicates that He probably spent as much time healing as He did teaching and preaching.

And Saint Matthew points out that Jesus' healing ministry filled out the prophetic picture of the Messiah found in Isaiah's great 53rd chapter: "Surely He took up our infirmities and carried our sorrows" (v. 4).

Though no longer with us visibly, Jesus is still the Great Physician. "Surely I am with you always," was His final promise. Through the skill of doctors, the care of nurses, the "miracle" of drugs and medical technology, along with the processes of nature, His healing comes to our sick bodies.

By serene trust and faith in the Savior who not only bore our sins but also "took up our infirmities and carried our diseases," we reach out and touch the source of all healing power.

O Great Physician, who once ministered to the multitudes, bringing health and peace and life, give all who are sick today a sense of Your nearness; bestow Your healing through the skillful hands at work in the healing arts. Amen.

183

A Trilogy of Hope

Speak tenderly to Jerusalem, and proclaim to her that her hard service has been completed, that her sin has been paid for. *Isaiah 40:2*

Most of us are not like cavalrymen on spirited horses who anxiously wait for the cry "Charge!" Most of us are ready for a word of comfort and hope. So it is good that the Scriptures picture God not like a field marshal pushing us into battle but more like a field physician bending over our wounded spirits and broken dreams to bring us calm and healing.

Isaiah 40:2 gives us three word pictures of comfort and hope. In the first one God declares: "Proclaim to her [God's people, the church] that her hard service has been completed." Each of us daily battles his or her sinful nature. The good intentions we formulate in the morning have usually faded away before noon. Our evil impulses tend to push the new man in us—the new nature in Christ—into retreat.

Then God steps forward and tells us that the decisive battle was fought at Golgotha. There Jesus, through His death and resurrection, won not only the battle but also the war. Our sins are forgiven. Death has been defeated. "Our hard service ['warfare' in some translations] has been completed." We live in peace. This is good news for us, and it is also the message our Lord wants us to share with the world.

Lord Jesus, Lamb of God, You have taken away the sin of the world. Grant us now Your precious peace. Amen.

The Peace of God

Peace I leave with you; My peace I give you. … Do not let your hearts be troubled. *John 14:27*

This was all our Savior had that He could leave to His disciples, but what a precious legacy—the peace of God! "Peace I leave with you; My peace I give you."

Peace does not come easily these days. Pressures from without and pressures from within disturb our peace. Our nerves are taut. We cannot relax. We are restless, worried, irritable. The burden and demands of work, the guilt of sin, the fear of death, and sometimes the fear of life—these wear us down. We have no peace.

Christ offers us His peace! He offers us the same serenity with which He went to Golgotha. He calms our troubled hearts with the same peace that stilled the Sea of Galilee and the fear-filled hearts of His disciples. He grants the same peace He breathed on His apostles when He commissioned them, "Peace I leave with you."

The peace He grants is the peace of a clean heart and a right spirit, the peace of guilt removed and sins forgiven, the peace of fellowship with God that gives us strength for every burden and sufficient resources for every task. It is the peace of God that passes understanding. Nothing can disturb it.

Grant us Your strength, O Lord, beneath the crushing load of life, and through Christ let us find peace in You. Amen.

Too Fearful!

I will trust and not be afraid. *Isaiah 12:2*

Trust and fear are opposites. The more we have of the one, the less we have of the other.

It is easy to fear. Cancer, nuclear weapons, recession, inflation, unemployment, tornadoes, marital and family problems—all these plus many others strike fear into our human hearts.

But we need not be afraid. The secret of overcoming fear is to know God better and trust Him more. In the Old Testament we note how wonderfully God cared for His people. In the New Testament we see how God has taken care of the spiritual needs of all people by sacrificing His Son for the sins of the world. In the entire Scriptures we read God's many promises to be our Keeper and the Lover of our souls.

In our own life we see the evidences of God's care. He has brought us to faith in Jesus, heaped many spiritual blessings upon us, and guided us year after year. He has cared for our earthly and physical needs.

The more clearly we see God's care for His people in the past, the more we will trust Him to take care of our present and future needs. The more we trust Him, the less we fear and the more we can face every situation in life confidently saying, "I will trust, and not be afraid."

Lord, drive out of my heart every fear, and let me trust in Your grace daily. Amen.

God, My Stronghold in Every Trouble

[God] alone is my rock and my salvation; He is my fortress, I will not be shaken. *Psalm 62:6*

Where do you go when troubles mount up? Do you head off into the hills to find some tranquility? Do you pile into bed and attempt to sleep it off? Is a bottle or a pill your hopeful refuge? Do you seek out a friend, or do you make an appointment with a counselor?

The psalmist knew trouble as well as you and I do. He experienced people who sought to destroy him—people who longed for his ruin. He even experienced the most hurtful of relationships: people who outwardly posed as friends, blessing him with their mouths, while inwardly cursing him.

Where did the psalmist David go with his troubles? He went to his stronghold—his God. He pictured God as a fortified city. There he would be safe; God would defend him.

You and I are reminded likewise to go to God as our stronghold. That is not to say that we should bypass friends and counselors, but it is to say that true power comes from God. He has already proven Himself the author of our salvation through Jesus Christ. He who gave us eternal life through His Son will surely protect us in the time of trouble, for He is our Rock, our Salvation, and our mighty Fortress.

Father in heaven let me flee to You in every trouble. Take me up and protect me. For Jesus' sake I pray. Amen.

Who Cares?

Martha ... said, "Lord, don't You care that my sister has left me to do the work by myself?" *Luke 10:40*

We are so quick to accuse God! Adam did it in the Garden, saying to God, "The woman You put here with me—she gave me some fruit from the tree" (Genesis 3:12). And the disciples in the storm-tossed boat asked Jesus, "Teacher, don't You care if we drown?" (Mark 4:38).

And now Martha, distracted with her noble intentions, frazzled by the housework, blames Jesus: "Don't You care?" When things don't go our way, sometimes we point the finger at God. "How could You let such a thing happen, God?"

It seems as if we think we deserve a life free from sorrow, and when we have problems, we become angry at such divine "carelessness."

And yet, it is God who cares the most. If we wonder about God's genuine concern for our ultimate good, we have only to look to Christ's cross. There we see our merciful God caring so much for us that He gave the life of His only Son to redeem us from our sins, including our distrust.

When life does not go as we wish, and we are tempted to accuse God of not caring, we remember the cross and know that God will always care for us. And we remember Christ's promise, "I am with you always, to the very end of the age" (Matthew 28:20).

Father in heaven, because of Christ's cross we know You care. Amen.

I Grow in Understanding

God's Therapy Is Good

Our light and momentary troubles are achieving for us an eternal glory that far outweighs them all.
2 Corinthians 4:17

When Luther visited a sick friend, he quoted the verse, "The Lord disciplines those He loves." "If that's the case," the friend replied, "I wish He wouldn't love me so much."

Sometimes life hurls us into a frenzy. We feel like saying, "Stop, world, I want to get off." At such times we should consider that God loves us too much to leave us as we are. He is intent on polishing us toward perfection. God, the master goldsmith, allows fiery trials to come in order that such impurities as obstinacy, a vengeful spirit, lack of faith, and self-love might be burned out and Christ's image burned in.

As both black and white keys of a piano are necessary for beautiful music, so bright and dark days, joys and sorrows, are needed to keep us in repentance and improvement.

Where there's trouble, God is needed; where God is needed, He is entreated; where He's entreated, His help is experienced; where His help is experienced, love and gratitude are excited; where love and gratitude prevail, there praise, goodwill, and joy reign. All this is ours because by faith "we have peace with God through our Lord Jesus Christ."

Lord, for sunny days and dark days we give You praise.
Amen.

Faith Moves Mountains

[Jesus said to them,] "If you have faith as small as a mustard seed, you can say to this mountain, 'Move from here to there and it will move.' " *Matthew 17:20*

Someone has said that *doubt* creates mountains. In this promise of Jesus we are assured that *faith* can move the mountains of doubt.

If it were possible for us to turn back the calendar just six months and then look forward once again, how many mountains would we see along the road that were put there by our doubts?

The anxious mother worries about getting the bills paid. The worried father is concerned about problems and new responsibilities at work. Tired students have lost sleep worrying about tests for which they have studied their best. Each one is afraid of a mountain that has been created by doubt. Yes, it is true that doubt *creates* mountains.

But faith *removes* them. Not just any kind of faith, certainly not faith in ourselves or in some kind of providence! The faith that moves mountains is trusting the heavenly Father, who has revealed His love for us by sending His Son into the world for our salvation. He has assured us that He will give us strength sufficient for each day. It is in His strength that we shall be prepared to move whatever mountains are set in our paths.

Lord, give me such a faith as this. Amen.

Power from God

Be strong in the Lord and in His mighty power. Put on the full armor of God. *Ephesians 6:10–11*

How much we rely on electric power in our homes! It can operate dozens of appliances to make life more comfortable and convenient. The light company makes a tremendous amount of power available. Yet we can choose not to use it. Then bulbs stay dark and appliances sit useless and silent.

Our Lord makes His mighty power available to us. He is anxious to pour it into our lives, but He doesn't force it on us. He waits until we are ready to receive and use it.

When we face drudgery, disappointment, or dismay, let us remember that God is with us. His almighty Spirit lives in us to strengthen us. We can be filled with the fullness of God! God has the power to do far more in us and with us than we ask or dream. Sometimes He lets us get weaker so that we turn to Him and rely on His strength.

Most of us have times when life seems more than we can handle. We may feel: I can't take it anymore; I can't stand it. We need to remind ourselves that God's strength is only a prayer away. We have constant access to this unfailing reservoir. Let us be strong and of good courage, aware that Jesus, the Lamb of God, has borne all our burdens.

Almighty Lord, fill us with Your power so that great things can happen in us and through us. Make us more useful to You. Amen.

Why Worry?

Do not be anxious about anything, but in everything ... present your requests to God. *Philippians 4:6*

The Holy Scriptures repeatedly warn us against the grievous sin of worry. It is an act of unbelief and distrust in God. When we worry, we accuse God of falsehood. God's Word says, "Fear not," but worry says, "You are lying, O God." As someone has said, "No matter what people may profess as to their faith, worry makes them practical atheists, because worry fears the future more than it fears God." This is quite a startling accusation, is it not?

And so in desperation we ask, "What is the answer to the problem of worry?" The most definitive answer is found in Romans 8:31–32, where we read: "If God is for us, who can be against us? He who did not spare His own Son, but gave Him up for us all—how will He not also, along with Him, graciously give us all things?" Here we are clearly informed that if God provided for our greatest need, eternal life and everlasting salvation through the doing and dying of Christ, then surely He is able to provide for needs that are infinitely small in comparison. If we trust Him for the greater, should we not also trust Him for the lesser?

Gracious Lord, deliver us from all anxious thoughts, and help us cast our anxiety upon You, for You care for us. Amen.

Worry

You, Lord, give perfect peace to those who keep their purpose firm and put their trust in You.
Isaiah 26:3 TEV

She tossed and turned. She could not get to sleep. That day her son had gone off to college, and she couldn't stop thinking about him so far away from home. "What's the matter?" her husband finally asked. "I'm worried about our son," she replied. "Did you talk to the Lord about it?" he asked. "Yes," the mother said. "Well, then, go to sleep," advised the father. "There's no sense in you worrying about him when the Lord is watching over Him."

Worry is a perfectly natural trait for sinful human beings. Unfortunately, it is most often a waste of precious time and energy. "Worry," it is said, "never robs tomorrow of its sorrow; it only saps today of its strength."

Fortunately, worry is not one of the characteristics of our God. Worry does not come from Him—"perfect peace" does! So the best way to overcome worry is to seek the divine rather than the human. Turn your worries completely over to the Lord Jesus Christ. He will exchange them for peace because through His death and resurrection, He also conquered worry. As Isaiah said, He will give perfect peace to those who trust in Him.

Forgive us, Lord, for wasting so much time and energy worrying. Help us to bring our worries to You and to receive Your peace. Amen.

Past, Present, Future

[God says,] "Those who hope in Me will not be disappointed." *Isaiah 49:23*

Hindsight is often 20/20 vision. When we look back, it is easy to recognize our mistakes and see what we should have done differently. Sometimes looking back at what we have done brings regret.

Not so with God's actions! When we look back at what God has done—in biblical history and in our personal histories—we see constant kindness and faithfulness. Joshua saw it, as did Abraham, Noah, Nehemiah, the apostle Paul, and countless other Christians throughout the history of the world.

The problem is that most of the time we can see how God has worked for good in our lives only in retrospect. We may be disappointed because we want to see immediate results. But in the light of eternity, this truth will be obvious to all: Those who hope in Jesus Christ will not be disappointed!

God's loving care never fails. Did He not send Jesus to rescue us from the condemnation we deserved? The history of God's faithfulness to His people—and to us today—demonstrates that grace and mercy are the core of His being and doing.

What God has done in the past is a pledge, a sign of His present and future work in our lives. His promises stand sure.

Lord, increase my faith and trust in You; I know You will not disappoint me. Amen.

Detour Ahead

We know that in all things God works for the good of those who love Him. *Romans 8:28*

Have you ever faced a detour? Recently, on a family vacation, we were forced off an interstate highway to avoid the scene of a terrible accident. In our lack of understanding and patience, we became frustrated. Yet the ensuing beauty of the rich farmlands, the abundant wildlife, and the people we encountered along the way made the detour a joy and blessing.

People face detours as unexpected events occur in their lives. Things don't go according to their plans. People get sick, jobs are lost, picnics are rained on, and friendships dissolve. Even though we don't always understand why these "detours" occur in our lives, we do know that God promises to be with us. He promises that in all things, in His time and in His way, He will make them turn out for our good.

Just as God turned the evil of the cross of Jesus into Easter victory, so He can take our detours and cause them to become blessings for us. We are assured in His Word that nothing or no one will ever be able to separate us from His love in Jesus. Even as we face detours, He is there to make them turn out for our good.

Dear Father, in life's detours help us to rely on Your guidance and presence. Amen.

Never Alone

Surely I am with you always. *Matthew 28:20*

The irony of a big city is that many people can feel all alone. They can rub elbows with large crowds and see hundreds of faces each day, yet their spirit cries out in pain.

Loneliness is not limited to any age. Young people can feel inadequate or unwanted. Older folks can dread the isolation of their apartment or nursing home. In all the in-between years this empty feeling in the spirit can leave its mark.

There are several sides to aloneness. Solitude expresses the glory of being alone. It is the voluntary isolation of the student, the artist, and the solitary fisherman. To be alone with one's thoughts can be a welcome change of pace. Loneliness, on the other hand, is a painful aloneness. It can be caused by conflicts between people, by separation, by death, or by a change of community.

In one sense, we are always alone. Before God we stand by ourselves. Faith or lack of faith is an individual matter between us and the Lord. On the other hand, we are never alone when we are with God by faith. He is the companion who understands, shares, and supports. Nothing can separate us from Him and His love.

Lord, help me be a friend to the lonely. Let me share Your unfailing love with those whose spirit cries. Amen.

Sharing Is Good Therapy

He who despises his neighbor sins, but blessed is he who is kind to the needy. *Proverbs 14:21*

Dr. William Menninger, noted psychiatrist and practicing Christian, was asked what he would do if he felt he were going to have a breakdown. The unexpected answer was, "I'd take my hat, go to the other side of the tracks, and find somebody who needs help. I'd help him, come home, and forget about the breakdown."

God urges us to share some of what we have from Him, for the good of others. In doing so we benefit also ourselves. God's laws are all for our good. When we ease another's burden, our own becomes lighter, too.

Giving of ourselves and of our possessions to help others, especially the less fortunate, is effective mental and emotional therapy.

The best advice that can be given to one who has lost his way in this confusing and frightening world, who can find no challenging purpose or meaning in life, is to learn to know, love, and believe in Jesus Christ, the Savior, the gift of a loving God, and to serve Him by letting His love shine through loving service to God and man. Then life becomes a triumphant adventure to the glory of God.

Ease our anxieties and confusions, O God, as we give of ourselves to ease the burdens of others. Amen.

The Changeable Weather

I the Lord do not change. *Malachi 3:6*

The weather changes suddenly and frequently in many parts of the world. One day it is sunny, but the next day it rains. It is warm one day but cold the next.

Our lives also are filled with change. A job promotion, our child receiving an award, or an unexpected word of kindness from a friend are examples of sudden happy events. However, even pleasant changes may require adjustments. Sometimes life suddenly seems to change for the worse. We learn we have cancer; a loved one dies; we lose our job. These events may make us wonder whether we can continue on life's journey.

With life swirling and changing around us, it is comforting to know that one thing is constant: God's steadfast love for us in Jesus Christ. The Bible describes how God always stands by His people. When God's creation became corrupted by sin, God immediately promised a Savior. The birth, death, and resurrection of Jesus fulfilled that promise. "Jesus Christ is the same yesterday and today and forever" (Hebrews 13:8).

No matter what happens, no matter how quickly events change, God promises never to leave or forsake us. That is an unchanging promise from an unchanging God.

Lord God, I know that You are my Helper. Increase my faith in Jesus so I will not be afraid. Amen.

The Life of Hope

Hope deferred makes the heart sick. *Proverbs 13:12*

The new life must be a life of hope. It must take the forward look that expectantly and confidently reaches out for the good things to come and draws on them for strength to face the present boldly and courageously. When there is no longer any hope or when the fulfillment of our hope is delayed, our heart is made sick, and we lose the will to carry on.

The ability to hope is one of the qualities that makes humankind different from the other earthly creatures of God. In it the Creator has given us another source of power and strength for the tasks of life. This is true for us especially in the new life in Christ.

The Christian can see ahead when the visibility is zero. It is hope that makes us persevere in a cause that seems doomed to failure. It is hope that makes us look for healing when we are desperately hurt and for improvement when a situation seems to be beyond repair. It is hope that makes us able to live with impossible people and to expect a change for the better even while the worst is before us. It is hope that encourages us to undertake tasks and assume responsibilities that seem to be beyond us. We need to hope. Thank God for the hope He has given us in Christ, our Lord and Savior! Pray God for more of it!

O God, in whom we trust, preserve us from despair and grant us a greater measure of hope. Amen.

Beyond Doubt

For forty days after His death [Jesus] appeared to them many times in ways that proved beyond doubt that He was alive. They saw Him, and He talked with them about the Kingdom of God. *Acts 1:3 TEV*

Have you ever doubted—doubted whether you would be able to pay the bills, find that new job, or even that Jesus really lived and died for you?

Thomas is probably the best-known doubter. He doubted that Jesus had really risen. Thomas said, "Unless I see the scars of the nails in His hands and put … my hand in His side, I will not believe" (Luke 20:25 TEV).

Knowing Thomas' doubt, Jesus appeared to Thomas and showed him His hands, feet, and side. Jesus asked Thomas to touch Him and see that His crucified body was indeed alive again. He told him to stop doubting and believe.

Jesus didn't abandon or forsake doubting Thomas; He convinced him. Jesus does the same for us. He comes to us through His Word, and through His body and blood in the Lord's Supper, to remove our doubts and convince us that He is indeed alive and with us. Jesus turns our doubts into confident faith so that, like Thomas, we exclaim, "My Lord and my God"!

Dearest Jesus, when we are full of doubt, show Yourself to us through Your Word and Sacraments, and assure us of Your loving presence. Amen.

Putting Life into the Old Bones

"If you can?" said Jesus. "Everything is possible for him who believes." Immediately the boy's father exclaimed, "I do believe; help me overcome my unbelief!" *Mark 9:23–24*

When the father of the demon-possessed boy says, "I do believe," he puts himself totally into Jesus' hands. He trusts Jesus to put him in touch with His healing power.

You will go to church on Sunday with the words in your heart and mind: "I do believe." You will say it in many ways throughout the service. You will be entrusting yourself to Him who suffered, died, and was raised again for you. Many people will find it important to hear you make this confession.

When the father cries, "Help me overcome my unbelief," he admits his faith is not what he wants it to be. He doesn't come with perfect faith, and he asks Jesus to increase it, knowing that only Jesus can do that.

You will not take perfect faith to church with you, either. You will take questions, doubts, concerns, and some unbelief with you. Your going will be important, though, for there you will hear the Word that puts new flesh on old bones, receive the Sacrament, and have your faith strengthened by the confession of others while you share your words of faith to strengthen them.

Lord, I do believe. Help me overcome my unbelief. Amen.

God Is Omnipresent

And surely I am with you always, to the very end of the age. *Matthew 28:20*

This promise constitutes one of the most precious realities of life. "I am with you always." There is never a single moment when we are alone.

Present with us believers wherever we are is this Jesus, our Redeemer, our ever-living Lord, our never-failing friend. He gave His life on the cross to make us His own. By faith we become His followers, saved by grace.

"I am with you always." More accurately, "I am with you all the days, to the very end of the age." As we live out our lives, our days vary. There are days of loneliness, days of frustration and worry, days of illness, days of success, days of bereavement, days of tragedy, days of disappointment, days of heartache, days of tension. We come face to face with good days and bad days, with happy days and sad days, days when we feel close to God and days when we wonder whether God will ever be near again, days when we feel strong and days when we feel weak, days when we are able to conquer temptation and days when we succumb to it.

Jesus said, "I am with you all the days"—every last one of them. Never for one moment will you be alone again. This never-failing presence of Jesus must be a source of constant strength to us Christians as we realize and enjoy the nearness of our Lord and Savior.

Lord Jesus, in everything we do and wherever we may be, help us be fully aware of Your gracious presence. Amen.

Being with Jesus

These men had been with Jesus. *Acts 4:13*

Peter and John were standing before the same priests who had put Christ on the cross. They expected to fare no better than their master. Instead of being silenced by fright, they went right on witnessing that only in His name could salvation be found. This took real boldness. Where did these uneducated disciples find it? "These men had been with Jesus." He had secured this courage for them by His suffering and death and was giving it to them by His abiding Word.

Christ gives us this same boldness. If He dwells by faith in our hearts, we shall stand up boldly to the problems and disappointments of life. Things do not always run smoothly. There are sorrows and adversities deep enough to defeat many people. They do not overthrow us; Christ gives us the strength to endure. By His power these are turned to our advantage and even made blessings.

We face an adversary worse even than the men faced by Peter and John. None is mightier or more deceptive than Satan. But Christ gives us boldness to stand against him, too. If we are with Jesus, Satan throws his fiery darts in vain. One little word can fell him.

If Christ is with us and we with Him, we have boldness on the Day of Judgment.

Lord, keep us ever near to Christ by Your Spirit so that His strength may be made perfect in our weakness. Amen.

God Is Love

This is how we know what love is: Jesus Christ laid down His life for us. *1 John 3:16*

Sometimes an adult tells a child, "God does not love you when you are bad." That is really not true. God always loves us. God loves us when things are going well and when things are going wrong. He loves us when in hurt and anger we ask why. God hates our sins but loves us sinners.

God could have remained in heaven cursing His creatures for spoiling His beautiful creation. Instead He laid aside His divine might and majesty for a while. In the person of His Son He took our human form and experienced our problems and pains. Finally, He let the forces of evil take His life. But He came back to life. By trusting in Him through the power of the Holy Spirit we can be sure of living with God forever.

We may be battered and shattered by life's blows. Some of our troubles may never go away. Many things puzzle us. We may think nobody cares. But God cares for us right now. Love gives, and God gave all. Through the cross—God's positive, permanent proof of His amazing love—He tells each of us clearly: "You mean a lot to Me. I really love you."

Gracious God, we praise You for Your wonderful love. Empower us to be like You: faithful and forgiving, willing to sacrifice and suffer for others. Amen.

When Trouble Comes

[God] will wipe every tear from their eyes. There will be no more death or mourning or crying or pain, for the old order of things has passed away.
Revelation 21:4

Troubles can cause us to question God's love for us. Saint Paul tells us in Romans that we can rejoice in our suffering because, being justified by faith, we have peace with God through our Lord Jesus Christ.

Sufferings can fit into the context of the primary goal God has for us—that we spend eternity with Him. If we will let them, our troubles can be helpful to us. Saint Paul says: "Suffering produces perseverance; perseverance, character; and character, hope" (Romans 5:3–4).

Trouble can teach us perseverance. We learn not to give up. This develops strength of character. And character produces hope. Biblical hope is the unshakable confidence in Christ that comes from having survived many troubles. And such hope, the apostle says, "does not disappoint us." Why not? Because we shall see our God face to face in His kingdom, where He will "wipe every tear from our eyes." Gone are death, mourning, crying, and pain. It is good to remember this when trouble comes.

Father, comfort me in my time of trouble and teach me the lessons You want me to learn. For Jesus' sake I pray. Amen.

Grief

Weeping may remain for a night, but rejoicing comes in the morning. *Psalm 30:5*

Perhaps you've heard the expression "Good grief!" Strange expression, isn't it? The two words are opposites. How can there possibly be such a thing as good grief?

Grief is very much a part of life. Sooner or later we all experience it. For each of us there are "nights of weeping"—times when we experience personal loss, professional setbacks, physical suffering, and other heartaches that cause grief.

Yet as Christians we know that grief is not permanent. Morning will follow the night of tears, and morning will bring rejoicing. That's what God has promised. Jesus promised comfort to those who mourn (Matthew 5:4). He also promised the blessings of hope, deliverance, courage, freedom, and a new day—life everlasting where there will be no grief. These things are good indeed!

As painful as grief is, it can help us to recognize God's promises and to claim them for ourselves. When it does, the morning dawns. And with the morning comes joy—a joy based on God's eternal love in the redeeming Christ, a joy that grief will never destroy. Thank God for the morning!

Lord, comfort us in times of grief and help us to see the joy You have promised to all those who believe in You. Amen.

Sorrow and Joy

You will be sorrowful, but your sorrow will turn into joy. *John 16:20 RSV*

Everything that we need to live is included in our Savior's final address and prayer on the night before His death. It is a complete map of life and history. Our Lord wanted to be sure that we would be able to meet every problem of life.

And so He also said many things about sorrow. He did not say that the Christian would always be happy, that life would be a bed of roses, that everything would always turn out as we wanted it. On the contrary, He said that we would have some sorrow in the world. There would be pain and tears. We would not always be happy.

He also said something, however, that no one had ever said with such power and truth: by faith in His atoning work, we could know, quietly and forever, that our sorrow would be turned into joy and that there would be a sure end for all our fears and a final disappearance of all our pain.

For the believing heart this is the great undertone of life. Under the crying of our sorrow there is the music of our joy in God. God may lead us through the gloom of a long and terrible night, but the morning will always come. And with it will come the return of joy—the deep, lasting joy of our faith in Him who does all things well. The last thing for the Christian, here or hereafter, will always be joy.

Dear Lord, help me to put my trust in You during the weeping of my nights of sorrow and remember that in You joy comes in the morning. Amen.

The Care-Less Life

In vain you rise up early and stay up late, toiling for food to eat—for He grants sleep to those He loves.
Psalm 127:2

One of the secrets of living the Christian life is learning how to live care-lessly, that is, to live without care, without anxiety, without fear. Such care-less living is precisely what God wants to give us, not because He is careless but because He is so care-full.

Life filled with cares is so hectic. Everywhere there seems to be something that just must be done. "There are not enough hours in the day," we fret. "I'll get up an extra hour earlier; I'll go to bed later," we say. But the worries of life don't become fewer. For all our care about life, we only work ourselves into a tizzy.

But God wants to give us a care-less life, one free from the anxieties that contribute to our stress-induced illnesses. "In vain you rise up early … for He grants sleep to those He loves."

Yes, even when we are sleeping, God is careful to give us what we need. The child of God can be care-less because God is care-full. We are His beloved, after all. And He has given us what we need most of all: forgiveness and love in our Savior Jesus Christ, even when we get all caught up in the cares and concerns of this life.

Dear Father, help me to live free of excessive cares. Amen.

No Need to Fear

**The Lord is my light and my salvation—
whom shall I fear?** *Psalm 27:1*

Why are so many Christians haunted by fear? Some live with fears they have never faced.

Worry is a form of fear. We do not like to admit that we are afraid we may lose our job, fail to get a promotion, or pass an examination. So we often disguise our fear by fretfulness over details.

A woman once gave a friend a motto that read, "Those who worry do not trust; those who trust do not worry." The friend was hurt because she resented the implication she was a worrier. But she had never realized that her excessive concern with personal problems spelled out the word *worry!*

At times we can become very much concerned about physical safety, spiritual development, school progress, etc. Worry can so upset us that we lose our grip on ourselves and go to pieces.

Why should Christians be afraid to stumble if Christ is the light that illuminates their paths? Why should they be afraid they cannot hold out against temptation and trial if God is the strength of their life? "If God is for us, who can be against us? He who did not spare His own Son, but gave Him up for us all—how will He not also, along with Him, graciously give us all things?" (Romans 8:31–32). God is all we need for life and growth and comfort and safety!

Let not worry take the joy of Your presence out of our lives, dear Lord. Teach us to trust You no matter how uncertain the future may be. Amen.

God with Us in the Fields of Life

He makes me lie down in green pastures, He leads me beside quiet waters. *Psalm 23:2*

We ought not overlook David's striking consciousness of God at work in the fields of life. We, too, can see Him there if only we look.

Often we are like the lady who took her first train ride to see her son. She had hardly gotten settled when she was up to check on whether her baggage was secure, to seek out the conductor to make sure she was on the right train, to summon the porter to bring a pillow, to find the water cooler, then to call the porter again to open the window, and on and on. The conductor called, "Jamestown!" It was her destination! She sighed, "If I had known the trip was so short, I would have taken time to enjoy the countryside."

There are two ways of living. We can be so occupied with immediate needs that we never really look at the life around us. Or we can pause, look up, and catch a view of God majestically providing for the needs of His flock.

While we are manufacturing imaginary needs, accompanied by frequent bleatings, the Good Shepherd is supplying our every want. God sustains our life and points the way to righteousness and eternal glory through the cross of Jesus.

Father of lights, from whom comes every good and perfect gift, and who has given Your Son that we might live with You in glory, fill our hearts with genuine gratitude. Amen.

Every Day a Grace Day

You were once darkness, but now you are light in the Lord. Live as children of light. *Ephesians 5:8*

We can resolve to make these choices:

Instead of being discouraged by what the world has come to, I will be encouraged by the grace and truth that has come into the world through the Lord Jesus Christ.

Instead of being fearful because I do not know what the future holds, I will be joyful because I do know who holds the future; God continues to care for me.

Instead of being perplexed for all the sin, I will be glad for all the grace of God for the sake of Christ.

Instead of being pessimistic for all the evil, I will be optimistic for all the good.

Instead of being dejected by the bad outlook, I will be delighted by the good up-look.

Instead of being gloomy for all that is wrong, I will be cheerful for all that is right and good and true.

We have a choice. We may "taste and see that the Lord is good," or we may eat the ashes of despair.

Saint Paul proclaimed, "Where sin increased, grace increased all the more … to bring eternal life through Jesus Christ our Lord" (Romans 5:20–21).

Dear Lord Jesus, my body and spirit glow in the light of Your grace and love. Amen.

Overwhelmed

**Jesus was sleeping. The disciples went and woke him,
saying, "Lord, save us! We're going to drown!"**
Matthew 8:24–25

We feel overwhelmed at times. A storm at sea, a blinding blizzard, a tornado, an earthquake—any of these can make us feel weak and helpless. But often it's other things that overwhelm us.

We get tired running around. We want to stop and catch our breath but can't. Some things looked so simple at first and so much fun: getting married, raising children, starting a new job. Then suddenly there we are—overwhelmed. We never dreamed it would be like this. When you add grief, pain, loneliness, frustration, and anger, the things that overwhelm us seem legion.

"Jesus was asleep." We think: If the Lord had been alert, it would not have happened. Unless we see Him standing there and doing something, we tremble. The winds and waves are too much for us. We cannot bear to have Jesus silent.

As a matter of fact, the Lord is often silent. Rare indeed are the times when He moves right in like a conquering hero. Why? Because whatever towers above us or threatens within us cannot hurt us. It will not overwhelm us. He is with and in us, and we in Him. The very grave could not contain Him. When this truth begins to overwhelm us, other things cannot.

Father, overwhelm me with Your love and power. Amen.

Your Strength

In repentance and rest is your salvation, in quietness and trust is your strength. *Isaiah 30:15*

A widow in our parish reads this verse from the inspired prophet Isaiah every day. That's a good way to begin every new day and a good way to begin a new week.

"In quietness"—the quietness of personal and private meditation! We need to escape from the clatter and clamor of this hurry-scurry, work-and-worry world. We need to meditate on the green and refreshing pastures of God's inspired Word. We need to gather with our fellow brothers and sisters in the sanctuary of our church for quiet worship.

Notice the word *confidence*. God's Word, the good news of the Gospel, can give us confidence, courage, and calmness. We need the comfort and companionship Christ brings to us. His death on the cross assures us of pardon for every distressing and destructive sin. Then comes strength—the strength and support that Christ's healing Gospel gives to our hurts, heartaches, and heartbreaks. So often we feel trapped by life—trapped by our job or by our bills or by our ill health. Let Jesus snap the trap by coming to Him for help and healing. He will give peace and rest to our souls.

Dear Lord Jesus, as we gather for worship, may the words of our mouth and the meditation of our heart be acceptable to You. Amen.

My Peace

Do not let your hearts be troubled. *John 14:1*

Our Lord's disciples, that last night together, were distressed and tense. They sensed that something was about to happen, but what it was they did not know. They were aware that the hatred of Jesus' enemies was hot against Him; yet they knew also that He was mightier than they. Still He had said that He was about to leave them, and He had said also that they could not follow where He was going. Therefore they faced something unknown and were filled with dread.

So we are sometimes fearful. We, too, are surrounded by the unknown. We, too, do not know from day to day what lies before us. Often we are afraid because we know that some things we particularly dread may happen. Like the disciples, we fear that it will be more than we can bear. We cannot even conceive what we should do if certain disasters were to occur. We are worried.

Life can, indeed, sometimes bring misfortunes. It did for those disciples in the sorrow-filled days "to come." Yet just as our Lord told them, He tells us: "My peace I give you. ... Do not let your hearts be troubled" (John 14:27). "Trust in God; trust also in Me" (John 14:1). No matter what happens, we cannot perish but are sure of our salvation through the cross.

Lord Jesus, help us believe in You. Speak to our hearts, too, and give us the grace not to be troubled. Amen.

Feed on His Faithfulness

Trust in the Lord, and do good; so shalt thou dwell in the land, and verily thou shalt be fed. *Psalm 37:3 KJV*

Some of life's most profitable lessons come from unlikely sources. Nancy, a poor woman with no financial security other than what she could earn by infrequent odd jobs, had a remarkable asset. She was a joyful Christian. One of her occasional employers was disturbed, however, that Nancy whistled and sang as she worked.

"Nancy," said the employer one day, "it is well for you to be happy now, but I should think that thoughts of your future would sober you a bit. Suppose you should have a spell of sickness and be unable to work; suppose we wouldn't need you anymore and you could find nothing else to do; suppose . . ."

"Stop!" Nancy cried, "I never suppose. The Lord is my shepherd, and I know I shall not want. Honey, it's all your 'supposes' that make you miserable."

The psalmist offers one thing that takes all the "supposes" out of a believer's life. "Trust in the Lord, and … thou shalt be fed." Saint Paul states this formula well: "He who did not spare His own Son, but gave Him up for us all—how will He not also, along with Him, graciously give us all things?" The eagle that soars in the upper air does not worry about how it will cross rivers. So it is with Christians.

Lord, give me sufficient confidence always to trust You.
Amen.

When the Lamp Burns Low

He will not ... put out a flickering lamp.
Isaiah 42:3 TEV

Recently a man who was guilty of a sinful habit and was terribly tortured by a guilty conscience wrote for help: "I don't want to stop doing it," he said "but I want to want to!"

Perhaps we should read that last sentence again. Behind it may lie the flickering flame of which Isaiah speaks above. The picture is that of a sputtering oil wick. It is burning so low and uncertainly that we expect it to go out any moment. But no says our gracious God. "I will stand by it. I will nurse it. I will enable it to shine more brightly."

Even the smallest faith is a gift of God's Holy Spirit, and even the weakest faith can lay hold on His greatest promises. We are not saved by the greatness of our faith; we are saved by despairing of our personal worthiness and by leaning wholly on Jesus Christ, our Savior.

Even a flickering faith is a saving faith. Sometimes even "wanting to want to" is evidence of a moving of the Spirit. Each of us has days when the lamp of faith burns low. Thank God that we have a Savior who "will not break off a bent reed nor put out a flickering lamp," but who will stand by us and nurse our wavering faith to health.

Lord, I believe. Help me overcome my unbelief. Let my faith, frail though it may be, always look up to You, O Lamb of Calvary! Amen.

In the Meantime ...

**Faith is being sure of what we hope for and certain of
what we do not see.** *Hebrews 11:1*

How's your faith?

It's sometimes difficult to be faith-full people, isn't it?
That's because faith, by it's very nature, cannot be proved.
It's the conviction of things that cannot be seen. If we could
prove what we believe, we would not need faith. The day
will come when faith will give way to knowledge and experience, but that day will not come until we stand before the
throne of God in eternity.

In the meantime ... we live by faith. And sometimes it
is difficult. Things happen in our lives that cause us to cry
out to our God, and we are confronted by His seeming
silence. We wonder, "Are you there, God?" Sometimes we
are overwhelmed by guilt, inadequacy, and our own sinful-
ness. We wonder, "Do You really love me, God?"

When our faith is put to the test, we can stand beneath
Christ's cross and view the visible proof of God's forgiveness and our redemption. Then our hearts proclaim, "You
are here with me, God. You do love me." And we receive
His power to live by faith in the meantime.

*Father, during difficult times, strengthen our faith in
Christ Jesus, Your Son and our Savior. Amen.*

God's Night

The day is Yours, and Yours also the night; You established the sun and moon. *Psalm 74:16*

We measure our life by active days. Though we spend one third of our life in sleep, such time does not seem to count. Many try to reduce that time in order to make life more worthwhile, more profitable. Manufacturers consider investment wasted if machinery stands idle for hours. Swing and night shifts are the accepted thing.

The night in which God gives His beloved sleep is still the Lord's. He who made the night never slumbers nor sleeps. He who prepared light and the sun in order to arouse life and make it active uses the night for the purposes of His creation, too. While we sleep, God's processes are active. We lie down worn and weak; we awaken refreshed and strengthened. Spend a sleepless night tossing on your bed, or foolishly in dissipating life, and you know you have missed the supply of strength.

Let us thank God for the night. When we lay ourselves down to sleep, He is alert to guard and to put in order what the day has spoiled. He is the God, who by His death and resurrection, has assured us that the night of death is likewise His. Trusting in Him, we face it without fear. We know that He will be there to rebuild and to reawaken to the great morning of heaven.

Teach me to live that I may dread
The grave as little as my bed. Amen.

God's Insomnia

He who watches over you will not slumber.
Psalm 121:3

God has the whole world, including you and me, in His hands. He who watches over us never sleeps. As it were, God is given to a divine insomnia. He has promised to be our keeper because He loves us with an everlasting love, and He will not fall asleep. But His insomnia is not the sleeplessness of worry, as ours often is, but the insomnia of faithfulness.

In the steady march of the years, some of us who were young and are now older "have never seen the righteous forsaken or their children begging bread" (Psalm 37:25). We have seen the morning break each day for many decades, and every dawn was new with God's mercies. Then why not share the benefit of our experience with those of younger years and let our lips be filled with praise? God has supplied every need according to the riches of His mercy in Christ Jesus.

Best of all, our mighty Maker, Provider, and Protector is also our Forgiver. God does not overlook or sleep through our sin; He suffers through it, according to His mercy in Christ Jesus. In Him God reconciled us. And now the outstretched hands of Jesus offer us the full supply of our most desperate need: forgiveness.

Lord, You hold us in Your hands. We thank You for watching over us and for supplying all our needs in Christ. Amen.

God Chastens His Own

The Lord disciplines those He loves, and He punishes everyone He accepts as a son. *Hebrews 12:6*

When Luther quoted this verse to console a friend who was ill, the friend countered: "Well, if that's the case, I wish He wouldn't love me so much."

Sometimes we feel that way. The love that lets us come down with crippling arthritis, virulent cancer, or painful angina seems a dubious love. But God assured us that He will make it all work out for good in the end. His love is at work.

Samuel Rutherford saw it this way: "When we come to the other side of the water, we will say, 'If God had done otherwise with me, I would never have come to this crown of glory.' "

These five biblical truths we must ever keep in mind: (1) God's chastenings are as much a part of His faithfulness as His blessings. (2) In God's plan cross-bearing and crown-wearing go together. (3) The love that chose us is also the love that chastens us. (4) Christ's love that purchased us purifies us. (5) The love that delivers us from death also disciplines us for life. Everything that God allows in the lives of His beloved and believing children is in keeping with His love for them.

O Holy Spirit, never let me waver from trusting that God loves me in Christ, no matter how hard His dealings with me. Amen.

Turn Burdens into Blessings

Before I was afflicted I went astray, but now I obey Your Word. *Psalm 119:67*

How can a good God, who loves us so much that He gave His Son for our salvation, be so rough on us? Many are asking that question. God doesn't mind that we ask the question, but He wants us to believe His answer. Our answers are often wrong; His are always right.

God allows affliction to purify the gold of our faith, to deepen our confidence and trust in the Savior who suffered to win our pardon. This much we know for sure: whatever draws us closer to God, however painful or hard to bear, is a hidden blessing for which we will be eternally thankful. This is God's explanation: "The God of all grace, who called you to His eternal glory in Christ, after you have suffered a little while, will Himself restore you and make you strong, firm and steadfast" (1 Peter 5:10).

God had one Son without sin. But He has had no son or daughter without suffering. It may be the cross now, but it will be the crown hereafter. Our gracious Lord has promised us that He will make all things work together for our good. The best and happiest way is to live as Jesus did: in everything trust our heavenly Father for guidance, strength, and eventual deliverance.

Dear God, when my turn comes to go through the dark valley, may the light of Christ guide me to glory. Amen.

221

Portrait of an Accessible Savior

As He went along, people spread their cloaks on the road. *Luke 19:36*

Sometimes presidents or heads of government mingle with the crowds, shaking hands with as many as they can reach. These are symbolic acts to show their accessibility to the people. There are other ways in which those who are in high office can keep in touch with the citizens.

Centuries before, our Lord declared His accessibility to the world by riding a colt into the capital city of Jerusalem. The slow-moving colt, the thronging crowd, the closeness of Christ to the people and they to Him—all this proclaimed constant accessibility to all people. He was accessible right after His transfiguration, ministering to a sick boy. On a less impressive occasion He was available to an ailing woman who had touched His garment.

The Lord's accessibility is a reality also in our time. The Scripture urgently invites us, "Cast all your anxiety on Him because He cares for you" (1 Peter 5:7). He cared enough to come as our Savior. He is close enough that we can "throw" our problems and concerns on Him. Christ's promise, "Surely I am with you always," is an unfailing guarantee of His immediate accessibility. Even before we reach out to clutch Him, His hand is extended.

Precious Savior, hold my hand as we walk together.
Amen.

In His Hands

While I was with them, I protected them and kept them safe by that name You gave Me. *John 17:12*

Some think they hold on to God by their faith. It is better to say that God holds on to them.

A father had a toddler of a son who was very stubborn. He was independent, and when they went walking in the ice and the snow, this led to problems. The most help the little boy would accept was to hold on to the father's little finger. Of course, as soon as they hit an icy patch, boom—down he went. Another icy patch and the scene was repeated. And again! The little tyke's small fingers just could not hold tightly enough.

"Here," said the father, "let me hold your hand." Finally the little boy agreed to the new arrangement. They hit an icy patch, and the father held on—no fall! It was better.

We do not hold on to God by our faith. He holds on to us. Jesus assures us: "I am the good shepherd; I know My sheep and My sheep know Me" (John 10:14). He gave His life for the sheep. And He assures us, "No one can snatch them out of My Father's hand." Thank God, He holds on to us! We are just not strong enough to hold on to Him. The psalmist declares that God's hand guides us and His right hand holds us (Psalm 139:1).

Father, thank You for sending Jesus to be my Shepherd, to find me and to bring me safely home to You. Amen.

Can God Be Fenced Out?

Who shall separate us from the love of Christ?
Romans 8:35

Many things separate us from God's love. Nothing can separate the love of God from us. A puppy can be fenced in with a bit of chicken wire a foot or two high. From his viewpoint the "wall" is insurmountable. His master, without effort, steps over the fence to bring food, water, and release. Who is separated from whom?

Saint Paul lists a number of walls that look monstrous to humankind—persecution, famine, want, danger, death itself. What walls they are! The hand of God must surely be restrained by them! Then with an easy stride God steps over them into the midst of humanity's need and helps and assures of His continuous presence. If we still doubt, He leads us to Calvary, where His Son hangs on the cross to take away the sin of the world. Faith assures us of His daily power to save from bodily danger and the power of sin. "I am with you always," says Jesus, to heal and to save.

God never leaves us, but we can leave God. On a church sign appeared the words: "If God seems farther away today than yesterday, WE have moved."

God will never leave us. He will not be fenced out. He tells us, "I will never leave you."

Lord, if we forget You, don't forget us. And if we leave You, don't leave us. We pray in Christ the Savior's name.
Amen.

Strength—Weakness

My power is made perfect in weakness.
2 Corinthians 12:9

What child has not called to his father, "Come and help me!" It may be to move a rock or to tighten a nut on a bicycle axle or to carry a picnic basket. The child has tested his own strength and found it to be lacking. He could not do what he wanted to do. Therefore he calls for someone who is stronger than he is to do it for him.

What a contrast when Dad's big hands get under the rock or on the business end of a wrench! His strength is shown for what it is in contrast to the weakness of his child.

We who are children of God frequently find ourselves in situations where weakness hinders our progress. "I wish I had a stronger faith," or "I hope I will be strong enough to resist" are confessions of weakness. Christians pray to God, their heavenly Father, to come and help, to get under their burdens and lift them, to meet the threats of Satan and defeat them. As this happens, the strength and power of God is shown, and we praise Him for it. What we could never have done, God has done in Jesus Christ, His mighty Son. Sin saps our strength, and we are weak and heavy laden. But strength and love pour down from the cross and into our lives. The power of our Lord's death and resurrection rescues, strengthens, and saves us.

Our Father in heaven ... the kingdom, the power, and the glory are Yours. Amen.

Too Impatient!

Wait for the Lord. *Psalm 27:14*

One of the hardest things to do in life is to wait. However, there are times when this is all we can do. We are hospitalized and must spend days, even weeks, waiting for strength and health to return. We are unemployed and have applied for work everywhere possible, and now can only wait. We seek to win loved ones to the Lord, and having spoken to them many times, we must wait. It is so hard to wait. It seems so useless. We wish there were something active that we could do. We become impatient.

We need the advice David gives: "Wait for the Lord." Just plain waiting is a waste of time. But "waiting for the Lord" is never misspent time. This means that we are to place ourselves, our life, and our problems into His hands. We can do this because we know He is interested in our well-being. He showed this in the sending of His Son, Jesus, to give His life for our eternal salvation. Knowing that God loves us that much, we can confidently place all our life in His hands and wait for His will to be done.

Here is the cure for our impatience. Remembering God's love for us in Jesus Christ, we can say, "Your will be done," and can know that His will is always a good and gracious will toward us. Then we can patiently "wait for the Lord." He does all things well.

Dear Lord, give us the patience to place ourselves trustingly in Your hands each day. Put our mind at ease as You abundantly forgive us all our sins for Jesus' sake. Amen.

Resting and Waiting

Be still before the Lord and wait patiently for Him.
Psalm 37:7

The secret to good rest is trust. If you don't trust the bed you lie down on, you will not rest very well. If you are vacationing and don't trust those whom you left in charge of your business, your vacation will not be very restful. If you don't trust the baby-sitter, you will find that the night off gave you no rest from stress, but only increased it. Trust is needed for rest.

Waiting on the Lord is the deepest level of trust; indeed, waiting and trusting are nearly synonymous in Scripture. No wonder that being still before the Lord—resting in Him—and waiting for Him are linked together in this psalm. One becomes rested as one waits on God. How is that? Well, waiting on the Lord implies that you trust that He can deal with what you give Him. If it is an enemy, He can take care of him. If it is a problem, He has the solution. If it is something pressing on your heart, He has the relief from every burden, help for every need, and strength for every occasion. He offers forgiveness to those who trust in Jesus' redeeming merit.

We are urged to put these concerns, burdens, and needs into His hands. Then we can sit back and wait. And we might as well enjoy the rest while we are waiting.

Father, here are my burdens; I'll rest and wait patiently while You handle them. Amen.

He Shares the Heavy Load

Come to Me, all of you who are tired from carrying heavy loads, and I will give you rest.
Matthew 11:28 TEV

God's heart often aches, too, just like yours and mine. He is such a caring God that He shares our heavy loads.

We know this because we find it so in the life of Jesus. His heart ached when told about the imprisonment of John the Baptizer, His relative and friend. His heart ached when He reflected on two unrepenting towns, Chorazin and Bethsaida.

His aching heart drove Him to prayer, and strengthened by prayer, He was moved to speak to all who, like Him, experienced an aching heart! "Come to Me, all of you who are tired of carrying heavy loads, and I will give you rest."

The very aching heart of God seen in Jesus, His Son, reaches out to embrace all who likewise hurt, whether over a son or daughter who will not yield to the Gospel or for any who are imprisoned in sin and darkness and will not repent.

And because God's heart aches with us, we who are burdened down are given relief and rest, for we know that He who is able to perform all things is likewise concerned, and we can move our heavy loads onto His broad back. Jesus, our Friend, bears all our sins and griefs.

Thank You, Savior, for sharing the heavy load of my heart. I know that You will give me peace and rest. Amen.

A Place for Burdens

Humble yourselves, therefore, under God's mighty hand, that He may lift you up in due time. Cast all your anxiety on Him because He cares for you.
1 Peter 5:6–7

A faithful paraphrase of these words of Saint Peter addressed to recent converts would be: "Lead a life of true humility before the Lord. He will lift you up in due time. Just cast your burdens on Him, for He is very much concerned about you."

The Christian who leads a life of true humility, a life of daily awareness of his or her dependence on the Lord, will know what to do with the inevitable burdens of each day—the worries, sorrows, and anxieties. The Christian will share them with the Lord, who has declared His personal concern for each believer.

The Scriptures again and again invite us to burden the Lord with our burdens. The psalmist urges: "Cast your cares on the Lord and He will sustain you" (Psalm 55:22). The Savior's entire earthly ministry was an open-armed offer: "Give Me your burdens, and I'll give you My peace." What an offer!

Have we learned to make that exchange in our daily lives? Christ's peace in exchange for our burdens! That offer still stands. All we need do is accept it.

Lord Jesus Christ, You are our Friend so faithful. You know all our weaknesses, and You bear not only our sins and griefs but also our burdens. We thank You. Amen.

God Turns Sadness into Joy

Just as the sufferings of Christ flow over into our lives, so also through Christ our comfort overflows.
2 Corinthians 1:5

No matter how deep the grief—or how heavy the burden and how depressing our loneliness seems—there is comfort, for in all our afflictions we know that Christ suffered to free us from sin, the greatest affliction. We are never out of the presence of God. His love is immediately at hand, ready to meet every need, to restore our spirits, to heal our minds, to bless us with the peace that passes all understanding.

Yes, God is always near to comfort and to turn sadness into joy. He guides us when we are at a loss to know how to proceed. He holds out His gracious promises when we feel inconsolable, telling us to trust in Him. In His divine, never-failing love He speaks to our sadness or sense of loss. He constantly assures us of His strength, made perfect in our weakness. He sends the promised Comforter, the Holy Spirit to be always near us.

Knowing that God never fails His own, we can let go of our fears and sorrows, trusting that under His guidance all things will work together for our good. Thanks to His love in Jesus Christ, we are sustained and comforted.

Lord Jesus Christ, we thank You for letting us share in Your suffering so that we may be comforted and find joy.
Amen.

God Wants Us to Have Joy

We write this to make our joy complete. *1 John 1:4*

At the heart of Christianity is joy. True, we are all sinners, and sin brings sorrow. We see our great loss in sin. We confess that we are "poor, miserable sinners."

But that is not all. Our defeat has been brought under the power of the Savior's victory. In Him our sins are forgiven. Through Christ and His sacrifice our whole problem of sin has been solved. Jesus has defeated Satan, who caused sin in the first place. Now Satan has no more power over us. We can go on our way with joy because the sinbearer is on our side. This is God's promise to all who are sorry for their sins and accept the Savior's forgiveness. God wants us to be sad only to be glad. The final note of the Christian religion is joy. Who can be joyless when they know they have a Savior who has conquered sin, death, and hell?

In the darkest night of His life Jesus prayed that His children might receive His joy. True, there is much sadness and heartbreak in the world. We are all disturbed by what the world has come to. But we must ever cling to what has come into the world through the Lord Jesus Christ, in whom we have triumph, victory, and joy. God expects every believer to live in joy.

O Lord Savior, keep us in the joy of our completed redemption. Amen.

The Lord Willing

If it is the Lord's will, we will live and do this or that.
James 4:15

Many Christians employ the custom of injecting into their future plans, whether in thought, speech, or writing, the symbol "D. v.," an abbreviation for the Latin equivalent of "The Lord willing."

It is a salutary custom. By it we acknowledge that humankind proposes, God disposes. We submit ourselves to the Lordship of Jesus Christ. We confess that our times are in His hands.

The apostle James encourages the habit. We do not know what tomorrow will bring, he reminds us. For life is a vapor that appears for a moment and then vanishes. We reach the end of life with unfulfilled dreams and unfinished plans. We can pursue our goals, carry out our plans, and continue our lives only as the Lord wills.

Another day fades into God's eternity tonight. What happened to the goals we set in the new year? What do we expect tomorrow?

Few things are certain. But this we know: that we are enfolded in the everlasting arms of a gracious Father. He has fulfilled His promises. We are still His forgiven children through the grace of Jesus. If our wills have had to be reversed, we know that His good and gracious will prevailed.

Lord, forsake us never, according to Your Word. Make our faith strong in Christ Jesus. Amen.

God's Time

When the time had fully come, God sent His Son.
Galatians 4:4

In the beginning God created time—days, months, years, centuries. Time is the measure of our lives. "How old are you?" "Can you come over next Saturday?" "How long will it take to do the job?" "How much time do I have, Doctor?"

Sometimes we try to bind God to our time frame. We want an immediate answer to prayer. We can't fit illness or emergency into the time schedule right now. It isn't fair when a life is cut short, we may think. But the Creator of time is above time. He told elderly Abraham and Sarah that He set His own unusual time for them to have a son.

We do need to measure time, to set goals and make good use of the days we have. But we also need to step back and take a look at God's time. In the sweep of eternity the daily pressures don't seem so important. And that's how much time each of us has—eternity. God sent Jesus (at His perfect time) so that we can live forever with Him.

Some of us will spend more time on this earth than others. Whatever the length, there is enough time to accomplish God's purpose for us. No life is wasted. That purpose becomes clearer as we take time for the Lord's work.

Thank You, Lord, for the gift of time. Help me to use the days You have given me on earth to Your glory. Amen.

Troubles from the Good Shepherd

The Lord disciplines those He loves. *Hebrews 12:6*

Despite troubles and sorrows we are still God's people through faith in the merits of Christ, who gained for us and freely gives us pardon for our sins. Yet we find ourselves asking, "If the Lord is good, why is it that I must endure hardship and pain?" It is not a sign that the Lord does not care, for "the Lord disciplines those He loves."

A traveler went to southern France, where many shepherds with their flocks could be found. He was sure he would find the shepherds leading their flocks to still waters and green pastures. But to his surprise he found many of them leading their flocks into rough and rocky places near the seashore. Many of the sheep stumbled and fell, and some were bleeding as a result of injuries sustained. Of course, the shepherd was there to give them help, but why was he leading them into such places?

A shepherd was asked this very question. He said, "We hate to bring our flocks into such places, but it is absolutely necessary, for this is where they can get the salt they need; they lick it from the deposits on the stones from the ocean waters."

Do not all of us need the salt of God's Word to purify our spiritual wounds? The rough road taking us to it leads to the healing Christ.

Savior, I follow on, guided by You. Amen.

Troubles Deepen Life

It was good for me to be afflicted. *Psalm 119:71*

None of us are fond of trouble. We look upon trouble as an intruder. We do not court trouble. We seek to avoid it. Yet the psalmist says: "It was good for me to be afflicted." Lives that are void of trouble usually are humdrum, shallow, stagnant. They lack salt.

Christian lives are not void of trouble. The Lord tells His followers that they will experience trials that will try their very souls. They will cry out in the agony of their soul: "Lead me to the rock that is higher than I" (Psalm 61:2). They seek refuge in God's promises, power, and love. They dig deeply into the Scriptures. They crowd the throne of God with their prayers as they confess: "Other refuge have I none." And God answers in His own way and at His own time to make all things work together for their good. The clouds soon pass; the sun shines again. Their faith is strengthened, their hopes are brighter, and a new song is on their lips.

Through their troubles Christians are helpful to others who are in trouble. Remember that in the Lord's service "only wounded soldiers will do." So the Lord equips us for better service to others wounded in life's battles.

Be still, my soul; the Lord is on your side. Amen.

The Glory of God's Preserving Care

In Him we live and move and have our being.
Acts 17:28

Under the grinding pressures of the life we make for ourselves, we sometimes become so impressed with the importance of what we are doing that we forget what God does. We begin to feel that unless we personally turn the wheels the world itself will stop in its course. The result is anxiety, fear, and the unhappiness of failure.

God not only created us, He sustains us as well. He did not merely wind up the universe, but He still controls and operates it. In fact, we and all things depend on Him directly and completely, for "unless the Lord builds the house, its builders labor in vain. Unless the Lord watches over the city, the watchmen stand guard in vain" (Psalm 127:1).

To the extent that we understand and accept this fact, we will see ourselves in the proper perspective. For one thing, it will lead us to a humble measure of our own importance. Then it will give us a sense of contentment with the role God assigns to us in our calling, at the same time sharpening our sense of responsibility to Him. And as we are aware of the governing and preserving activity of God in all the events of our life, even our critical times, we shall find our fear giving way to confidence in the faithful care of our God.

Into Your hand, O God, we commit our world, our life, and all of our concerns. We trust Your wisdom, Your power, and Your love, in Christ Jesus. Amen.

Perplexed? Yes
In Despair? No

We are … perplexed, but not in despair.
2 Corinthians 4:8

Why are we perplexed? Because, in spite of our highest dreams and best intentions, evil seems to dog our steps. We are perplexed because, in a paraphrase of Saint Paul's words, "when we would do good, evil is present with us." We are perplexed because as our world grows smaller, its people are growing farther apart. We are perplexed because we are lost people—people with the power of the sun in our hands but with the darkness of night in our hearts. We are perplexed because our civilization is a structure of contradictions. It is capable of building missiles to climb to the stratosphere, but these bring us no nearer to heaven. We can build airplanes that fly with the speed of sound, but we have no wholesome place to go.

Perplexed? Yes. But why are we not in despair? We do not despair because, in the last analysis, the world's affairs are not in the hands of humankind but in the hands of God. We are not in despair because the Gospel has the last and truest word: The God who created us and who judges us is also the God who in Jesus Christ has received us as His own beloved children. "He has given us new birth into a living hope through the resurrection of Jesus Christ from the dead" (1 Peter 1:3).

In the midst of life's perplexities, O Lord, keep us in hope and faith in You. Amen.

The Hug of God

I have loved you with an everlasting love; I have drawn you with lovingkindness. *Jeremiah 31:3*

There comes days in the life of every one of us when the love of God seems merely an abstract term—His love seems irrelevant to our daily living.

But that is not the way our Lord wants us to regard the promise and the offer of His love. He is eager that we not only acknowledge His love, but that we remain in daily awareness of it. Again and again He reminds us: "I have loved you with an everlasting love; I have drawn you with lovingkindness." Again and again He tells us that His relationship to those who put their trust in Christ as Savior is that of a father to his children—an ongoing, day-to-day relationship.

The love revealed in the Gospel is more than a kindly gesture; it is the hug of God, His reassuring arms around us. In days of darkness or distress, in nights of pain and sorrow, may we hear His loving voice: "Fear not, for I have redeemed you; I have summoned you by name; you are Mine" (Isaiah 43:1). Yes, He is our God. He loved us so much that He gave His only-begotten Son to die for us. May we always feel His loving presence near us!

Jesus, Lover of my soul, keep me strong in my faith in You. Amen.

Seeing God's Hand

I, the Lord, ... will make you to be a covenant for the people and a light for the Gentiles, to open the eyes that are blind. *Isaiah 42:6–7*

These words are part of the first of four poems in Isaiah called "Songs of the Suffering Servant." They paint a portrait of the servant who is the Savior of all nations. At our Lord's Baptism these words find fulfillment as Jesus begins His ministry of "doing good and healing" (Acts 10:38).

It is to open our blind eyes that Jesus came—our eyes that grow blind to those around us in need, our eyes that fail to see the guiding hand of God in our life. It is for us, who by nature are dead and blind to God, that He sent His servant, our Savior.

Jesus is the light to the nations, as aged Simeon declared in the temple, and He came to open our blind eyes. In our Baptism we have been called by God's Holy Spirit and enlightened with the Spirit's gifts so that we may see the hand of God in Christ Jesus reaching out to touch, forgive, and heal us. His is the hand that guides and protects. Without His hand on our shoulder, we grope and stumble in darkness, but with it we find the way to everlasting peace.

Lord, take my hand and lead me
Upon life's way; Direct, protect, and feed me
From day to day. Without Your grace and favor
I go astray; So take my hand, O Savior,
And lead the way. Amen.

(From *LBW* © 1978. Used by permission of CPH.)

239

Shoulders for Burdens

The Levites carried the ark of God with the poles on their shoulders. *1 Chronicles 15:15*

In an age that has perfected mechanical devices of all kinds for carrying loads, we are apt to forget the homely wisdom of the Yiddish proverb: God gave burdens, also shoulders. The Levites counted it an honor and a privilege to carry the ark of the covenant upon their shoulders.

The shoulders of God's people of old were also for bearing suffering, as the psalmist declared: "Yet for Your sake we face death all day long; we are considered as sheep to be slaughtered" (Psalm 44:22). In the New Testament God's people are also encouraged to bear sufferings for Christ's sake, yes, to find joy in being exposed to "the painful trial" through which they are participating in the sufferings of Christ (1 Peter 4:12–13).

Discipleship under Jesus is a burden which is not to be escaped. To be mocked, abused, and rejected because we walk with our Lord is to "share Christ's suffering." None of this is easy, but it is all necessary. For this God has given us the shoulders of faith—of faith in Christ's sufferings for us. Our faith is lifted by the promise: "My yoke is easy, and My burden is light" (Matthew 11:30).

God's grace is sufficient for us today, as it has always been for those chosen by Him to extend His Word and work into the world.

Lord, give us shoulders equal to Your burdens. Amen.

Crucial Tests of Life

My Father, if it is possible, may this cup be taken from Me. Yet not as I will; but as You will. *Matthew 26:39*

We can face crucial tests of life in several ways. We can pray to be spared the anguish they may impose on us. Or we can ask for the necessary courage and faith to accept the challenges they place before us.

When Jesus in the Garden of Gethsemane was confronted with "the cup"—His mission of dying for our salvation—He prayed earnestly: "If it is possible, may this cup be taken from Me."

As disciples of Christ, we can also pray: O Father, may this cup—this suffering of body and mind, this critical surgery, this painful task, this demanding challenge, this heavy responsibility—may this cup be taken from us!

But can we continue with the crucial test of our faith as expressed in the phrase "yet not as I will"? If it is not possible for the nails and the cross to be removed, do we too say, "Yet not as we will; but Your will be done, heavenly Father"?

God's will was done by His Son. He did put the cup of our guilt to His lips so that our "cup" might run over with His forgiving love and with the power He grants to trust in His gracious will, especially in the crucial tests of our life.

Heavenly Father, strengthen my faith, that I too may pray, "Yet not as I will, but as You will." Amen.

The Glory of Fulfillment

The time had fully come. *Galatians 4:4*

Only God decided when the hour had come for which the world had been waiting. When in His judgment all the conditions were right, when time had woven all the threads of the centuries into the pattern of His design, when the events in the history of the nations had reached the point that He had predetermined—then, not before and not after, the time had fully come, and then God sent His Son.

There is a glorious majesty in the thought of God's timing of His acts. He is not to be pressed into hasty action. Until His hour has come, humankind must wait. Nor can He be persuaded to postpone His plans. When His measure of the days and years is filled, there is no more delay. The Lord is His own counselor, and He acts when He decides.

This is most significant for our own life and experience. Because our judgments are clouded as a result of sin, we can so easily become impatient and demand premature action that would distort the balance of our lives. Or we can be slow and late in our timing and again disable the mechanism of events in which each part must mesh perfectly with all the rest. There is a readiness for all things that is known only to God and the determination of which must be His alone.

Grant us, O Lord, patience to await Your fullness of time and a confident trust in Your judgment for Jesus' sake. Amen.

I Grow in Patience

How Long, O Lord?

The fruit of the Spirit is ... patience. *Galatians 5:22*

The prayer of many a contemporary person seems to be, "Dear God, I pray for patience. And I want it right now!"

Someone has remarked that a woman who has never seen her husband fishing doesn't know whether or not she has married a patient man. Still another declares, "If you're too lazy to start anything, you may get a reputation for patience."

What is the patience that the Holy Spirit gives? It is, in part, the gift we human beings need because we cannot look around corners or, more importantly, cannot see around the next day.

God's Spirit gives us a gift that overcomes our limited gaze into the future and helps us to endure. Patience is the certainty that we are in God's good hands. It gives us the strength to wait and see because we know that the guarantee of God's promises is always the final word. In Jesus Christ, our Lord and Savior, all of God's promises find their "yes" (2 Corinthians 1:20).

Patience is not a "do nothing" attitude. It is an active assertion created by God's Spirit to take hold of the future without fear. Our future is in God's hands.

Heavenly Father, all ages are continually in Your sight. Give me patience when the future is not clear. Remind me that my times are in Your hands. Amen.

Faith for the Storms

Who shall separate us from the love of Christ?
Romans 8:35

At La Guardia Airport in New York City there is a sign that reads, "Runway Reading 134′M. Recheck your compass." Before a pilot lifts his jet off the ground, he can check whether his compass is correct. The flight may run into a storm, and poor visibility would make it particularly necessary for him to rely on his instruments. If he is to reach his destination, the compass must be working properly.

Sooner or later we meet storms in our lives: financial setbacks, poor health, death, and many other problems. Often the troubles are so great that we don't know what to do.

What a blessing a strong faith in God is, especially in such days! It is a wonderful comfort to know that He is in control and no burden will be more than we can bear. Even though the going is rough, we know there is eternal joy ahead. The conviction that God loves us keeps us steady and gives meaning to our lives.

We must draw closer to God before trials come. Life is not just a stormy journey to be endured. It is a gift to be enjoyed and used in the service of Him who came to serve and to give His life as a ransom for many.

Thank You, loving Father, for Your assurance that nothing can separate us from Your love. In every storm of life draw us closer to You and bring us safely home. Amen.

You Can Take It!

I have learned the secret of being content in any and every situation, whether well fed or hungry, whether living in plenty or in want. I can do everything through Him who gives me strength.
Philippians 4:12–13

"I can't take it anymore." That's what the electric company worker said when she asked for a transfer. For 11 years she had been answering customer complaints. Many calls were angry, some abusive, others pathetic.

Most of us can sympathize with her. We live under stress, too. People disappoint us, and things disgust us. It's not only the major catastrophes that get us down. Often it's a series of small matters.

Despite all the potentially defeating factors that gang up on us, we can live victorious lives. We may tell God frankly that we can't take it without His help. We must stop challenging God's goodness and wisdom by asking why. We must concentrate on the solution. God never promised to exempt us from all the trials and tears of this life. But He does promise to be with us. We ask Him for strength, patience, and courage. We expect Him to answer our prayer. We live in such a way that we're part of His answer. God is a wise Father. He does not do for us what we can do for ourselves. Beyond that He takes over. We can depend on Him.

Dear Lord Jesus, thank You for being the way to eternal life. Help us believe that You can always make a way through life's troubles even when there seems to be no way. Amen.

Teardrops to Diamonds

Consider it pure joy, my brothers, whenever you face trials of many kinds, because you know that the testing of your faith develops perseverance. *James 1:2–3*

"The Lord disciplines those He loves" (Hebrews 12:6). When we realize that afflictions serve as steppingstones to glory, we no longer ask, "Why me, Lord?" but "Why *not* me, Lord?"

Afflictions can hurt or help. The key is to view them from the vantage point of Christ's own cross. Jesus Himself bore the cross before entering His glory. By His grace, we who follow in His footsteps will tread the same path.

God allows burden-bearing to increase our reliance on the sufferings of Christ for our salvation, to polish us toward perfection, to intensify our prayer life, and to bring us closer to Himself. Our adversities are not punishments to pay for our sins. Jesus Himself bore all our punishments for us: "The Lord has laid on Him the iniquity of us all" (Isaiah 53:6).

God will see to it that we gain more than we lose. Bitter tears now will turn into glistening diamonds, mournful sorrows into jubilant song. We should remember our Lord's promise: "In this world you will have trouble. But take heart! I have overcome the world" (John 16:33).

Dear Lord, when troubles arise and shadows fall, remind me that You are preparing me for the glory ahead. Amen.

Affliction's Blessings

Consider it pure joy, my brothers, whenever you face trials of many kinds. *James 1:2*

Is it really possible to count it joy when trials come? Can we be happy about something that makes us unhappy? Usually we cry, "What did I do to deserve this? How long will this trial last?"

To make tribulation "work for us" as Paul said, we'll have to look at it this way: If we lose a dollar and in our search for it find $100, our unhappiness in losing the lesser would be offset by our joy in finding the greater.

The burdens God sends are intended not to get us down but to lift us up, not to make us stumble but to make us soar. Whatever draws us closer to God, however painful or hard to bear at the moment, is a hidden blessing. Trials sweep away the debris that has cluttered life with things that hide God from our eyes. The shore is swept clean by the storm, and we get a new experience of the ocean of God's grace.

The One who led us into the dark valley is our friend. He has gone all the way to the cross to have us as His own. He leads us into the dark valley, not to leave us there but to train us there. When we come out, we will be better for it: closer to God and nearer to heaven.

Lord Jesus, when the path gets dark, help us to tighten our grip on Your hand and to hold on until we come back into the light. Amen.

Oh, Blessed Singular!

Look, the Lamb of God, who takes away the sin of the world! *John 1:29*

Have you ever thought of how comforting it is that the Bible frequently uses the word *sin* in the singular—sin instead of sins? Some may think it strange that a point should be made of this "accident" of grammar.

But, praise God, we are dealing here with more than an accident and with more than grammar. We are dealing, rather, with a profound theological truth.

While it is true that Christ died for our individual sins (hatred, slander, greed, etc.), it is also true that He took our whole load of sin (our sin in bulk, as it were) and nailed it to His cross. Notice the wording in the text quoted above: Christ "takes away the sin of the world"—the whole ugly heap of it! That is the significance of the singular.

When our tortured conscience frightens us with the remembrance of a certain sin and we wonder in the stillness of the night, "Can God ever forgive me for that sin?" His precious Gospel answers, "Yes! Christ assumed our entire guilt. He paid our debt in full. He took away the sin of the world—including mine." Oh, blessed singular!

Guilt no longer can distress me; Son of God,
Thou my load Bearest to release me.
Stain in me Thou findest never; I am clean,
All my sin is removed forever. Amen.

A New Creature

If anyone is in Christ, he is a new creation.
2 Corinthians 5:17

God's promise to make a new creation out of a sin-loving person holds for everyone, even though he or she may be the most loathsome sinner. There is not one of us who deserves any such consideration from God. Yet Jesus declares there is hope and promise for every one of us.

The same Lord who could forgive Aaron for molding an idolatrous golden calf; the same Lord who could forgive David his adultery and murder; the same Lord who could forgive Peter after he cursed and denied Him; the same Lord who says through Paul: "If anyone is in Christ, he is a new creation" offers the promise of a new life to everyone who believes in Christ as his or her Savior. All the old weaknesses, the old habits, the old sins—all these can pass out of our lives if we are in Christ.

What does "in Christ" mean? It is the opposite of living outside of Him, against Him. It means to be united with Him in faith. It means to believe in Him who was crucified for us and who freed us from the eternal punishment of our sins. It means to renounce the devil and to be ready to serve Jesus only as our King. And one glorious day, to be in Christ will mean to be in heaven.

Lord Jesus, make of us new creations by Your love and forgiving mercy, for we trust only in You. Amen.

Our Burdens

Cast your cares on the Lord, and He will sustain you.
Psalm 55:22

The psalmist is referring to burdens on the heart, not on the back. We all know that mental burdens are worse than physical, and spiritual burdens are worse than both. These words, however, open up a golden opportunity to do something with our burdens.

We should know that burdens are inescapable. They come to high and low, rich and poor, saints and sinners, old and young. We can no more dodge them than we can fly by waving our arms.

Burdens bring temptations. We are tempted to think God is unconcerned. We are tempted to sit in the brew of self-pity. We are tempted to become bitter toward life and people.

David advises us to "cast your cares on the Lord, and He will sustain you." We notice that the first part of this passage is coupled with a promise, namely, "and He will sustain you." This is the key to the understanding of the first part of the sentence. Our Lord promises to sustain us. The burden may still remain, but the weight, the drag, the bitterness, will be gone. So it was in the life of the apostle Paul, who complained of his burden, but the Lord said: "My grace is sufficient for you" (2 Corinthians 12:9).

Lord, keep us from becoming embittered under the burdens of life. For Jesus' sake strengthen and support us day by day. Amen.

Enough Is Enough

Each day has enough trouble of its own. *Matthew 6:34*

We have a way of trying to peer over God's shoulder and then of trying to take things out of His hands by putting them into our own. The trouble with this is that we then try to make ourselves bigger than we are and God smaller than He is. This is not good for us, for it vastly overrates us and our abilities. Nor is it to the glory of God, for it grossly underrates His wisdom and power.

But there is another trouble, too. We may try to take upon ourselves burdens that God never intended to come on us at all. We spend our strength, not just on the carrying of the real load of the present as God permits this present to come upon us; instead we reach out for imaginary loads as well.

We forget something, too: strength to bear comes from bearing. Under the wisdom of God the strength we shall need to bear the burdens of the future come from our experience with the burdens—and with God's faithfulness—of the past. God alone sees the end from the beginning; and from that beginning He has made provision for the end. Therefore the apostle Paul tells His Christians to place their problems and their future in the lap of God and to leave them there.

O unforgetting God, let Your mercy and power give peace to our present. Amen.

His Resurrection

Declared with power to be the Son of God by His resurrection. *Romans 1:4*

That there was an awesome aspect in the crucifixion of our Lord, something beyond the human in this Man who hung there, was evident even to the centurion and his soldiers. They said, in awe and fear: "Surely He was the Son of God!" (Matthew 27:54).

There is also an awesome aspect to Jesus' resurrection. There was awe enough when our Lord called back to life the dead bodies of others. He spoke, and the dead heard Him and arose. Yet this awe reached its greatest height when Jesus Himself arose from the dead. For He had said: "Destroy this temple [of His body], and I will raise it again in three days" (John 2:19–21). This He did by His power and by that of "the glory of the Father."

So in days when the odds seem all against us and our strength fails and our security is shaken, we need to know that He who loved us unto death does not love us helplessly. With a love that is as strong as it is tender, as almighty as it is compassionate, He stands at our side. In days when all seems lost, as it seemed long ago to His followers, let us remember the risen Christ, who by His resurrection was declared to be the Son of God who loved us and died for our sins and sorrows. In the world to come we shall have an endless, glorious life with Christ.

Strong Son of God, be our faithful and compassionate Friend forever. Amen.

Darker the Night, Brighter the Star

The Lord disciplines those He loves. *Hebrews 12:6*

Why does God use our blackest hours to come to us with healing in His wings? That is when the great roadblock to redemption gets broken down. Sooner or later we have to face the uncomfortable fact that what keeps redemption from "drawing nigh" is the high opinion we have of ourselves and of our ability to manage on our own.

The sacrifices that God desires are not an impressive array of Christian qualities. The sacrifices of God are a broken and a contrite heart. When something breaks down in the way we handle things, when we have to cry with the speaker in 2 Chronicles 20:12, "we do not know what to do," or join the helpless man in John 5:7: "I have no one to help me into the pool when the water is stirred," then we should look up and lift up our heads, for we will find redemption coming over the horizon. The light of God's saving love in Christ has dawned. It is morning in our lives.

That's the thing about the dark: light looks so much better in it. When you feel the earth shake, you can sing, "On Christ, the solid rock, I stand." When you are tempted to give up hope and throw in the towel, reach out and look up and lay hold on Him who is our "strength in time of trouble."

O Christ, Light of all the world, shine out of trouble to illuminate our way. Amen.

253

Expect Great Things

Zacchaeus, come down immediately. I must stay at your house today. *Luke 19:5*

So often we find that our God gives us blessings far beyond our expectations. That's the way it was with Zacchaeus, the little man in the sycamore-fig tree. He was a man of questionable reputation and character. But when he heard that Jesus was passing through town, he wanted at least to get a glimpse, and so he climbed the tree to see over the crowds lining the street. Imagine his surprise when Jesus stopped, looked up, and said: "Zacchaeus, come down immediately. I must stay at your house today." Not only did Jesus visit, but salvation came to the house of Zacchaeus that day.

Zacchaeus' problem was that his expectations were far too small. He was willing to settle for just a glimpse of Jesus, while the Lord had far greater things in store for him. It wasn't that Zacchaeus was so deserving but that the Savior was so gracious.

Our Lord still invites us today to seek and expect great things from Him. In His loving heart are the greatest gifts imaginable—forgiveness, hope, life everlasting, as well as all that we need to support our body and life day by day. And we should seek and expect nothing less than what He promises.

Come, Jesus, Friend of sinners, abide with me. Amen.

God Will Provide

My God will meet all your needs according to His glorious riches in Christ Jesus. *Philippians 4:19*

The idea that God will provide for all our needs is perhaps one of the hardest concepts to communicate to people. We pride ourselves in being independent and not requiring any support from anyone else. We would rather do without than be indebted to others for their help. We have become so self-sufficient that at times we even exclude God from our list of helpers.

And yet God wants to help us with our problems and needs. He wants us to call on Him and, rightly understood, put Him to the test. Not only that, but He can solve our problems and provide for all our needs. We merely need to ask. He is always eager to hear from us. As our gracious heavenly Father, He is always ready to pour out His blessings on those who come to Him acknowledging their dependence on Him.

Saint Paul, writing to the Romans, says: "He who did not spare His own Son, but gave Him up for us all—how will He not also, along with Him, graciously give us all things?" (Romans 8:32). There is no doubt that He will do this. Those who have put their trust in Him have found Him to be faithful and true in every way.

We thank You, O Lord, for graciously providing for all our needs, particularly for our salvation in Christ Jesus, our Lord. Amen.

Jesus, Our Healer

Which is easier: to say, "Your sins are forgiven," or to say, "Get up and walk"? *Matthew 9:5*

Our Lord performed a double cure on the paralyzed man: He healed his soul by forgiving his sins and He healed the sickness of his body. For Christ, the one was as easy as the other. In fact, He said He would prove His power to forgive by making the paralyzed man walk again. And He did just that.

Apart from demonstrating His divine power, it is evident that Jesus had genuine concern for the sick man. He was concerned about his real trouble: sin. As the Good Physician He remedied the cause by pronouncing forgiveness. Then in compassion He also took care of the bodily illness by doing a miracle. At other times, too, Jesus showed His total concern for total persons, helping them in their spiritual problems, in their bodily ailments, in their mental and emotional distresses.

Our Savior recognizes our problems, even better than we do. He senses what causes our troubles and how it affects us. He is concerned about us altogether. Even when we cannot understand what He says or does, we can trust that it is for our welfare. This trust is rooted in the love He showed us by redeeming us. We show our confidence in His love by coming to Him in every need and by bringing to Him others who need His healing.

Heavenly Physician, Your concern for our good prompts our praise. Help us proclaim Your love to all people. Amen.

Nothing Impossible

I am God Almighty; walk before me and be blameless.
Genesis 17:1

Our God fulfills every promise He makes. He can do this because He is almighty.

When elderly Abraham and Sarah were promised a son and heir, they found it hard to believe. To them it seemed impossible. Sarah even laughed at the possibility. But the Lord reminded them of His almighty power with the question, "Is anything too hard for the Lord?"

When Mary was told that she was to become the mother of the promised Savior, she asked the angel how this could be. Gabriel explained that the Spirit's power would bring this about. Then he told her that her cousin Elizabeth was also expecting a son in her old age, and he explained, "There is nothing God cannot do."

Jesus, God's Son, showed His almighty power by healing the sick, stilling storms, raising the dead, and doing other miracles. He showed that He is a friend who even today can act miraculously in answer to our prayers. Consequently, we keep on hoping even when our situation seems to be hopeless. Despite the most desperate circumstances, we know that with Him all things are possible. Above all, we rejoice that we are kept by the power of God in the true Christian faith to salvation.

Almighty Lord, keep us strong as we trust that You can deliver us from every trouble. Amen.

Not Now

As the heavens are higher than the earth, so are My ways higher than your ways and My thoughts than your thoughts. *Isaiah 55:9*

God often says the two little words "Not now." When we remember that, we have caught one of the deep secrets of the Christian life. He has said them to every one of us who has asked Him for something that we wanted very badly, to every soul that has carried the heat and burden of life.

God has His own timetable for us. When we think that the hour for joy has come, He may say, "Not now," and lead us into the valley of the shadow. When we feel that we should see the fulfillment of some cherished plan, He whispers, "Not now," and allows us to experience disappointment and failure.

It is the very heart of the Christian life to know that His ways are always good. They were good when He waited 4,000 years before He sent His only Son to redeem us. They were good on Good Friday and Easter and Pentecost. In His own time He does all things well.

Not now! When we know the meaning of these little words, we can know the joy and peace of the obedient and surrendered heart. We can know that darkness may be our darkness before His dawn. He loves us forever, deeply and tenderly, even when He says, "Not now."

Dear Lord, help us to remain confident of Your love for us even when You tell us, "Not now." Assure us of Your promise to bring good out of even our dark times. Amen.

When the Cloud Tarried

When the cloud remained over the tabernacle a long time, the Israelites obeyed the Lord's order and did not set out. *Numbers 9:19*

Here was a test of obedience. It was easy to break camp when the fleecy folds of the cloud were gathering from off the tabernacle and moving before God's people. Change is usually pleasant, and there is excitement in traveling, in moving on to the scenery of the next stopping place.

But the waiting, that is something else. However uninviting and oppressive this spot, however trying to flesh and blood, however irksome to impatient dispositions, however exposed to danger the Israelites were, there was no option but to remain and wait.

God often keeps us waiting. The psalmist had the same experience: "I waited patiently for the Lord." But it had its reward, for "He turned to me and heard my cry" (Psalm 40:1). What God did for His saints of old He does for those who in all ages have found Him in Jesus, the Savior from sin. All the while there is the painful waiting. We want to move on from discomforts and unpleasantness. But the cloud of the divine presence remains there. God wants us to wait and, while we wait, to remember that He is in the cloud. He is our guide on life's way.

Grant us patience, Lord, to wait as You prepare to lead us and bless us in Your own time and way. Amen.

Formula for Happiness

Delight yourself in the Lord, and He will give you the desires of your heart. *Psalm 37:4*

The Persians have this advice: If you have two coins, use one to buy bread for the body and the other to buy a hyacinth for the soul. We need more in life than eating, dressing, making money, and paying bills. Jesus said: "Man does not live on bread alone, but on every word that comes from the mouth of God" (Matthew 4:4). An animal eats and is satisfied, but we have a soul, and that needs food, too. So God comes to us with this formula for happiness: "Delight yourself in the Lord and He will give you the desires of your heart" (Psalm 37:4).

In other words: Lift your spirit into the world of spiritual values! Discover the heavenly treasures that are there for you! There is forgiveness of sins, life and salvation, joy and peace, and the promise of an eternal life in the new world. Can anything be better than that?

If we live on the side of these Christian positives, we will overcome the enslaving negatives of worry, fear, doubt, and despair. In God Himself we have the secret of serene delight, a feeling of security in His grace, peace through His love, and confidence in His promises. All that was purchased for us when Christ gave His life for us we pray.

Holy Spirit, help us to live in the joy of salvation and the lavish promises of God. In Jesus' name we pray. Amen.

The Secret of Joy and Peace

May the God of hope fill you with all joy and peace as you trust in Him. *Romans 15:13*

Many people seem to think and sometimes actually feel they have found the secret of joy and peace in faiths and philosophies other than that of New Testament Christianity. That people may receive certain uplifting influences in adhering to false religious beliefs when life treats them well is understood, but these things collapse when people are tested by the deeper sorrows of human experiences.

There can be no real joy or peace such as Paul refers to in any but a Christian heart; for until the sin problem has been solved, there can be no right relation with God; and there is no solution of the individual sin problem apart from Christ. Only in Him is there atonement for sin and reconciliation with God. Only in Him do we have access to the throne and find ourselves "accepted in the Beloved."

How happy we should be that we have such joy and peace that comes from trusting in Jesus, for it will outlive the grave, outlast the years, and outshine the sunset.

We rejoice that God in pure grace has opened our eyes to see, our minds to know, and our hearts to possess that which we never deserve to see or know or possess. And certainly, we are to be prayerfully concerned for those who as yet have not found this "joy and peace" that comes with "trust in Him."

Lord Jesus, increase our joy in believing and make us earnest in our prayers for those who do not yet know You. Amen.

261

It Might Have Been

Forgetting what is behind and straining toward what is ahead, I press on toward the goal to win the prize for which God has called me heavenward in Christ Jesus. *Philippians 3:13–14*

The things that are behind us—wasted opportunity, wasted talent, wasted time, wasted years—clearly remind us of the words of John Greenleaf Whittier: "For of all sad words of tongue or pen, The saddest are these, 'It might have been.' "

We look back to the days gone by and say: "Oh, if I hadn't done this"; or, "If only I had used the opportunities I had." Or we might say: "I might have lived life on the highest plane, yet I was content to sink into cheap and easy living." Many are settling for the second best in life when they might have had the best.

We cannot call back the years that have passed, but out in front of us, God willing, are other years, still unused, unmarked, unmarred. The important thing is what we are doing with the moment we have now. "It might have been" is gone forever; "it can be" is with us right now. We cannot make of ourselves persons of power, but there is a power in Christ to mold us into what we ought to be. Our sins? They are washed away through Christ's precious blood. The abundant life? It is ours the moment we come to faith in Christ as our Savior.

O Holy Spirit, we commit ourselves in surrender to You, to follow Your prompting and leading. Amen.

Two Days Not to Worry

Who of you by worrying can add a single hour to his life? *Matthew 6:27*

Worry is like a rocking chair: it gives you something to do, but won't get you anywhere. Sometimes, however, it's hard not to worry when we have problems with health, family, finances, or the like. And many people find themselves bearing not just one worry, but three—troubles they have had, troubles they have now, and troubles they expect to have.

There are, however, at least two days of the week about which there is no need to worry. One of those days is yesterday. It's gone, and you can't call it back. It was your day, then, with its peril, pain, and mistakes. Now it's God's day of forgiveness for yesterday's blunders. God grants such forgiveness because Jesus carried all our sins to Calvary's cross.

Another day about which there is no need to worry is tomorrow. It's beyond our mastery. Tomorrow is God's day, yet to be ours.

There is a terrible weariness in carrying the remorse of yesterday and the fear of what tomorrow might bring. But such worry doesn't have to be ours, because those are God's days. Leave them to Him. He has promised to "hurl all our iniquities into the depths of the sea" (Micah 7:19).

Father, this is the day You have made. Help me rejoice and be glad in it; for Jesus' sake I pray. Amen.

No Comparison

I consider that our present sufferings are not worth comparing with the glory that will be revealed in us.
Romans 8:18

There are times in the life of every one of us Christians when we think we cannot continue. Pain, agony, loss of a loved one, loneliness, divorce, sickness, unexpected events, and other unpleasant experiences like these discourage us.

In the midst of pain, agony, and sorrow we may readily think that God is causing us to suffer too much, that He has gone past our limit. This can never occur. God reminds us and comforts us through these words of Saint Paul: "He will not let you be tempted beyond what you can bear" (1 Corinthians 10:13).

Even though it is true that "we must go through many hardships to enter the kingdom of God" (Acts 14:22), the apostle reminds us that all our sufferings here on earth are not worth comparing to the great happiness that awaits us in heaven.

Because Jesus is our Savior, we know that God is not punishing us for our sins. He punished His Son on the cross. God now offers and gives us the power to cope with all our sufferings. Our goal is heaven. What a wonderful home awaits us! This is great encouragement for all of us. The best is yet to come!

Lord God, heavenly Father, may my life always reflect Paul's words, For me to live is Christ and to die is gain. Amen.

Who Does He Think He Is?

The Lord said to Job: "Will the one who contends with the Almighty correct Him? Let him who accuses God answer Him!" *Job 40:1–2*

Have you ever asked questions like these: Why is God doing this to me? Why did God make me like this? Why doesn't He answer my prayers? In effect we may be saying: He has no right to do this. Who does He think He is?

When we question the wisdom, goodness, or fairness of God, we put ourselves in the position of judge. How limited our knowledge is! How often we are wrong! Yet we expect God to follow our instructions and measure up to our expectations.

God doesn't answer our faultfinding questions. We couldn't understand His reasons. His thoughts are as far above ours as the heavens are above the earth, the prophet Isaiah declares.

Being sure of certain unchanging truths helps us cope with our unanswerable questions. God is wisdom. He makes no mistakes. He knows all things, even the future. God is love. Christ's cross is permanent proof of that. Whatever He wills is always best. God is all powerful. He is in control. God is just. Evil only appears to win. In all things our Lord works for good with those who love and trust Him.

Dear Lord, when we ask why, move us also to ask what. What do You want us to learn? What are we to do? O Lord, we believe. Help our unbelief. Amen.

God Keeps His Promises

Does He speak and then not act? *Numbers 23:19*

A covenant is a contract, a pledge, a promise. It should not be given or taken lightly. Society is dependent upon its trust in promises and pledges.

In the Bank of England can be seen ashes of bank notes burned in the Chicago Fire. Applying chemicals to the ashes, the bank learned the serial numbers and the value of the notes burned and paid the money to the owners.

If people go to that length to keep their pledge, how much more can God be trusted in His promises! God made many promises to His people in the Old Testament. The most precious were the prophecies concerning the Messiah. From the Garden of Eden down to the days of John the Baptizer, God's people found courage and strength in the hope of a Savior. These Messianic promises were the Gospel in the Old Testament.

God keeps His promises! He has gloriously fulfilled His pledges to send the Savior. On Calvary's cross Jesus was sacrificed for our sins. On Easter morn God raised Him from the dead as promised. Our God does what He says He will do. God's promises should strengthen our faith in God's mercy and goodness.

O God, help us to lean heavily upon Your Word of promise. We ask this in Jesus' name. Amen.

The King Is with Us

Surely I am with you always, to the very end of the age. *Matthew 28:20*

During the wars between the Spanish and the French, the Spaniards, surrounding their foes, sent an insulting note to the French commander: "Surrender! We are more numerous than you." The general fastened his reply to an arrow and shot it into the Spanish camp: "Surrender? Never! We have our king with us!"

Our three greatest enemies—the devil, the world, and our flesh—are constantly asking us to surrender, to do their will. But we refuse to do it; our King is with us!

Jesus Christ is Lord of lords and King of kings. He overcame sin, death, and the devil for us. Through His suffering, death, and resurrection He made us more than conquerors.

God promises through the prophet, "Though the mountains be shaken and the hills be removed, yet my unfailing love for you will not be shaken" (Isaiah 54:10). No matter what our circumstances in life may be, we know that our King has promised to be with us. He keeps His promises.

Surrender? Never! Because Christ has overcome our enemies for us, we can overcome them with His help in our daily life. "If God is for us, who can be against us?" (Romans 8:31).

My King, help me to trust in the power of Your presence and the presence of Your power. Amen.

Our Benefactors

Throw your net on the right side of the boat and you will find some. *John 21:6*

Certain people have helped us along life's way. Often we are unable to repay them and can only say thank you! Perhaps someone has encouraged you, stood by you during hard times, or shared their material blessings with you. Such generous friends are benefactors.

Jesus is our Benefactor in the fullest sense. He did the greatest amount of good for others by dying and rising for the salvation of the world. On this occasion after His resurrection, He directed His disciples, who had not caught a thing all night, to let down their empty nets on the right side of the boat. Miraculously, they hauled in 153 large fish. And when they came to shore, He had breakfast waiting. What a gracious host!

Though now Jesus is in glory, having conquered death and the grave, He remains concerned about the earthly problems of His followers. He knows our failures and defeats, our worries and needs. He exercises His divine power for the good of His church, promising, "Do not be afraid, little flock, for your Father has been pleased to give you the kingdom" (Luke 12:32). He purchased us with His precious blood so we may serve Him in righteousness, innocence, and blessedness. Our Benefactor will supply all our needs!

Thank You, Lord Jesus, for benefactors along life's way. Help us to pass on deeds of kindness. Amen.

A Godly Person Is a Caring Person

Carry each other's burdens, and in this way you will fulfill the law of Christ. *Galatians 6:2*

"Mind your own business" is not a biblical maxim. "Bear one another's burdens" is.

We have a caring God. He cared enough to send His Son for our redemption. He wants us to possess and to express His spirit of caring. If we want to be like Him, we must care for one another.

God has put us in community so that one may help the other into heaven. He directs: "Brothers, if someone is caught in a sin, you who are spiritual should restore him gently" (Galatians 6:1). We can almost never truthfully say, "It's none of my business." God has made it our business. It is never true that we can't do anything about a problem. We can always pray, and that may be the best that we can do.

Of his caring friends Saint Paul said, "They have refreshed my spirit." Even he needed the care of loving Christians. He wrote, "Be kind and compassionate to one another, forgiving each other, just as in Christ God forgave you" (Ephesians 4:32). God directs: "Above all, love each other deeply, because love covers over a multitude of sins" (1 Peter 4:8).

Dear Lord, let every contact with every brother or sister in Christ be a love contact. Amen.

A Friend in Deep Water

When you pass through the waters, I will be with you.
Isaiah 43:2

People are instinctively afraid of misfortune. The billions upon billions of dollars in insurance companies bear mute testimony to that fact.

You and I, however, have an assurance that is higher and wider and deeper than all the puny props that man can build to hold back the floodwaters of adversity. We know that no matter how great the misfortune or how stark the tragedy our God is there—right in the midst of calamity. Listen to His assuring words: "Fear not, for I have redeemed you … You are Mine. When you pass through the waters, I will be with you; and when you pass through the rivers, they will not sweep over you. … For I am the Lord, your God" (Isaiah 43:1–3).

A devout Christian who had just been informed of the death of his son remarked: "Whenever my tragedy becomes baffling, I lay it against Calvary." There is the real insurance against despair in the midst of misfortune. If the almighty God of heaven loved us so much that He gave His only Son into the "calamity" of Calvary, then surely He will permit no tragedy to come to us that would rob us of the full enjoyment of His Gospel promise. Disappointment and heartbreak, these may come. But not despair! We have a friend who walks beside us in deep water.

Lord, be with me in the day of adversity. Amen.

Perfect Peace

Peace I leave with you; My peace I give you.
John 14:27

Swimming in the ocean waves can be fun but also treacherous. What do people do when a rolling wave is about to break on them? Amazingly, diving under the water works best. There is more peace under the turbulent wave than on the surface.

For many people, life seems like a giant wave. Everything seems so topsy-turvy. Things don't seem to go right; there is no peace anywhere in life. And those people don't know where to turn.

Beneath the surface of our human agony, there is One who offers true and lasting peace. Jesus Christ gives us a peace that is different from the world's peace. His peace is a gift based on His love, shown clearly when He died for us on the cross to take away our sins. There He suffered the full horror of sin's crashing wave. Because our sins are forgiven, we have peace with God and with each other. We have the assurance that nothing or no one can pull us away from Him.

Even though there are big waves all around us, beneath the surface of the turmoil is God's promise that He is there to bring us through. The result is a blessed peace.

O Lord, You are a God of peace. Bring peace to me through Your Son, Jesus Christ. Amen.

God Is God

Be still, and know that I am God. *Psalm 46:10*

Ours is a noisy age. Radios blare. Telephones jangle. Brakes squeal. Planes roar. Machines grind. That may be a factor, more potent than we realize, in making ours such a tense, restless, nervous, and neurotic age.

Whatever the reason, or reasons, we are highstrung and excitable. A trifling upset becomes a major catastrophe. A minor disappointment takes all the joy out of life for weeks. A shrinking world has tightened the noose of apprehension. Worries and fears have multiplied. Life is intolerably fast. There are times when rage and frustration almost make us scream.

Through all this feverish turmoil and confusion rings the commanding voice of God: "Be still." All our fretting serves no purpose. All our anxieties merely raise blood pressure. God still is God. He rules and controls. We are His children. His pardoning love is sure. The cross is its eternal guarantee. "He who did not spare His own Son" will never fail nor forsake us. Whatever happens must be for our good. So He has promised. Though He slay us, yet will we trust Him.

Whenever we read His Word or go to His house to worship Him, He will speak to us words of cheer and peace, of hope and strength. What a privilege to be the children of a God who is God!

O Father in heaven, speak peace to my soul and pardon to my heart, and give me rest through Jesus Christ, my Redeemer. Amen.

Don't Worry!

Do not worry about your life, what you will eat; or about your body, what you will wear. *Luke 12:22*

The housefly raced madly back and forth across the screen door searching frantically for a way out. But the fly was so shortsighted it did not notice the door was open and it could easily have flown to freedom.

Sometimes we Christians act like frantic houseflies. We buzz about, busily looking for a way out, for solutions to problems. We flit about getting as much done as possible. Then, as if today's busyness were not enough, we may panic thinking about tomorrow: What happens when I grow older and cannot work? What if I get sick?

We may be too worried to be aware that the Lord has opened the door to freedom for us. "Do not worry about your life." When we remind ourselves that the Lord who loves us is also in control of all our tomorrows, we are free to live today effectively.

This does not mean that we can sit around twiddling our thumbs waiting for the Lord to provide for us. The Lord expects us to work if we want to eat. But He wants us to be joyful in our work and not let worry drain our energies. Let us work as if everything depends upon us, and let us pray as if everything depends upon God!

Dear Lord, when we are tempted to worry, help us to remember Your promise to provide for our need. Amen.

We Can't Go Wrong

We know that in all things God works for the good of those who love Him. *Romans 8:28*

Paul wrote the above words to the Romans out of a conviction based on his own experience. We, too, believe that God works in all things for our good. He works for our good in the big and beautiful things like providing us with godly parents and good childhood training, a sound education and stimulating employment, good friends and faithful neighbors. We generally expect good things to produce other good things.

When Paul says "all things," however, he includes also unpleasant things—the little irritating things like a subway train five minutes late or a nasty remark from an unkind person. He means also the larger disappointing things like loss of employment and increasing loneliness; great and crushing things like broken health and impoverishing medical expenses.

Yet all things do not work together for good for all people, but only for those who "love God." Thus the Christian first looks into his or her own heart and asks, "Do I love God?" The answer will be: "Of course, I do. Surely I have to admit that at times my love is a roaring flame and at times a tiny flicker. But I love God!" Such a Christian can be sure that all things will work together for his or her good. Even the Christian's mistakes are not necessarily his or her undoing, for God can overrule them and make them serve the greater good.

God, I love You. Let everything turn out to my good. Amen.

I Grow in Understanding

If

Lord, ... if You had been here, my brother would not have died. *John 11:21*

One day the word was brought to Jesus that Lazarus was sick. Before He arrived, Lazarus died. When Jesus finally came, the sisters chided Him: "Lord, ... if You had been here, [our] brother would not have died." *IF!* The sisters were trying to change what happened to what might have happened. In the wise providence of God it was according to His will that Lazarus died. It was also His will that he should be raised by Jesus from the dead.

We, too, are tempted to say: "If this would not have happened" or, "If I had not done this," thinking that everything would have been changed. Instead of looking only at what happened or only at what we did or left undone, we should try to see what purpose God may have had in mind.

Again, we so often torment ourselves with sins of the past: "If I hadn't done that." Whatever we may have done, as long as there is sincere repentance in our heart, we know there is cleansing in the blood of Christ. So let's not try to reconstruct our lives upon an *IF.* Rather, let us place our trust in Christ, believing that "in all things God works for the good of those who love Him" (Romans 8:28).

Lord, give us faith, that in everything we trust in Your will for our lives. Amen.

God's Word Is Power

My Word ... will not return to Me empty, but will accomplish what I desire and achieve the purpose for which I sent it. *Isaiah 55:11*

There are many fascinating forces at work in nature. The staples of our lives—food, clothing, and shelter—are the result of these forces.

The greatest power, however, is the Word of God. It created the world. When God spoke in the beginning, our world came into existence out of nothing. That Word is still active and powerful today as God speaks to us through the Scriptures. The Holy Spirit accompanies that Word and is active through that Word. As the Law this Word stirs the guilty conscience. As the Gospel it creates faith in the Lord Jesus as personal Savior. It changes the lives of people. It makes them alive to God. It glows with peace, joy, and hope in the many dark corners of life.

When God gave this Word to our world, He wanted it to produce these blessings. We may read our Bibles out of a sense of duty and be bored by the process. When we read it, however, as the Word of God to us, it becomes a power for our lives. The promises that God makes to us will accomplish that which pleases Him. God's promises are deserving of our trust.

Lord, strengthen us with the power of Your Word so that we may more firmly believe in You and do Your will. Amen.

Strive for Holiness

Make every effort to live in peace with all men and to be holy; without holiness no one will see the Lord.
Hebrews 12:14

Spiritual growth is exhilarating. How can we grow spiritually and become more holy and dedicated to God's will? We do this only by the power of God's Spirit.

Jesus teaches us to pray for the Holy Spirit. "If you then, though you are evil, know how to give good gifts to your children, how much more will your Father in heaven give the Holy Spirit to those who ask Him!" (Luke 11:13). The Spirit works through His Word. Daily we need to meditate on that Word so that God's thoughts and truths can control our thinking and govern our actions.

As we open our lives to the influence of the triune God, we grow spiritually. We pray more for others, forgive more easily, and have more peace within. We are less money-minded, less worried, and more grateful. We are less jealous, less critical, and more understanding. We are less stressed, less harried, and more cheerful. We will never be all that we ought to be, but we can make progress. Each of us can say with conviction, "By the power of Christ's Spirit working through the Gospel, I can and will be better than I now am."

Spirit of the living God, thank You for giving us faith in our crucified, risen Savior. Help us to strive for holiness. Amen.

If You Are the Son of God

If You are the Son of God, tell these stones to become bread. *Matthew 4:3*

"If You are the Son of God"—this was Satan's ultimate weapon against Jesus. There was no doubt about the nature of this weapon. It was intended to separate Jesus from His Father and to leave Him defenseless for the final kill.

We do well to take note of this assault against Jesus. For in that He was tempted, we are all tempted. In that moment our dreadful accuser seeks to bring us under divine judgment. The evil we have done, the goodness we have attempted but never achieved, the virtues we have imagined but not carried out—all these arise to condemn us. But in the very moment when all seems lost, our Lord stands in our place. He is God's man for us; He is the faithful and obedient Son in whom we are judged to be faithful and obedient children of God, for He obeys, suffers, and dies for us.

Saint Paul concludes: "There is now no condemnation for those who are in Christ Jesus" (Romans 8:1). We are no longer separated from our Father. Reconciliation and peace with God belong to us. No ifs or buts remain. There is only this good news: "We are God's children. Now if we are children, then we are heirs—heirs of God and co-heirs with Christ" (Romans 8:16–17). Tempted with Christ, we have also conquered with Him.

Thank You, Lord, for making us sons of God. Amen.

Broken Dreams

Like a dream he flies away, no more to be found.
Job 20:8

The above words were spoken by Zophar, a friend of Job, to describe the fading life of a wicked man. They have meaning also for the Christian, for the Christian is not only a saint but also a sinner. The words speak to us as the end of each day forces us to add the subtotals of our life. The question we must answer as we take stock is not so much what lies ahead but what lies behind us.

At a time like this we dwell on our weaknesses and shortcomings, our sins of omission and commission. We recall also our unrealized hopes, unfulfilled longings, frustrated ambitions, and shattered dreams. Where have we gone wrong? What has really happened to change us in ways we did not anticipate and did not want? Sometimes we can pinpoint our answers with accuracy. More often than not, the answers are vague and elusive. We are left with two impressions—very definite and very devastating: one, we have failed; two, we are under judgment for our failure.

Now is the time to listen to and believe the Word of God: "But with You there is forgiveness" (Psalm 130:4). There is forgiveness because God made His sinless Son to be sin for us "so that in Him we might become the righteousness of God" (2 Corinthians 5:21). That word gives us a new start for the week ahead. It bids us continue with Christian living—with our hopes and dreams.

Lord, have mercy upon us. Amen.

Peace with God

We have peace with God. *Romans 5:1*

A father and son are spending a night camping. The boy has pictured many possible dangers, but he feels that his father is stronger than any threat. His little heart may dread all sorts of evils. But he knows that his father is with him, and this gives him courage. In the midst of all his uneasiness he feels secure.

Before God we always remain children. The threatening dangers are greater than our strength. Take God away, and sickness becomes a never-solved why, death a fearful venture into the unknown. Our sins rob us of confidence. Our troubled conscience will not let us alone. We dread the judgment to come.

But what a difference it makes when we know that there is unmeasured strength to defend us, an impregnable refuge to which we can turn! We have all these when we have faith in Christ Jesus. He has proved the love that God has for us by going to the cross in our stead. There He proclaims peace to all who will accept it.

This peace with God is more than a tranquil feeling. It is a peace that God has established and that He has transmitted to us through our Lord Jesus Christ. This peace is our first and best treasure.

> *You only, dearest Lord,*
> *My soul's delight shall be;*
> *You are my peace, my rest.*
> *What is the world to me! Amen.*

The Joy of His Peace

Peace I leave with you; My peace I give you. ... Do not let your hearts be troubled. *John 14:27*

These words of Jesus deserve to be written indelibly and unforgettably in our hearts: "In Me you may have peace. In this world you will have trouble. But take heart! I have overcome the world" (John 16:33).

The only truly happy people in the world are those who have the peace of Christ in their hearts. They have a secret peace of which the world knows nothing.

To illustrate this truth, we may think of beautiful Yosemite Valley in California. High up between the peaks and crags, storms rage in wild fury, but in the valley below placid calm prevails. Here the flowers bloom, graceful trees cast their shadow, and songs of birds fill the air. Greater is Christ's way of peace in every believing heart. Here in God's valley we enjoy the peace beyond understanding, the breezes of hope that gently blow from the peaks of paradise.

"God hates heavy and sorrowful feeling and loves cheerful hearts. He has sent His Son to cheer up our souls in Him. The apostles, prophets, Christ Himself, exhort us, yea, command us to rejoice and be glad" (Luther).

Lord Jesus, for the spicy breezes from the heavenly shore I thank and praise You. Amen.

We Have a Lord Who Heals Us

Praise the Lord, O my soul … who forgives all your sins and heals all your diseases. *Psalm 103:2–3*

We have a Lord who is our great Healer. What a priceless blessing we enjoy if we have been granted a sound body and good health. Most often we fail to appreciate that gift until we lose it.

If we should lose it, what shall we say? Can we still enthusiastically bless the Lord? In seemingly endless pain and suffering, can we still bless Him who has promised to heal our diseases?

While our Lord walked this earth, He spent much of His ministry in healing bodily diseases. He has the same power to heal any and all of our illnesses today. But He may refrain from lifting such crosses when, in love, He has a purpose for allowing us to continue to suffer. His answer to our prayers may be a gentle and loving, "No, not yet."

But above all and without exception, He can and He will heal that which is in the greatest need—our souls. He won our forgiveness at the cost of His own blood. When He forgives our iniquities, then we are truly whole. When our souls are healed, we can bear disease and pain, disability and weakness in whatever measure He allows. For in Him we have a vision of eternity. Through the life He gives us we can see the glory of life eternal and be forever healed.

Jesus, our Lord, may Your glorious promise of life eternal fill even our pain and weakness with Your glory. Amen.

Glory through Affliction

**For our light and momentary troubles are achieving
for us an eternal glory that far outweighs them all.**
2 Corinthians 4:17

The news is always a lesson in suffering. It tells us about sickness and disease, automobile accidents, train wrecks, and plane crashes that cost human lives. There are floods, famines, earthquakes, criminal violence, and the bloodshed of war.

What do all these things mean? Are we the victims of fate, the playthings of chance? Is there a vast indifference at the heart of the universe? Some say that whatever power may direct our lives, it is completely blind or at least beyond our understanding.

The Bible gives us a far happier view of life. It says that He who is called the supreme being of the universe is a wise and good God, who has a deep, personal interest in His people. Under His gracious control even affliction has value for us.

If we are in Christ, we can find meaning in our tears, purpose in our pain, and sense in our suffering. In Christ we too can say: "Our light and momentary troubles are achieving for us an eternal glory that far outweighs them all." Christ was afflicted that we may be glorified.

*Lord Jesus, help us to understand that in all things You
work for the good of those who love You. Amen.*

Barely Alive

A bruised reed He will not break, and a smoldering wick He will not snuff out. *Matthew 12:20*

A grocer throws out the soft peaches and the wilted lettuce. An employer discharges the incompetent worker. We discard the inferior.

God isn't like that. He gives His attention to the weak, the brokenhearted, the enslaved, and the faltering ones.

Our faith may have been so buffeted by temptation that it's barely alive. We may be ashamed to face God because of the grave sins we have committed. God's grace reaches out also to those whose moral and spiritual condition seems to be hopeless.

The Gospel of God's redeeming love in Jesus is for all who are like a bruised reed or a smoking wick. God's power can undergird the faltering ones and give the floundering ones strength.

All who trust in Christ are God's children, and He reaches out His hand to them when they are almost down and out. He turns the bent reed into a flourishing plant and changes the smoking wick into a bright light. God never discards the weak as useless. No soul is worthless in His sight. Jesus died for all, including the weak and wavering. In His love and mercy He restores the weak.

Gracious Father, thank You for the assurance that You will not cast us away when we are spiritually weak and almost dead. Amen.

The Life-giving Savior

Jesus answered him, "I tell you the truth, today you will be with Me in paradise." *Luke 23:43*

We could never find a greater depth of despair and hopelessness than we find in the two criminals crucified with Jesus. With their lives ebbing away in a fiendishly cruel execution, their hearts were filled with hatred and their mouths with curses. What a prelude to eternity!

But suddenly for one of the thieves, there was hope where no one could have dreamed of hope. Suddenly, he knew that beside him was his Savior and Redeemer, his Lord and God, who was bearing even his sins. Hardly daring to hope, he turned to his Savior and asked for help. He received help, incredible help.

For Christ it made no difference that the thief's life was one of crime, one in which little if any good had ever been accomplished. Our Lord saw his repentance, and He saw his faith. And that was sufficient. The thief's dying moments had been a prelude of horror to a horror greater still. Now those moments became a prelude, agonizing still, but to an eternity of glory.

When our sins overwhelm us and seem too great to be forgiven, we too can turn to our Savior in repentance and faith and receive from Him the same promise of forgiveness and never-ending life.

Jesus, our Savior, when our last hour comes, may we not doubt but firmly believe Your life-giving promise. Amen.

God Is a Personal God

Fear not, for I have redeemed you; I have summoned you by name; you are Mine. *Isaiah 43:1*

There are comparatively few true atheists in our day. Nearly everyone believes that there is a God. But there are many practical atheists—people who live without God or as if there were no God.

God, we Christians believe, is an intensely personal God, deeply and vitally involved in everything that happens in our life. So deeply personal is God's involvement that even the very hairs of our head are all numbered.

This means that whatever might befall us today—the illness, the bereavement, the trouble, the accident, the promotion, the salary raise—is much more than merely a result of chance. God not only knows what is happening but also is concerned about it. He has a vital stake in our entire life.

You see, He has redeemed us. So intensely warm and personal is His relationship to us that He even has called us by our name. He lives in our home. He is at our side. He is with us really, personally, the very moment when we need Him most. That is why Jesus came to earth, when we were lost in sin and dead to God, to redeem us so that by faith in His atoning blood we might be saved. Today He calls us: Come and be healed.

Lord, help me respond with a thankful and grateful heart to Your love and involvement in my life. Amen.

Importance of the Individual

Jesus said to him, "Today salvation has come to this house." *Luke 19:9*

We thrill when we read of Jesus' preaching to the multitudes in Judea and ministering to the thousands gathered by the Sea of Galilee. We behold with glad hearts the crowds that thronged about Him in Capernaum.

But how refreshing it is to also read in the Gospel record that amid the multitude in Judea He was not too busy to heal one leper! Or surrounded by the hungry crowd of people who came to hear Him preach by the Sea of Galilee, Jesus found time to use one boy to bless them all. And in the crowded house in Capernaum He stopped to heal one man who was let down through the opened roof.

Although besieged and mobbed by the multitudes, Jesus never lost sight of the value of one soul. How comforting it is to read of His conversation with a single Nicodemus; of His visit with one woman at the well; of his personal interest in little Zacchaeus in a sycamore tree; of the thief to whom He said, in view of His atoning death about to take place, "Today you will be with Me in paradise"! And regarding each one of us this is spoken: "There will be more rejoicing in heaven over one sinner who repents than over ninety-nine righteous persons who do not need to repent" (Luke 15:7).

Lord, thank You for Your personal interest in us and for what You did to bless us throughout eternity to come. Amen.

In God We Trust

Trust in the Lord forever, for the Lord, the Lord, is the Rock eternal. *Isaiah 26:4*

A young girl awoke from her fitful sleep and cried out in the darkness. Her nightmare had sent shivers down her small frame. She felt alone and helpless. But as she cried out, she heard the familiar sound of her father's footsteps. She saw her bedroom door swing open and saw the face of her concerned father. He stepped to her bedside and gently brushed the hair from the young girl's face. The little girl smiled contentedly. There was nothing to fear; her father would protect her from the dangers of the night.

Our trust in God is similar to the little girl's trust in her father. When the trials of life lead us into situations that are as fearful as the nightmare of a little child, God asks us to trust in His continual protection.

God has always kept His Word. He promised to send the Savior to die for our sins and to rise again, and that promise was fulfilled. Through and in His Word we can see His loving face before us and feel the gentle touch of His hand. We are assured that God will use our trials and tribulations to our advantage. This is the everlasting truth on which our trust can rest.

Dear Lord, we thank You for always being with us and for being our everlasting strength. Amen.

The Everlasting Arms

The eternal God is your refuge, and underneath are the everlasting arms. *Deuteronomy 33:27*

When we were babies, our mothers carried us in their arms. When they wearied, as we grew heavier, our fathers carried us in their arms. In the arms of either we felt secure. Now those arms are no longer underneath us. In a sense we are now "on our own."

Do we, then, no longer need arms underneath us? Quite the contrary. In our adult life we find ourselves time and again in situations in which we realize our utter helplessness and recognize, more than we could in our childhood, the need of strong arms to support us. "Lo, I sink, I faint, I fall" is the anguished cry that tells of our fears.

What a comfort, then, to know that the eternal God is our refuge and that underneath us in the storms of life are His everlasting arms! Whatever may be the nature of our distress, even when we brought it on ourselves by our own sinful folly, He will not fail us. For this eternal God is also our Savior. He has loved us with an everlasting love. He loves us to the end. "Jesus Christ is the same yesterday and today and forever" (Hebrews 13:8). To Him let us go in every hour of need, assured that He will hear us as we pray:

Other refuge have I none;
Hangs my helpless soul on Thee.
Leave, ah, leave me not alone,
Still support and comfort me! Amen.

I Am with You

Do not fear, for I am with you; do not be dismayed, for I am your God. I will strengthen you and help you.
Isaiah 41:10

Here we have one of the many comforting "fear nots" in the Scriptures. When we say to a little child, "Don't be afraid," or to an adult, "Don't worry about it," we mean good for that person. But we often don't have the power to make the threatening thing go away. The dark room is still there. Our friend still needs the surgery.

But when our Lord says, "Do not fear," He has the power to either make the source of our fear disappear or to calm our quaking hearts so completely with His presence that our fear seems to have left us, and we are at peace.

"I am with you," says our Lord. Everywhere, every second, He knows where we are, and He is there to sustain us. He can see us through every crisis, every peril, every want.

Since He is our God, we need never be dismayed. He gives strength; He helps us; He upholds us with His righteous right hand. With His divine power Jesus Christ defeated Satan and all his cohorts. Nothing can harm His redeemed, whom He purchased with His own precious blood. His victory is our victory. His promise holds: "I am with you always, to the very end of the age" (Matthew 28:20).

Lord Jesus, I will not fear, for You are my Savior. You will help and strengthen me. Amen.

Jesus Was Puzzled

He replied, "You of little faith, why are you so afraid?"
Matthew 8:26

Experienced seamen plied the boat on the Sea of Galilee the night Jesus slept in the stern. At first they all held up bravely, but eventually they grew tired and weary. We can well imagine them looking at the sleeping Jesus and saying to themselves, "Won't He ever wake up?" At last, frantic with fear, they said, "Lord, save us! We're going to drown!"

The noise of the wind and waves didn't bother Him, but when the disciples turned to Him with a desperate prayer, He awoke and asked, "Why are you so afraid?" Before they could answer, He rebuked the wind and waves, and there was a great calm. It's a fact, isn't it, that these men, who could have given many excellent reasons for their fears a few moments before, were silent now. Their fears were positively foolish in the presence of Jesus, who acted in calm confidence.

"Why are you so afraid?" Do you understand the lesson that Jesus wants to teach with this question? How often, like the disciples, we struggle against odds in our lives, forgetting to turn to Jesus, who always stands ready to help! Remember, if God so loved us that He gave His own Son to die for us, how shall He not with Him freely give us all things!

Lord, increase our faith so that we may not be afraid in life's storms but confidently look to You. Amen.

Portrait of a Provider

Jesus then took the loaves, gave thanks, and distributed to those who were seated as much as they wanted. *John 6:11*

When some of our fellow human beings have insufficient food, we sometimes dismiss their plight quickly and say, "It is their own fault; they have been careless." We ought to remember that we, too, on occasion were so engrossed in nonessentials that we have neglected the necessary.

The multitudes that followed the Master "saw signs," and their curiosity became aroused by the miracles. They forgot the time of day and the place—uninhabited hills devoid of markets. In facing the problem of feeding the multitude, human resources could declare only the inadequacy of "eight months' wages" and "five small barley loaves and two small fish." But Christ, the provider, was not only the first to recognize the problem, but already He had the solution in mind. His gifts, then and now, are superior, unmeasured, and satisfying. The multitude "all had enough to eat" while the remaining fragments "filled twelve baskets." What providence!

Even when we are careless and inept, even when we are unconscious of our needs, even when we pursue lesser goals, Christ cares for us and graciously meets our needs. O wondrous love! That same love moved Him to lay down His life for us.

Jesus, Bread of life, You came down from heaven to provide for all our needs. Nourish our souls with Your Word. Amen.

Peace through Trust

You will keep in perfect peace him whose mind is steadfast, because he trusts in You. *Isaiah 26:3*

Trust is demanding. Trust challenges our own competence. Trust is humiliating since it recognizes our dependence on the one we trust. So what's so good about trust?

Christian trust is rewarding beyond measure. For one thing, it takes an honest look at what we really are and makes us know ourselves and our need for help. That, then, leads us to look to Him in whom we trust to supply our wants and make up for our shortcomings, whether they be our inability to stand before the throne of God's justice or our weakness to bear life's burdens and our inadequacy for our tasks. Trust says with Saint Paul: "My God will meet all your needs" (Philippians 4:19).

And from this there comes into our hearts and lives God's own perfect peace, a peace that He Himself sends us through faith in His Son, the peace that will keep our hearts and minds in a security that is known only to one who trusts in Him.

So the new life in Christ is a life of trust. That is where we must begin to live. And in the measure in which we trust Him who loved us and washed us in His blood we shall be able to live out that new life to His glory and in His service.

O Lord, we need to trust in You for all things. Grant us such trust, and through such trust give us Your own abiding peace through Jesus Christ, our Lord. Amen.

A Great Feeding

They all ate and were satisfied. *Mark 6:42*

What a miracle! In a remote place Jesus blessed five barley loaves and two fish. The crowd was fed, and 12 baskets full of scraps were gathered.

But for many this was no doubt not the greatest "feeding" of the day. Many had followed the master to a remote spot. Then Jesus fed them with His Word. Their hunger to hear was so great that nothing mattered—not time, place, or physical needs. They wanted to be nourished by the Word and have their spiritual hunger and longing filled. Jesus, the promised Savior, did just that. They saw His saving love in action. The Messiah was to feed His flock like a shepherd. They knew the joy of a promise fulfilled.

What is your need today? Jesus is there to multiply your joys and diminish your sorrows. His miracle of feeding can be great for you. He promises to still the hunger of those who long for what He has to offer: forgiveness, peace, salvation, the life in Him. He is there to fill their inner emptiness. He brings the sure hope of heaven to those who are seeking fulfillment and purpose in life.

Are you hungry? Are you seeking? Feed on Jesus, and you will find eternal satisfaction. Come to the Bread of life, and your spirit will hunger no more.

Dear Jesus, continue to feed me and help me grow in knowledge and love of You. Amen.

Life in the Midst of Death

Who shall separate us from the love of Christ? Shall trouble or hardship or persecution or famine or nakedness or danger or sword? *Romans 8:35*

Life is never far from death—a beat of the heart, a stray bullet, an accident, a blood clot. That is why over-treasuring the earth is considered foolish in biblical thinking.

This world has its place. It was made by God and is available for our needs, comfort, and leisure. It is to be used to honor the Giver, to be treasured as gifts are treasured. But it is not to be *over*-treasured. It has no enduring place with us or with God. When *over*-treasured, it easily becomes an end in itself rather than a gift from God.

God's greatest gift to us is faith in Jesus, for by it we are made heirs of life in Him—of eternal life on a level of existence that we cannot comprehend from our present vantage point. It is an inheritance once squandered by sin but now offered anew in Jesus, whose suffering, death, and resurrection open the door to a heavenly inheritance that goes far beyond anything we presently know. Keeping this inheritance in view gives us the right perspective on what we now have. Troubles in this present life are not so huge as to blot out Jesus' promises.

Be my protection, my strength, my guard, my hope,
O Lord. Amen.

Evening with Christ

Jesus came up and walked along with them.
Luke 24:15

The story of Emmaus is like the gentle sound of a distant church bell ringing for evening prayer. The walk down the road in the falling twilight, the invitation "Stay with us, for it is nearly evening; the day is almost over," and the sudden vision of the living Christ is one of the most beautiful stories in the entire sacred record.

But the greatest beauty of the story is that it is a picture of an abiding reality. It is not a bit of ancient history; it is a living story of something that is happening as long as the world stands. The believing heart is never alone. Christians never walk a lonely road. Always and forever there is beside beside them the sound of marching feet and the touch of unseen hands. When our Lord said, "Surely I am with you always," He meant exactly that. He would never leave us alone. Where we walk, He walks. Where we suffer, He suffers. Where we live, He lives.

Our time is a time of appalling loneliness. Surely, the deepest need of our hearts today is for a friend stronger and greater than humankind, whom time does not change nor death take away. And we can find Him at the foot of the cross and at the door of the open tomb.

Abide with us; with heavenly gladness
Illumine, Lord, our darkest day;
And when we weep in pain and sadness,
Be Thou our Solace, Strength, and Stay. Amen.

You Are Never Alone

Surely I am with you always, to the very end of the age. *Matthew 28:20*

What is loneliness? It is a child whose parents are about to be divorced, a youth not accepted by the group, an aging person in a society that worships youth, a mourner coming home for the funeral of a loved one. All of us are lonely at times.

Jesus suffered the ultimate loneliness. In Gethsemane His friends deserted Him. On the cross even His Father abandoned Him. He experienced total separation from His Father for our sake, so that trusting in Him, we might never be forsaken.

How can we deal with loneliness? As a first step we may pray, "Lord, use my loneliness for Your good." We may be lonely, but we are never alone. God is always with us. As we recognize His presence, we can daily draw strength from Him through prayer and meditation on His Word.

When alone, we can make good use of our time. We may read a good book, develop a skill, follow a hobby, or do some physical exercise. Rather than indulging in self-pity, we can take an interest in people. We might write or visit someone or volunteer for work in the church or community. We are only as lonely as we choose to be.

O God of mercy, help us to rejoice in Your presence and to cheer others who are lonely. We pray in Jesus' name. Amen.

God Is Omnipotent

For nothing is impossible with God. *Luke 1:37*

Nearly everyone would be willing to agree that religious faith is a good thing and that God can and does help us in the many problems of our life. But too often the impact of this truth does not reach down into the very center of our lives.

We confess readily enough that we believe that God is almighty, but in our daily living we fail to understand that the omnipotence of God is an actual reality. If we believe in God, as we say we do, and if we believe that with God nothing is impossible, then this ought to make a difference in our entire outlook on life.

For one thing it ought to make a difference so far as our fretting and worrying is concerned. There is not a single circumstance in life about which God is helpless, and it does not matter what that circumstance may be. It may be an emotional problem or a physical illness. It may be a terrific loneliness because of bereavement, or it may be financial distress or problems of insecurity or of adjustment. It may be the need of protection from sickness or accident or even death. With God nothing, absolutely nothing, is impossible. Even when humankind was lost in sin, held firmly in the clutches of Satan, God stepped in and sent His Son to make full atonement for us. His blood cleanses us from all sin.

Good Lord, more and more help us understand the power of Your omnipotence working in our lives. Amen.

On Thin Ice?

Therefore we are always confident. *2 Corinthians 5:6*

Is our confidence level always where it should be as Christians? One winter in pioneer days, a man named Jake needed to cross a frozen river. Not being sure of the thickness of the ice, he began crawling cautiously on hands and knees. He was some distance from the shore when a team of horses pulling a heavy wagon came rumbling by. The driver was singing merrily. How foolish Jake felt, creeping along fearfully when he could have been dancing his way across the solid ice!

If we think we are on thin ice as we travel through life, we will creep along as timid and worrisome souls. The message of Jesus Christ, though, is that the ice is far thicker than we think. God's love and power will always hold us up. God created the universe by His word. He redeemed us by giving the life of His Son for our salvation. His Holy Spirit lives within us to sustain us.

Fears, worries, and doubts will always plague us, but our God is stronger than all of these. His words and promises in Jesus Christ, our loving Savior, do keep us confident. We can approach each day with optimism. We are not on the thin ice of our own strength, but on the solid Rock that is Christ.

Lord God, heavenly Father, give us the confidence in Christ that makes for joyful living. Amen.

Go, Jump into the Jordan

Go, wash yourself seven times in the Jordan, and your flesh will be restored and you will be cleansed.
2 Kings 5:10

Elisha spoke the above words to the Syrian general Naaman. And they were offensive words to the general. He had traveled a great distance to Elisha, expecting the prophet to spectacularly heal him of his leprosy. But all the man of God told him to do was: "Go, jump into the Jordan." Of all the nerve! How on earth can a dip in the muddy Jordan cure a man of leprosy? The outraged general was about to return to his Syrian home in a huff when his servants persuaded him to give it a try. What did he have to lose? So off he went to the Jordan, did as the prophet commanded, and wonder of wonders, he was healed.

The lesson is abundantly clear: God works His wonders in a very unspectacular fashion, in the little things—in a little land, in a little baby, on a little hill called Calvary, in a little water (Holy Baptism), in a little bread and wine (Holy Communion). In all of this God is great and strong to save, help, and heal.

And think what He can do with just your little faith—bring you at last into His own presence. Think, too, what He can with just your little love—heal the hurts of a suffering world.

Lord God, help us to remember that it is the little things that count. Amen.

The Greatest Expression

Dear friends, let us love one another, for love comes from God. Everyone who loves has been born of God and knows God. *1 John 4:7*

The greatest expression of love is giving. Divine love led to the divine gift: "God so loved the world that He gave His one and only Son, that whoever believes in Him shall not perish but have eternal life" (John 3:16). By the Spirit's power, we grasp the depth of Christ's love for each and every one of us. It was love that prompted Christ to go to the cross to pay for our sin and the sin of the whole world.

This divine and heavenly love leads us to give to others. The greatest gift we have to share is the Gospel of Jesus Christ. And the amazing thing is that even if we give it away 10 times each day, we still have it. In fact, the more we give it away, the more we may appreciate it and cherish it for ourselves. God promises that everyone who expresses Christ's love has been born of God and knows God.

Love is giving for the world's needs,

Love is sharing as the Spirit leads,

Love is caring when the world cries,

Love is compassion with Christlike eyes.

Lord Jesus, help me to share Your love in words and actions. Amen.

Depend on God's Promises

He is faithful. *1 John 1:9*

There are many passages in the Scriptures that speak of the faithfulness of God. Yet people tend to always question whether God is dependable. We think of the people in the Old Testament. God had promised a Savior already to Adam and Eve in the Garden of Eden. Yet He took many centuries to fulfill that promise. People began to ask, "Will He keep His promise?" The problem became so great that when Jesus, the Savior, did come, they could not accept Him. But come He did! God is faithful; He keeps His word.

Jesus promised that when He would be buried, He would rise in three days. He did!

God promises that if we will confess our sins, He will forgive us. He does!

Jesus has promised that He will return to this earth to take us to the heavenly home. He will!

Have you been bearing a burden for a long time? Jesus has promised to help, and He always keeps His promise. He will help!

Through the prophet Isaiah the Lord says, "What I have said, that will I bring about; what I have planned, that will I do" (Isaiah 46:11). Whatever your situation today, be encouraged by God's promise of faithfulness.

Lord, grant to us steadfast faith in Your promises. Amen.

The Gift of a Caretaker

Cast your cares on the Lord, and He will sustain you.
Psalm 55:22

Problems! Worries! Burdens! Nobody wants them. Few escape them! Still fewer know what to do with them. In our fast-changing times, it seems, they keep piling up beyond our ability to cope with them. Problems move in from so many directions—health, job, family, etc. Then there are often the much deeper, more wrenching problems of soul and spirit, the "fightings and fears, within, without," as the hymn has it.

What's to be done? The basic answer is in the short text above, which could be matched by many others in Scripture. They say, "Stop trying to carry your burdens all by yourself; lean on the Lord Jesus." Your God—the God who made you, redeemed you, and through His Holy Spirit called you as a member of His family—offers Himself as your personal Burden-bearer.

Cast all your cares on Him! How? By taking them to Him in serious prayer, talking them over with Him, and reading His comforting promises in Scripture and believing them. His hands are strong, and He has been in the burden-bearing business for a long, long time. "Oh, what peace we often forfeit; Oh what needless pain we bear," unless we trust Jesus to bear all our sins and griefs. Then what joy is ours!

Thank You, heavenly Father, for caring about us. Help us leave our burdens with You. Amen.

The Shepherd's Love

He tends His flock like a shepherd; He gathers the lambs in His arms and carries them close to His heart; He gently leads those that have young.
Isaiah 40:11

When a frisky young lamb continuously strays from the flock and the shepherd's guiding, the shepherd may have to resort to disciplinary measures to correct bad habits. But when the lamb is ailing or lost, he drapes it over his shoulder and carries it home. The lamb becomes very attached to the shepherd and depends on him for all its needs. When the lamb recovers and the shepherd releases it, usually it no longer wanders, but follows the shepherd closely.

Because Jesus, our Good Shepherd, loves us, He may permit us to experience pain and suffering in order to keep us from straying from Him. When the sinful world injures us, He gathers us up in His arms, holds us tenderly, and teaches us our dependence on Him, so that when He puts us on our feet again, we will follow Him more closely.

We are precious indeed to our Good Shepherd. He gave His life to save us from the devouring wolf, then took up His life again. In love He cares for us, leads us in God's paths of righteousness, and guides us to heaven's eternal shelter.

Good Shepherd, thank You for loving us stubborn and frisky lambs, and leading us in tender mercy. Amen.

In Strong Arms

The eternal God is your refuge, and underneath are the everlasting arms. *Deuteronomy 33:27*

"What thought has been most comforting since the sudden death of your wife?" John replied, "When situations get intolerable, I picture Jesus, the Good Shepherd, carrying a helpless lamb. I know I am that lamb. I know Jesus will carry me." John is a responsible, capable man, but he recognized his need for help and where to get it. Eventually he was able to go on with his useful life, a stronger man for his sorrow.

God's children are not immune from the trials and troubles of the world. We are subject to many of the same griefs that plague all humankind. But we are sure that our loving heavenly Father, who through Christ rescued us from the eternal penalty of our sin, is also concerned about us as we face problems and tragedies.

We can talk over our fears and frustrations with our ever-present, always-listening Lord. His promises give comfort and courage. With the power of His Spirit within us, we can meet the challenges of life with strength and confidence.

The Lord wants us to stand on our own feet, to "stand firm." But we know that when our strength fails, He will carry us through.

Lord Jesus, we know that You will enable us to handle anything that happens to us. Though troubles surround us, with Your arms around us, we can carry on. Amen.

Life's Purpose

I have brought You glory on earth by completing the work You gave me to do. *John 17:4*

Why are we in this world? We are born, we play our part, we die. What is the purpose of this fleeting life? Why are we here? The age of the atom lends emphasis to such questions and fills us with frustration and fear.

The whole tenor of our text tells us that God did not put us on this earth by accident. No one lives unto himself. We are living for God's good, great, and gracious purpose. With Him, life in time leads beyond time. Life on earth prepares for life in heaven.

This is no life in pious idleness. Here also Christ is our example: "I have brought You glory on earth by completing the work You gave me to do." There is purpose enough for any and every follower of Jesus to be able to say in the end: I have completed the work God gave me to do, to work with and for Christ.

God's Son lived on earth in obedience to the Father's will. This will is to save the world. Before He walked to Calvary, our Lord spoke a prayer of farewell for His friends which outlined life's glorious purpose: "This is eternal life: that they may know You, the only true God, and Jesus Christ, whom You have sent" (John 17:3). For this mission Jesus lived and died, and in this awesome purpose we are fellow workers with Him.

Gracious Savior, whose will with the Father is one, we thank and praise You for the gift of life eternal. Amen.

Section II

Prayer

Time Out for Prayer

Evening, morning and noon I cry out in distress, and He hears my voice. *Psalm 55:17*

Scripture urges us to pray without ceasing. We are to have a prayerful mind throughout the day. It is our means of communicating with our Lord. Prayer provides us with an outlet for our anxieties and uncertainties as we present our needs to Him. It also is an avenue for presenting the needs of others to Him. Knowing that He promises to hear and answer our prayers encourages us to be less selfish and more sympathetic towards others.

We have time without number sinned against the holy will of God. Through Christ Jesus, however, God blots out all our transgressions and remembers them no more. That puts our mind at ease. That removes the sting of guilt. Having been restored to a right relationship with God, He invites us to bring our hearts' desires to Him in prayer and promises to hear us.

Through our prayers we recognize God's lordship over our lives. We know that God is everywhere, and therefore we know that God is with us wherever we go. Acquainted with every situation of our lives, He is our help in every trouble.

Let us then continue morning, noon, and night to go to our heavenly Father in Christ and receive new strength and continued encouragement to go on in His name.

Heavenly Father, in Christ Jesus we come to You as children of Your grace and ask You to protect us from sin as You pour out on us Your blessings. Amen.

Morning

We count our many blessings, naming them one by one. Thank You, Author of every good and perfect gift, for the morning—each new day, waiting for the record that our lives will write on it; for health, if we have it, and hope if we do not; for the little graces of life we usually take for granted; for food and friendship, respite, and people who work for our comfort and protection; for forgiveness for yesterday's failings and to cover today's mistakes; for our present estate and for life everlasting as our goal. Thank You, God, especially for Your mercy in Christ, our Savior. Amen.

Evening

Heavenly Father, we come to You for forgiveness. As we look over the past day, we can see where we have sinned. Forgive us for the sake of Jesus. Forgive us also for the sins we do not remember. Fill us with peace that comes down from above. You told us to come to You when we are weak and tired. So, Lord, we come. We seek Your rest and refuge. You have promised to hear our prayers. Now give us the faith to trust in Your promises. Grant us all that we need, both physically and spiritually, for we ask it in the name that is above every name, the name of Jesus Christ. Amen.

Ask

Ask and you will receive, and your joy will be complete. *John 16:24*

"Ask, and you will receive, and your joy will be complete." In His last sermon our Savior had much to say about prayer. To our hurrying and forgetful time His words come like a voice from another world. It is certainly true that we do not pray often enough and hard enough. We need to hear His pleading: "Ask, and you will receive."

All truly Christian prayer lives in the shadow of the cross. By His redeeming life and death our Savior has given us the great power to speak to God, confidently, as children speak to their father. Prayer allows the believing heart to draw near to God, to have Him walk with us, to speak to Him, quietly and warmly, at any and every hour, in all the conditions of life. It is one of the highest privileges we have on this side of heaven.

When we pray, we are face to face with the Creator and Ruler of the universe, who holds the stars in their courses and controls the vast distances of space. We speak to Him from all the loneliness and hate and unbelief of this present world. And across all that—the distance of space and sin— we can talk to Him. We can tell Him about the pain in our heart, the disappointment in our life, the hurt of a toothache, or the sorrow of death. There is no greater power and privilege than that. It lifts the roof from life and opens the windows toward heaven. When we pray, we draw as close as we can to our listening and waiting Savior.

Dear Jesus, help us to bring all our concerns, both large and small, to You, for You love to answer prayer. Amen.

Morning

Dear Father, when we survey our lives, we see not only success and achievement but also broken dreams, regrets, and the deeds of our evil nature. We find ourselves appalled by our weakness but also amazed by Your patience, Your protection, and Your sustaining presence. We see You as One whose hand is lifted to respond to our needs, to fulfill our prayers, to strengthen and support our faith, to heal us in body, mind, and spirit. Remember those who have great need of You, and help us all to discover rhyme and reason for our lives, to find joy and peace in serving You and others. We ask this for the sake of Jesus Christ, our Lord. Amen.

Evening

Dear Father, You are truly our only refuge and strength. Your strength is made perfect in our weakness. In times of trouble we cry to You, and we hear the reassuring answer of a voice saying: "Be still, and know that I am God." In the quiet of this evening hour, let us hear that voice again. Assure us continually that You are in the heavens and that all is well with us. Give us the strength and courage to face the future in and with You. Make us increasingly able and always willing to live our lives entirely for You. Guide us in setting our goal of unselfish service ever higher. We ask these blessings in Jesus' name. Amen.

More Than Power Unlimited

When you pray, say: "Father, hallowed be Your name."
Luke 11:2

God not only cares for us with a concern that far surpasses that of any earthly father, but more—He is a father with unlimited power. He holds all the might of heaven in His hands. With God all things are possible! We bring our needs before Him confidently. There is no problem too great for Him. He can turn evil to good ends. He can untangle the crossed lines of our lives.

We have a friend who possesses "power unlimited." Let's tell Him just what needs to be done!

But wait. Ponder these words in all their fullness before proceeding. "Father, hallowed be Your name" is more than power unlimited. He is also perfect wisdom. His thoughts are not our thoughts. His wisdom is so superior to ours that His ways are to us often a puzzle past finding out.

In the presence of His perfect wisdom, our knowledge, our notions, our solutions to life's problems are often childishly wide of the mark. It would be a disastrous day if God would let our limited knowledge direct and control His unlimited power.

Faith in our Father is more than faith in His concern and power. It is also faith in His infinite wisdom. One of the joys of faith is that we do not have to rely on our wisdom when we pray. We can rest easy in the knowledge that He knows best.

Lord, as we pray, give us the grace to desire Your wisdom as much as we desire Your power. Amen.

Prayer in Sickness

Gracious God, my heavenly Father, I come to You in my hour of need, knowing that You are ever near and ready to help me. Grant me an ever deeper trust in Your presence and in Your power to meet my personal needs, knowing that You have also promised to give me all things that will work for my present and eternal good. Give me the joy of sins forgiven. Let me see in my illness the glorious opportunities to walk closer to You, to meditate even more on Your precious promises to me, and to live even more as Your child. In Jesus' holy name I pray. Amen.

Evening

After the busyness of the day, O God, it is time to pause and to converse with You, our ever-waiting Father. We lay before You all the burdens we have accumulated today: the problems for which only You have the solution, the care of our loved ones and of all people whose needs You alone can provide, the hurts and pains and guilt that only Your forgiveness and peace can soothe. In wonder we recall Your love for us, the compassion that we never exhaust, and the promise of glory that shall be ours through Jesus Christ, our Lord. Keep us through the night hours, and grant us a peaceful and refreshing sleep. In Jesus' name we pray. Amen.

Prayer in Sickness

Evening, morning and noon I cry out in distress, and He hears my voice. *Psalm 55:17*

When sickness strikes, we have special reason to come to God in prayer. He has said, "Call upon Me in the day of trouble" (Psalm 50:15). Sickness or an ailment requiring surgery can bring on a day of distress. Then it is time to pray more fervently, as it is said of Jesus in Gethsemane when "He took up our infirmities and carried our diseases" (Matthew 8:17): "And being in anguish, He prayed more earnestly" (Luke 22:44).

In our prayers we will certainly want to thank God for all His benefits to us. The greatest of all kindnesses is the gift of salvation in Jesus Christ, our Sinbearer. In Him we have forgiveness of sins and the promise of eternal life. Then so much else prompts our thankfulness: support from family members and friends, medical care from doctors and nurses, mail and get-well cards, time to read and reflect. All this prompts us to give thanks.

As we pray the more fervently and frequently, we have this assurance: "He will hear my voice." We have the promise of our Lord's presence and nearness right here in the sickroom: "The Lord is near to all who call on Him, to all who call on Him in truth. He fulfills the desire of those who fear Him; He hears their cry and saves them" (Psalm 145:18–19).

I am trusting You, Lord Jesus;
Never let me fall.
I am trusting You forever
And for all. Amen.

Prayer in Time of Illness

Gracious Father, I know that You watch over me. You know my sickness better than I do. Give to the doctors and those who attend me knowledge and understanding that I may receive the needed treatment. You also know why I am going through this suffering. Give me the faith to accept the suffering and pain as right and good for me. I trust in Your divine power. You can make me well. My healing or continued sickness I leave to Your will for me. I do ask You to give me the faith to accept Your will and find comfort in Your direction for me. Into Your hands I commend myself as I pray in the name of Jesus. Amen.

Prayer for Those in the Healing Arts

Lord Jesus Christ, Physician of our bodies and souls, we thank You for the men and women—physicians, technologists, orderlies, nurses, and aides—who care about our health and who serve us when sickness strikes. We thank You especially for those who minister to us out of Christian faith and love, convinced that they are Your instruments and servants. Bless them in their work by day and by night, and heal us through the medications they administer. "Thou, O Christ, art all I want; More than all in Thee I find. Raise the fallen, cheer the faint, Heal the sick, and lead the blind." Amen.

Pray On!

The eyes of the Lord are on the righteous and His ears are attentive to their prayer. *1 Peter 3:12*

In an age as skeptical as ours quite a few people question the relevance of prayer. In a time so full of pressing needs—worldwide hunger, ongoing wars, the threat of overpopulation, pollution, energy shortages, and the like—prayer can seem rather innocuous. To some it appears harmless, but hardly meaningful.

Perhaps we as Christians do not feel quite so negative about prayer. But it appears that on many occasions even Christians will spend a great deal more time worrying about things than they will praying about things. It might be necessary for us to take a moment to rediscover prayer.

Our text tells us quite plainly that God's ears are open to our prayers. We need not pray in a stiff, formal fashion, for prayer is conversation with God. He will hear prayers that are spoken in the name of Christ, and He will answer them. Sometimes He has to say no. Even earthly fathers have to weigh and consider the requests of their children. But when God says no, He gives us something better than what we prayed for. That's why we pray: "Your will be done," for God always hears and answers our prayers in a way that is best for us.

What a privilege prayer is! Therefore let's bring all our requests, both small and large to our Lord in prayer, for as the hymn writer reminds us, "His grace and power are such None can ever ask too much."

Lord Jesus, teach us to pray without ceasing. Amen.

Morning

Dear Lord, we praise You for giving us the assurance of eternal life, which is ours forever because of Jesus' sacrifice. Everything we are and have in this life is a gift from Your hand. We thank and praise You for Your generosity. Often we take our blessings for granted or look with envy at others. Forgive us for times when we complain and grumble. Open the eyes of our faith so that we may recognize that You are in control of this world and of all that life may bring. Then we will have no anxious thoughts, no worry about what may or may not happen today or all our tomorrows. In the name of Jesus Christ we pray. Amen.

Evening

For granting us another opportunity to hear Your Word, to sing Your praise, and to enjoy the company of fellow believers we give You thanks, O Lord. Strengthen our desire to serve You and not our worldly possessions, to trust in You and not in ourselves. Remove from our hearts all anxious thoughts and useless worry. Increase our faith in You and our confidence in Your fatherly care, so that our sleep will not be disturbed by fretful questions about what we shall eat, drink, and wear. We place ourselves completely in Your care, assured that we shall awake in the morning to walk another day with You. Keep us in Your grace for Jesus' sake. Amen.

The Answer Is en Route

Before they call I will answer; while they are still speaking I will hear. *Isaiah 65:24*

A widow, her young son, and her invalid daughter moved to a poor part of London. They had formerly lived in comfort, but because of the death of her husband, they had to move.

The day came when their resources were exhausted and their meager income would no longer stretch. That evening, while mother and son knelt beside the bed of the invalid daughter, they committed their need to God. The next morning the mailman delivered a letter. In the envelope was the equivalent of a week's wages. It had come from New Zealand. The benefactor had heard of the husband's death and had been moved to help the woman and her children. The letter went first to the village where they had lived, then finally reached London. Five months after leaving New Zealand, it arrived in London the morning after the family prayer.

Although God is fully aware of our need, He still delights to hear our voice. His answer often predates our call, and help is on the way before our prayer ascends. God supplies all our needs, including forgiveness in Christ, our Savior.

Dear Savior, help us never act as though prayer were unnecessary, but remind us that it is effective because You have promised to hear us. Amen.

Evening

Almighty Father, our constant Helper and Provider, hear us for Your tender mercy's sake. Help us at all times to draw near to You in praise, thanks, and petition. Teach us to seek Your face at all times, in times of triumph as well as in times of trouble. We trust that in Your own way and in Your own appointed time You will fill all our necessities and needs. Teach us perseverance in prayer, and patience in awaiting its fulfillment. Make us daily aware not only of our own but also of our neighbor's needs. We come to You in firm trust and confidence as we seek these blessings. We ask it in the name of Jesus, our Intercessor. Amen.

Prayer for the Unemployed

Lord God, our heavenly Father, we come to You in behalf of those who because of handicaps are unemployable, as well as those who because of economic conditions have no work or only part-time employment. Take them into Your divine care and keeping. Assure them of Your love and favor. Let them not lose hope. To all who cannot work give a sense of fulfillment in serving with the leisure time at their disposal. Do not let them and their families suffer want or deprivation. In due time grant them again gainful employment, and make us Your instruments to this end. Hear us for the sake of Jesus, our Lord. Amen.

Big Prayers

Open wide your mouth and I will fill it. *Psalm 81:10*

There's a story of a little fish in the Mississippi River who was afraid to take a drink lest he use up all the water and suffocate.

Sometimes we pray like that—afraid we may be asking God for too much. God's power is limitless; His resources are inexhaustible; His promises are all-embracing. Jesus said that if we believe we will receive whatever we ask for in prayer.

This "whatever" is as all-embracing as the "whoever" in John 3:16: "God so loved the world that he gave his one and only Son, that whoever believes in him shall not perish but have eternal life." In a hymn John Newton encourages us: "You are coming to your King, Large petitions with you bring."

We can come to the throne of grace with our smallest trifles and our biggest problems. This is Jesus' promise: "If you remain in Me and My words remain in you, ask whatever you wish, and it will be given you" (John 15:7).

Nothing is too hard for the Lord. He can grant all our prayers, the big ones as well as the little ones. He who gave us His son as the greatest gift is able to do immeasurably more than all that we ask or imagine.

Lord God, give us the confidence to bring also our big troubles to You in Jesus' name. Amen.

Prayer for the Sick

Grant to those who are sick, O Lord, the healing that comes from You. Bring wholeness to those who suffer from any kind of sickness and disease. Be with them when the burdens of life seem overpowering, and grant them grace to trust in You in the times of their adversity. Keep them from giving up hope in their sickness. Remind them that You care for them. Help them cast all their cares on You, for you will deliver them. Because You came to bear their grief and carry their sorrows, assure them of Your forgiveness. Lord Jesus, if it is Your will, restore them to health. Amen.

Prayer for the Sick

Hear our prayer, O God in heaven, as we beg You to show mercy and compassion to our dear one who is ill. We come to You for healing and help because You are the Great Physician of our souls and bodies. Grant strength in place of pain, faith in place of doubt, trust in place of fear. If it is Your will, O Lord, grant our loved one a prompt return to regular life and service. Above all, give to each of us a tenacious and resilient faith in Your forgiving love, made possible by the bitter suffering, death, and resurrection of Jesus Christ, Your Son and our only Savior. Amen.

The Spirit Is with Us When Prayers Come Hard

In the same way, the Spirit helps us in our weakness. We do not know what we ought to pray for, but the Spirit Himself intercedes for us with groans that words cannot express. *Romans 8:26*

The flame of faith does not always burn with the same intensity. The great London preacher, Charles Spurgeon, preached for over 30 years to an average of five thousand people every Sunday morning and five thousand people every Sunday evening. Yet this man of God frequently had to fight great moods of depression.

God does not abandon His children when the soul is disquieted and cast down. When the question arises, "Where is your God?" the believer can answer, "His Spirit is with me, even now interceding for me with 'groans that words cannot express.'"

The work of the Holy Spirit is not limited to bringing about a state of repentance. When He comes creating faith in Jesus as Savior, He stays to intercede. This does not mean that He substitutes prayers on behalf of those who refuse to pray or pray indifferently. But one of the most glorious aspects of His presence as the promised Comforter is that He is with us speaking unutterable words as we pray to the Father.

All thanks to God that our ability to express the depths of our conflicts as well as the breadth of our love is always refined and enlarged by the Spirit within us.

We thank You, heavenly Father, that in our prayers we always come before You with Your Spirit at our side. Amen.

Morning

Holy Spirit, this is Your day. I know that all that I am as a child of God I owe to You. You caused faith to bloom and grow in my heart. You have given me strength to continue in that faith. And when I have failed to live according to God's will for me, You have brought me the assurance of the forgiveness that Jesus earned for me.

Now I pray that You will fill me with an even greater measure of faith, strong enough to triumph over every storm of life. Open me to receive every gift and every grace You desire to give me. Empower me to live out this life of faith to which You have called me. In Jesus' name I pray. Amen.

Evening

Lord God, we bring our joys and our sorrows to You. Even though we know that we ought to rejoice in Your mercy, sometimes we find ourselves depressed. So, Lord, we bring our sadness to You and ask that You fill us with joy. We bring our doubts and ask that You give us faith. We bring our weaknesses and ask that You give us strength. We bring our questions and ask that You give us answers. We bring ourselves and ask that You remake us. Fill us with Your Holy Spirit that we may be sure of Your presence, Your power, and Your willingness to help. We ask this for Your love's sake. Amen.

Claiming His Good Gifts

Ask and it will be given to you; seek and you will find; knock and the door will be opened to you.
Matthew 7:7

God has great gifts for us. The best gift He has already given: His Son, who by His sacrifice on the cross earned our forgiveness and opened heaven for us. Then there are the gifts of food, clothing, and all that goes with living.

However, we may lack some of the things we need and would like to have. Why is that? Could it be that we don't have some good things simply because we don't ask for them? Saint James tells us: "You do not have, because you do not ask God" (James 4:2).

God has promised to hear our earnest prayers. The Bible makes this plain. The woman of Canaan asked the Lord to heal her daughter, and she was healed. Lepers who sought the Lord's help were cleansed. The disciples called on Jesus in the storm, and "He got up and rebuked the winds and the waves, and it was completely calm" (Matthew 8:26). The thief on the cross asked Christ to remember him when He came into His kingdom. His prayer was heard. Jesus took him into paradise that very day.

These and many more examples from the Bible are in accord with Jesus' promise: "Ask and it will be given to you; seek and you will find; knock and the door will be opened to you" (Matthew 7:7).

Dear Lord, we know You hear all our prayers. Teach us to seek from You the good things You want us to have. In Jesus' name we pray. Amen.

Prayer for the Sick

Lord Jesus Christ, we know You have pity on the sick. We remember that while You walked the roads of Palestine You cured the deaf, the blind, the lame, and the lepers. Help us to believe You are present now in a very real way. Lord Jesus, look in mercy on [mention persons by name]. Reach out Your gracious hand and grant a healing. Increase the wisdom and skill of doctors and nurses who minister to the sick as Your instruments. Use us to demonstrate Your love in cheering, visiting, and caring for the sick. Above all, we ask for spiritual healing for the sick and for us through Your Word. Amen.

Prayer for God's Healing Power

Almighty God, Giver of life and health, look in mercy on all who are sick and who suffer in body and mind. Remember those who must undergo surgery. Be with the handicapped and the infirm, with the aged and those at the point of death. Bless, O God, the ministrations of everyone who gives them care. Let Your healing power restore them to health, or ease in their ills. Let Your lovingkindness be their solace and comfort. Give them strength that they may endure their affliction with patience and courage. If it be Your will, make them well, that they may serve You with thankfulness. Amen.

Prayer Gives Strength

Pray continually; give thanks in all circumstances, for this is God's will for you in Christ Jesus.
1 Thessalonians 5:17–18

It is good to begin and end each day with prayer, thanking God for His love, guidance, and provision for all our needs. It is in keeping with God's will that we talk to Him also during the day for then we feel His power sustaining us. "Pray constantly," writes Saint Paul.

When we make prayer a thoughtful habit, we have the assurance of God's presence with us. He will enable us to carry on in the face of trial, to have adequate strength to lay aside our burdens and fears. God wants us to trust Him completely that He will help us meet the challenging circumstances and make them steppingstones to greater blessings in life.

As we become constant in prayer, we feel a continual flow of spiritual vitality and inspiration, for God supplies us with strength. In answer to our requests He will show us the right way to proceed. Regardless of appearances to the contrary, God answers prayer. In His love and wisdom He provides everything needful for today and the future. Having given us His Son as our Savior, He will grant also lesser gifts.

Heavenly Father, hear our prayer as we come to You with our needs. We pray in the name of Jesus, Your Son. Amen.

Morning

Our heavenly Father, we thank You for the rest of this past night. We feel renewed and refreshed and are ready to face the challenges and opportunities of this new day. As we begin this day, fill us with love and zeal for our work. Help us to carry out our vocation with compassion and commitment. We pray for others. Heal those who are bruised and broken in body, mind, or spirit. Fill those who are empty and lonely with the assurance of Your abiding presence. Make us willing and able to minister to the needs of people here and elsewhere, bearing witness by word and deed to the redeeming love of Jesus Christ, our Lord. Amen.

Evening

At the close of another day, O God, we come before You, thankful for Your many blessings. Insofar as it has been a peaceful day, we are truly thankful, knowing that peace is a rare treasure. Insofar as this day has been a day full of challenges, grant us the strength of mind and spirit to manage all well. Where blessings have abounded, move us to respond as capable stewards. Where difficulties have cast a shadow, help us handle them well so that even they may work together for the good of Your kingdom and to the glory of Your holy name. Hear us for Jesus' sake. Amen.

Letting God Know Our Requests

In everything, by prayer and petition, with thanksgiving, present your requests to God. *Philippians 4:6*

The heavenly storehouse is full of God's gifts and blessings. This overwhelming abundance would be ours if we would but storm the gates of heaven with our prayers.

All of us have our needs and wants. Our problems often seem like insurmountable obstacles on life's road; they are hindrances to our happiness. We may not be able to do anything about them, but God is almighty. He can move mountains. And He would do so if we but make our requests known to Him in prayer.

Solomon prayed for wisdom, and he received it. Hannah prayed for a child and became the mother of a great man of God, Samuel. Saint Paul's request for relief from his thorn in the flesh was denied, but instead he received strength to bear his burden. That was something even better for him than what he had desired. That is how God answers prayer. He is "able to do immeasurably more than all we ask or imagine" (Ephesians 3:20). He has given us His Son to be our Savior. "Will He not also, along with Him, graciously give us all things?" (Romans 8:32). Indeed He will. In answer to prayer He will open the storehouse of His bounty.

Heavenly Father, what a privilege it is that we can carry everything to You in prayer! Hear us for Jesus' sake. Amen.

Morning

Gracious Lord, our Father in heaven, let this be our comfort, that You are fully aware of what it is that threatens to shatter our hearts. Let this be our encouragement, that You are competent to handle any emergency and to resolve every problem. Let this be our assurance, that though we may walk in danger this day, we do not walk alone but are constantly in Your company. Let this be our prayer, that this day we again commit ourselves, body and soul, into Your loving hands. Guard and guide us as we assume our work. We ask this in the name of Jesus Christ, our Lord and Savior. Amen.

Evening

At the close of this day we thank You, Father, that we can take all of our cares to You and leave them there. We know that with You all things are possible. Give us faith always to hold Your hand and to trust You. Grant us Your Spirit in such measure that nothing will ever get us down. Help us to let go of every anxiety, knowing that in You there is always hope and help, for in Christ You have promised to give us all good things. Make us grateful for life, health, and all our being and give us grace to recognize You as the Source of all life. Lead us to commit to You the faithfulness You have a right to expect. In Jesus's name we pray. Amen.

When Trouble Comes

Be self-controlled and alert. Your enemy the devil prowls around like a roaring lion, looking for someone to devour. *1 Peter 5:8*

One thing we all have in common is trouble. Every person is a bundle of trouble. Put a few of those bundles together and trouble grows.

Our troubles usually send us into emotional wheelspinning on the worry road. This never helps. It offends God and hurts us, but it never solves the problem.

God's way is best. Instead of giving way to fear, worry, and anxiety, we are to assert an action of faith. The first step is to get God into our problem. Here is the way: Quietly, confidently, ask God to help you bear the trouble and live with it until you have learned the intended lesson and He Himself takes it away. Thus prayer becomes the place where burdens change shoulders.

We confidently go to God because we know His love for us in Christ Jesus. We know that He will help us in our troubles, through our troubles, out of our troubles. In this way they become steppingstones instead of stumbling blocks. Instead of getting us down, our troubles lift us up, for whatever drives us to God in trust and surrender always brings victory.

Holy Spirit, help us convert every care that comes to us into a prayer that goes to God. Let the troubles of life lift us up to Jesus, our Lord. Amen.

Evening

Our gracious God and Lord, it has been a day of challenges, many and varied. It has had its share of frustrations and disappointments, as well as its sorrows and joy. You have permitted our faith and our confidence to be tested so that we might be led to seek Your help and guidance, and through them to be strengthened for new efforts tomorrow. Help us at this hour to lift up hearts so that we may be able to see the discipline of Your love and the sustaining peace of Your forgiveness. So may we rest in the assurance that we are ever in Your loving care because of Jesus Christ, in whom we find our peace and joy. Amen.

Evening

O God, we bring our hearts to You as they are, and ask You to make them as they ought to be. Create, therefore, a clean heart in us, and renew within us a right spirit. Detach our minds and our thoughts from earthly things, and raise them to the love of Your heavenly riches. May we love You above all things and in loving You love our fellow human beings. Grant us release from the cares of the day and the terrors of the night. Lighten our burdens and our troubles by taking them upon Yourself. Light our lamps of faith and hope in the darkness of this world. Keep us from harm and preserve us unto Your heavenly kingdom. Give us a quiet mind that hears You speaking to us in the silence of this evening hour. In Jesus' name we pray. Amen.

Praying in Chains

**I thank my God every time I remember you. In all my
prayers for all of you, l always pray with joy.**
Philippians 1:3–4

Elsie was quite a woman. By age 92, she was worn
down. Now confined to a bed, she may as well have been in
chains. She felt like a prisoner, unable to do anything
worthwhile. Until now her life had been full of activity and
service, especially for her church. Her world now revolved
around the bed from which she could not move.

But Elsie could pray! Waiting for the Lord to call her
home, she continually offered up prayers for anyone and
anything that came to mind. Not only did her prayers benefit an untold number of people, but she, too, was blessed.
In those prayers, the loneliness of her confinement was
replaced with an intimate fellowship with Jesus, the friend
who had borne all her sins and griefs.

Saint Paul found out this secret long ago. When he was
in chains, he spent much of his time praying. He experienced the same blessing Elsie and countless others have.

The same is true for us. When we find ourselves confined, pray! Even in chains that imprison, there is freedom
and intimacy with Jesus. Have you discovered and enjoyed
His presence?

*Dear Jesus, my Savior, thank You for the fellowship I find
with You in my moments of prayer. Amen.*

When Confined

The walls of confinement press heavily upon me, O Christ. You who appeared to Your disciples behind closed doors come also to me and set my heart and mind free. When I am discouraged because I cannot work or move about, remind me that all things, also my disabilities, work together for my good, for I love You. When loneliness overtakes me, comfort me with Your presence. Help me to pray often for all who need Your mercy. Show me how I can serve You with the gifts, talents, and powers of mind I have. Keep me faithful, whatever my lot in life, until I shall see You, my Lord and Redeemer, face to face. Amen.

When Confined

Lord, it is frustrating and lonely to be unable to move about freely. I wish I could visit relatives and friends more often. I do thank You for those who visit me, especially those who bring Christian comfort through their words and deeds. I cling to Your promise that nothing can separate me from Your love in Christ Jesus, and that You are with me always. Open my eyes to the wonderful opportunities I have to pray, meditate on Your Word, and bless others through my witness to my Savior. Keep strong my trust in You as my God and King, the One who grants me life and salvation for Jesus' sake. Amen.

Prayers of Thanksgiving

Give thanks to the Lord, for He is good. His love endures forever. *Psalm 136:1*

Psalm 136 calls believers to give thanks for many reasons, the main one being that God's gracious love—His forgiveness and mercy in Jesus Christ—endures forever. Similarly, Saint Paul admonishes us to "give thanks in all circumstances, for this is God's will for you in Christ Jesus" (1 Thessalonians 5:18).

How can we give thanks when we are sick, lose our job or a loved one, or find ourselves in other sad circumstances? The answer is that God still loves us. In bad times God draws us to Himself in a special show of love and reveals Himself as a mighty and merciful helper. He is there when we sorely need Him, and our problems often make us appreciate His love more.

An uplifting experience for us Christians is to begin our daily prayers with thanksgiving—with thanks to God for His Word, for our Savior and the Spirit-created faith in Him, for our church, our family and friends, our health, hope, money, home, automobile, and other blessings. Not all Christians will have the same list of blessings, but all will have a long list. Praying with thankful hearts comes from the conviction that God is good and that His love for us in Christ endures forever.

Dear Father in heaven, make us thankful for all our countless blessings. In Jesus' name we pray. Amen.

Morning

We seek, dear Lord, to come before you to offer You our total praise. You are the author of the daily blessings we enjoy. You are the source of the moments when we are at peace, the times when we see through the dark glass of our humanity to glimpse the promise and the majesty of our eternal destiny. You save us and protect us daily from threats of which we have no knowledge and from menace about which we are not even conscious. For all Your graces to our souls and bodies, those of our families and friends, we give You thanks. In Jesus' name we pray. Amen.

Evening

As this day draws to its close, we thank You, Lord, for the blessings it has brought us: a home to dwell in, family and friends to cherish, work to fulfill our calling, air to breathe, nutritious and delicious foods to eat, healthy exercise, and simple pleasures. And more than these, You laid down Your life that we might enjoy eternal life with You. Instead of a sense of winding down, Lord, lift us up to thank and praise, to serve and obey You our whole life through until we come to praise You with angels and archangels and all the company of heaven to the glory of Your holy name. Amen.

Ask, Seek, Knock

Ask and it will be given you; seek and you shall find; knock and the door will be opened to you.
Matthew 7:7

God has given to us the privilege of prayer. Because of Jesus' death on the cross, our sins are forgiven and our relationship with the Father is restored. We can talk with Him about our problems, praising Him for His mercy and abundant blessings.

Have we prayed often for a relative who doesn't know Christ, for healing, or for a new job? Whatever the prayer, we can be confident that God hears us. Our Savior desires that we talk with Him about all our concerns—to ask, seek, and knock. He wants us to be persistent. He speaks in a parable about a man who, during the night, went to a neighbor and got what he wanted—bread for a visitor—because he kept asking.

Praying diligently is hard. Satan likes to put obstacles in our way. Our sinful human nature causes us to forget to pray. We try to work out problems on our own. But God's Word reminds us that God is the One we must rely on. God has told us that without Him we can do nothing.

Let's continue praying! What a privilege to take all our cares to the God who has promised to answer!

Heavenly Father, we thank You for the privilege and power of prayer in Jesus' name. Amen.

Evening

At Your invitation, dear Father in heaven, we gather this evening to seek, to knock, and to ask in the name of Jesus Christ, Your beloved Son. We pray not only for ourselves but for all who call You Father, for the welfare of Your suffering church, and for the cause into which You have enlisted us. We pray for all in authority. Grant them wisdom to govern righteously. We pray for those distressed by illness and for those who care for them. Fill with Your Spirit the weak and the joyless. And bring into Your family of believers all who are still without hope and without Christ. Amen.

Prayer by One Who Is Ill

Merciful Father, I come to You, acknowledging my sin and unworthiness. Still I trust Your promise for Jesus' sake to hear my prayer and to give me whatever needful blessings I ask in His name. I implore You to lay your healing hand on me. Add Your blessing to the ministrations of doctors and nurses and to the medicine that I am receiving during this time of my illness. If it be Your will, renew and restore my health and strength. I commend myself into Your gracious care and keeping. I ask that through the presence and power of Your Holy Spirit You would keep me strong in faith. Grant this for Jesus' sake. Amen.

He Hears the Feeble Cry

Before they call I will answer; while they are still speaking I will hear. The wolf and the lamb will feed together, and the lion will eat straw like the ox.
Isaiah 65:24–25

There is a distinct tonal quality in each voice. Friends call on the phone, and after only a word or two we recognize the speaker on the other end of the line. As blind Isaac identified Jacob, the younger of his twin sons, by his voice, so we know the familiar sound of a family member speaking with us.

Our recognition of voices, however, is very limited, especially when compared with the staggering ability of God. His ears detect the feeblest cry. The multitude of voices that rise up to Him never overtax the switchboard of either His omniscience or His grace.

It is not the pleasing tone of voice or the persuasive petition that causes God to listen. He hears the repentant sigh of the sinner, the sobs of the hurt spirit, the whisper of the soul in need, and the groan of the one in pain.

God hears even before the words are formed in the larynx and on the lips. He understands when the first impulse of faith in Jesus Christ, prompted by the Spirit, comes into being. And when His children gratefully respond to His goodness, the echo of their praise delights His heart.

My faith is so shallow! Teach me, Lord, to pray. Amen.

Prayer in Sickness

Gracious Lord, I need You at all times but especially in time of sickness and pain. I need Your forgiveness, for I am stained with guilt. I need Your strength, for I am weak and weary. I need Your comfort, for I am worried and upset. I need Your healing. Without Your blessing, all other help is in vain. Be near me now, merciful Lord, with all the blessings Your grace alone can provide. Then I know that all will be well with me, and this sickness will be to Your glory and my greatest good. Keep me patient, cheerful, and hopeful. I await Your answer confidently, for I know it will come from Him who loves me, my Savior and my God. Amen.

Prayer by One Who Is Sick

I'm depressed, dear Lord, and I'm tired of being sick. When I think of all the things I could and should be doing, I get discouraged. Lord Jesus, You understand what suffering and pain are like. Thank You for enduring misery and agony to free me from the burden of my sins. Thank You for loving me. Thank You for providing people to help me. Renew their strength. Lord, keep me from complaining so much that I turn others away. Help me to show those around me that I'm confident in Your love. Only You can heal me, Lord. If it is Your will, make me well. I believe, Lord. Increase my faith. Amen.

Let Go! Let God!

When I am weak, then I am strong.
2 Corinthians 12:10

The kitten cried pitifully as it clung to a branch high in the tree. The climb up had seemed so simple; the way back down, impossible. Standing on a ladder, the man grabbed the cat with gloved hands. He brought it, yowling and clawing frantically, down to safety.

Sometimes we face situations that look impossible. Even though we do the best we can, sometimes our best isn't good enough. Problems get bigger. Troubles get worse.

With feeble faith we cry, "God, can You do anything to right what's wrong?" We may fail to recognize His answer. We may not like His solution. We protest, "Not Your will, O Lord, but mine!"

Our great God is a loving rescuer. Once He sent His Son to deliver us from our greatest dilemma, the eternal consequences of sin. Jesus suffered and died in our place. We have to trust in Jesus to be saved.

We can entrust Jesus with our other problems, too. We turn our cares over to Him. Prayer changes things. It changes us. We gain faith, wisdom, courage, power, and peace.

God is listening. He answers. He has not promised that we'll have no headaches or heartaches. He does promise to be with us. We know somehow that in all things He is working for our good.

Thank You, Lord, for loving us so much. Amen.

Prayer by the Sick

Look with mercy and compassion upon me, O Lord, for I am ill. I believe that You can lay Your hand upon me and I shall live. Have pity upon me for Jesus' sake, and forgive my many sins and transgressions. Renew my strength and restore me to health again, if it is Your will. Make me to know that all things must work together for good to them that love You. I pray You, bless the means that are being employed for my recovery. Be at my side, and assure me that You are mine—and I am Yours—in time and in eternity. Help me to keep the eyes of faith on Calvary's cross, looking up to Jesus Christ, the Lamb of God, who gave His life for me. Amen.

Prayer amid Trials

Lord, we are weak, but You are strong. Give us Your strength to endure the problems of life. Help those who are suffering through illness, from the loss of a loved one, or from emotional problems. Especially we pray for any who are involved in alcoholism, depression, or drug abuse. Keep them and us strong through faith as we continue to look to You, our Rock. Turn our hearts toward You, for You hear our cries for help. Your love sustains us. You lift us and offer us the comfort of Your Word, giving us the power of Your Holy Spirit within us to give us strength. In Jesus' name we pray. Amen.

Beauty While You Sleep

In vain you rise early and stay up late, toiling for food to eat—for He grants sleep to those He loves.
Psalm 127:2

A marvelous truth is hid in this sentence. The psalmist is really saying: "He gives to His beloved in sleep." God gives many things to His beloved in sleep: angels to guard their beds, vitality for waiting tasks, fields growing in the silent darkness into tomorrow's bread.

But the highest gift that God gives to His beloved in sleep is the beauty of Jesus. There is something remarkable about the last thought we think before we fall asleep. All through the night that thought continues to work in our subconscious mind. It permeates our inner self. It becomes a part of us.

And what is the last thought of a child of God? It is a thought of prayer, of Jesus who hears prayer. Then we enjoy sleep—transforming sleep. Through the still hours of the night the Holy Spirit uses that last thought to keep us close to the Lord Jesus. "Those who have the gales of the Spirit," says Brother Lawrence, "are carried forward even in sleep." Did we fall asleep last night with a prayer and with a thought of Jesus?

When the soft dews of kindly sleep My wearied eyelids gently steep, Be my last thought how, safe from harm, I rest within my Savior's arm. Amen.

Evening

It is not night, O Lord, if You are near. Though the shadows have lengthened and the night has fallen, remind us, O Lord, that it is only dark where we are. You are our eternal sunshine and light. You do not grow weary and need to sleep. You do not repose in order to be renewed. You are eternal in strength and can therefore always protect, strengthen, and watch over us. You are the God of renewal, energy, and might. We rest content then, O Lord, for Your watchful eye is on us and on all whom we love. We trust that You will strengthen us for the day ahead, that we may glorify You; through Your Son, Jesus. Amen.

Evening

Gracious Savior, Your boundless love has brought us to the end of another week. Forgive us wherever we have strayed from Your path. Bless our household this night and all our loved ones, near and far. Be with them and with us as a mighty shield and fortress. Cause Your angels to encamp round about us while we wake or sleep and ward off whatever might harm us. Speak peace to our souls, O Lord, and let us spend this night in quiet, restful slumber. And when the morning breaks, let us arise refreshed and in good health, ready once more to worship You in the fellowship of Your church. In Your name we pray. Amen.

Praying for Others

Brothers, pray for us. *1 Thessalonians 5:25*

We find Saint Paul continually praying for the Christians entrusted to his care. He names them before God and fervently asks the Father to fill their needs. But Saint Paul does not stop here. He realizes that he is his brother's keeper. He sees himself as the servant of God's grace. For Paul this means that he is an agent God uses to help and keep Paul's neighbors. So a part of Paul's prayer for others is a prayer for himself. He prays, and he asks the prayers of all Christians—"Brothers, pray for us"—that God would give him the strength to be the answer to his neighbor's prayer.

There are times and conditions when we fervently ask God to come to our loved one on wings of healing. We beg Him to give them the courage they need for the difficult hours of their lives. We plead with Him to give them strength to choose the right.

This is good, but let us pray for ourselves at the same time. We are our brother's keeper. Perhaps the courage our friend needs for his dark hours can best be given by God through us, if only we would pray God to make us strong to help. Perhaps the guidance, the understanding, and the help our friend needs can best be given by God through us.

Some of our best prayers for others are those fervent prayers we say for ourselves.

Lord, teach us the value of helping others by praying for ourselves. Amen.

Morning

Refreshed by Your Word, Lord God, we begin this day by praising Your name. Whatever our tasks, wherever they may lead, let us meditate on Your wonderful works. Let us be aware of people, working with us and around us. Let us be strong for those who lack strength, be comforters for those who sorrow, and be helpers for those who need assistance. Let our joy in Jesus be a light in that section of Your vineyard where we live. We move into this day confident that You hear and answer our prayers; through Jesus Christ, our Lord. Amen.

Evening

Gracious Lord Jesus, another day in our lives has ended. We bring before You all our problems, pains, and broken relationships that need mending. Help us, heal us, forgive our sins, and make us instruments of Your peace. Open our hearts to live for others, not worldly things. Help us be generous, mindful of the many people who are homeless, suffering, without families, and institutionalized. Bless all caregivers, endowing them with skills and compassion so that Your brothers and sisters may be comforted in their needs. Enable us to also support them. Refresh us this night so that we may serve You faithfully in the days ahead. Amen.

Be Thankful

Speak to one another with psalms, hymns and spiritual songs. Sing and make music in your heart to the Lord, always giving thanks to God the Father for everything, in the name of our Lord Jesus Christ.
Ephesians 5:19–20

God gives us what we need to be joyous people. He gives us reason to move around with a song in our heart.

There's so much for which to be thankful. Let's rejoice that when we wake up in the morning, we are able to get out of bed and have something to get up for, such as a meaningful day with family or job or friends.

But even if we are sick or distressed or alone, we have the daily assurance that God loves us so much that He gave His Son to redeem us. God brings us to saving faith in Jesus and keeps us in it. God gives us strength equal to our days and their challenges, and He promises to let nothing separate us from His love in Christ. What a life!

How shall we express our thankfulness? By reflecting God's generous goodness. By saying thank you to people around us and by saying thank You to God. We show our thanks in what we think and say and do. We join with fellow believers in worship as we praise the Lord.

Heavenly Father, help us to realize our blessings, to feel Your loving presence and care, and to give thanks for them all. Amen.

Morning

Lord Jesus Christ, grant that all through this day my heart may be filled with the joy of salvation. On the ground of what You did for me on the cross give me the peace beyond all understanding and the golden hope beyond all describing. Let Your love set my spirit ablaze with praise and thanksgiving. Let faith, love, and hope so fill my heart that there will be no room left for gloom, doubt, fear, and discouragement. Lord, it is my earnest hope that all things I say and do today will glorify You. In the light and power of Your presence let me preach the living sermon of contentment under Your care. Amen.

Evening

Praise be to You, our Father in heaven, for Your lovingkindness to us this day in Christ Jesus. Help us each day in this year to remember that through Jesus You have adopted us as Your children and made us heirs of Your glory. Some of our days, dear Father, bring struggles for us. But trusting in Your promise of deliverance, we ask You to keep our hearts and mouths singing songs of joy and peace despite the troubles and storms of life. In Your Son, Jesus Christ, we have a heavenly peace that passes all understanding. In His name we pray. Amen.

Portrait of Fearful Disciples

He replied, "You of little faith, why are you so afraid?"
Matthew 8:26

The above question of our Savior is still a valid one for us today. Our fears have many sources: nature's devastations, the economy, the job market, health, social pressures, foreign enemies, neighborhood violence, personal guilt, and many more. Our Lord's power to still any of our restless seas has not diminished.

The storm threatening the disciples was real. They were veteran fishermen experienced on this sea. Yet they were so frightened that they said, "We're going to drown." They didn't seem to remember what it means to have Christ with them.

It wasn't the storm that awakened the sleeping Savior; it was the prayer of His frightened disciples. His response was immediate and was directed at the real problem: anxiety. He first stilled their hearts, then addressed Himself to the storm. The storms of life unsettle us because our hearts are not firmly anchored in Him.

Wherever Christ is, there life's storms become a great calm. In His presence and by His almighty power tempests turn to peace, winds of sorrow become gentle breezes of comfort, seas of doubts become quiet harbors of faith.

Lord of the storms, quiet our restless hearts and anchor them firmly in You, our Rock, our Rest. Amen.

Morning

Lord Jesus Christ, go with me through this day. Be present now in these first hours of the day as I consider what I must accomplish. Time, O Lord Jesus, is a sacred trust from You. It is one gift You have given equally to us all. Help me to use my 24 hours in such a way that You are glorified. Grant others to see my faith in You through my work, my attitude, and my conversation, Lord. You bring to my day the power that stills storms, the care that heals illness, and the love that dies for another. With You beside me I approach this day with great confidence and hope. In Your name I pray. Amen.

Prayer for the Sick

O Christ our Lord, whose word stilled the stormy sea, during times of distress, pain, and anxiety quiet our troubled thoughts. Be near us so that in the calmness of Your presence we may hear You say: "Peace, be still!" Impart wisdom, strength, and grace to all doctors, nurses, and technicians so that they may be the channels of Your healing and restoring power. Grant us grace to place ourselves in Your hands, for You are our true Physician. Draw us closer to You and lift us to the higher life. Hasten the day, when with renewed health, we may return to Your house to praise You, and to Your world to serve You. Amen.

Ringing of the Bell

At that time men began to call on the name of the Lord. *Genesis 4:26*

A minister was present in the hospital while the surgeon performed a difficult operation on a parishioner. He saw the doctor bowing his head before entering the operating room. After the operation, the minister asked whether he always prayed before an operation. The physician said, "A surgeon cannot do miracles alone. While I am operating, I feel God is so near to me that I never know where my skill leaves off and His begins."

Prayer is mentioned in the Bible thousands of times. It is never too late to pray. King Hezekiah was ill and even was told by God's prophet Isaiah that he would not recover. Yet he did not give up hope, but cast himself on God's mercy and prayed fervently. What happened? God changed His mind, promising to heal Hezekiah, give him 15 more years of vigorous life, and rescue him from the attacking Assyrians. What a dramatic illustration of the power of prayer to stir the compassion of our gracious God!

We are moved to pray to Christ because He is near and dear to us. Look backward—see Christ dying for you; look upward—see Him pleading for you at the Father's right hand; look inward—see Him living in you; look forward—see Him coming for you.

I believe, Lord God, that You answer prayer. Amen.

Prayer in Sickness

Heavenly Father, look upon me in Your mercy and grant me Your help. In my illness give me a patient and cheerful spirit. Draw my heart heavenward to think upon Your love and the treasures that are eternal. Grant me the peace of salvation purchased for me with the blood of Jesus. When this illness has served Your good purpose, restore me to new health. If it be Your will to lengthen my days, let me spend them in grateful service to You. Bless those who minister to me, and keep my loved ones in Your gracious care. Extend Your healing hand to others who are ill. In Jesus' name I commit myself into Your loving hand. Amen.

Prayer after Surgery

Merciful Father, You have fulfilled Your promise to be with me in the hour of fear and pain. When I was weak and helpless, You gave me strength. I called on You in my distress, and You delivered me. You blessed the surgeon's skill and safely brought me through the operation. All my sins and weaknesses You forgave for Jesus' sake. Gracious God, continue to shower Your favors on me, and if it is Your will, grant me full and speedy recovery. Give me patience in the days ahead and let all my thoughts dwell on Your goodness. I cast all my cares on You. Hear my prayer for the sake of Jesus Christ, my Lord and Savior. Amen.

Where Did Everyone Go?

Jesus asked, "Were not all ten cleansed? Where are the other nine?" *Luke 17:17*

Ten men, afflicted with leprosy, pleaded with the Lord Jesus for healing. God's mercy heard their cry and gave them physical wholeness. Nine went their way so taken with what had happened that they completely forgot to praise the One from whom all blessings flow. One came back, bursting with thankfulness. It was then that Jesus asked the questions.

Thankfulness is a human problem. Once we receive what we earnestly seek, our inclination is to rush to life's corner, there to frolic with our gift, excluding everyone and everything else. If what we desperately sought looks common—like sleep, food health, protection—there is hardly an awareness of blessing, let alone words of thanks.

"Every good and perfect gift is from above," writes Saint James (James 1:17). God pours down His bounty to satisfy our every need. He does this not because we deserve it or because we seek His goodness. He responds because we need it. His special gift, desperately needed, is forgiveness. He offers it to us from the fullness of His love, not our worth. "While we were still sinners, Christ died for us" (Romans 5:8).

For all this goodness we can only echo the psalmist, "Oh, give thanks to the Lord."

You have given us everything else, Lord. Dare we ask for one thing more, a thankful heart? In Christ's name we do. Amen.

Thanksgiving for Healing

Almighty God, who heals our diseases and gives us new life, we return to give thanks to You for the answer to our prayers. You have restored us and given hope once again. Help us to take this gift as a sign of Your constant care. When we are discouraged, remind us of the times when You acted in our behalf. Especially help us to see that the life of Your Son given for us on the cross is the healing that gives all life meaning. Lead us now to live healed lives through Jesus Christ, our Lord. For this and all that we have received in His name, we give thanks and praise. Amen.

Thanksgiving for Recovery

Lord, You always do all things well! You are the One who forgives all our iniquities and heals all our diseases, crowning our lives with lovingkindness and tender mercies. Thank You for relieving me of my illness and permitting me to experience the power of Your restoring love. And now I gladly accept with gratitude the word You once gave to a healed man: "Go ... and tell them how much the Lord has done for you, and how He has had mercy on you." You have indeed done great things for me! "O Lord, open my lips, and my mouth will declare Your praise." In Jesus' name I pray. Amen.

Our Confidence

This is the confidence we have in approaching God: that if we ask anything according to His will, He hears us. *1 John 5:14*

People who have confidence in themselves are not afraid to speak up. Sometimes confident people pose a threat to those who are unsure of what to say or do in response to a challenge. The latter may wonder where confidence comes from.

For the Christian, confidence comes from the assurance of God's Word. There are more than 8,000 promises in the Bible. There is only one thing God cannot do and that is fail to keep a promise He has made.

When He promises rest to all who come to Him, they receive rest. When He assures His people of His abiding presence, they know that He is very near at all times.

Of God's many promises in Holy Scripture, the one from which we can gain special confidence is this: If we ask anything according to His will He will hear us. No request goes unheard. No God-pleasing prayer goes unanswered.

Jesus brings our requests before His Father in heaven and intercedes for us. This is our confidence: "If we know that He hears us—whatever we ask—we know that we have what we asked of Him" (1 John 5:15).

Thank You for hearing our prayers, Lord, and for giving us the promises that give us confidence. Amen.

Morning

Heavenly Father, we praise You for the gift of life, and for the joys and opportunities that each day brings. Help us to live this day in such a way that we can exclaim with the psalmist, "This is the day the Lord has made; let us rejoice and be glad in it." Forgive us, Lord, when we live out our days in near despair, as though life were something to be endured rather than enjoyed. Comfort us with the promise that this day, as in all our days, we will experience the truth that all things work together for good to them that love You. With Jesus beside us, we know that we will be blessed. Amen.

Morning

How grateful we are to You, O God, for bringing us to the beginning of another day. You have sent Your holy angels to protect us from all harm and danger. You have granted us another day to live for You and to serve our fellow human being. We live each day confidently, knowing that we belong to You, our heavenly Father. You have promised to be with us, and we know You keep Your promises. Help us to cast all our anxiety on You, for You care for us. You have proven this to us through the forgiveness of our sins and the peace we have received through the death and resurrection of Your Son, Jesus Christ, our Savior and Lord. Amen.

Topical Index

Author Acknowledgment

A

Julius W. Acker

Daniel P. Aho

Theo. E. Allwardt

Bernhard H. Arkebauer

B

Herbert F. Beck

Norbert V. Becker

Victor L. Behnken

David S. Belasic

Carl W. Berner

Eugene R. Bertermann

Bruce W. Biesenthal

Charles R. Birner

Frederick G. Boden Jr.

Paul A. Boecler

Diane Boehm

Clarence H. Born

Eldon L. Brandt

Victor L. Brandt

Harold H. Brauer

Luther C. Brunette

C

Stephen J. Carter

Lois Mae Cukel

D

J. H. Deckman

Paul W. Devantier

Albert Doerffler

Richard T. DuBrau

Henry C. Duwe

E

Lewis E. Eickhoff

William H. Eifert

Richard C. Eyer

Stratford Eynon

F

Henry E. Fuelberg

G

Albert W. Galen

Ernest L. Gerike

A. Leroy Gerner

Delmar J. Glock

Herman W. Gockel

Daniel F. Goerss

Richard J. Gotsch

William Griebel

Jeanette L. Groth

H

Victor F. Halboth Jr.

Paul M. Heerboth

Bernard H. Hemmeter

John E. Herrmann

Frederick C. Hinz

Richard T. Hinz

Raymond C. Hohenstein

David W. Hoover

Lynn C. Hoy

Harry N. Huxhold

J

Richard A. Jesse

K

Dennis A. Kastens

Alma Kern

Herbert M. Kern

Barry J. Keurulainen

Elmer C. Kieninger

Oscar J. Klinkermann

George Koenig

William A. Kramer

Justus P. Kretzmann

O. P. Kretzmann

Arnold G. Kuntz

L

William A. Lauterbach

Herbert F. Lindemann

Louis P. Lochner

Henry C. Lubben

Elmer O. Luessenkop

Karl E. Lutze

M

Ray F. Martens

Elmer E. Maschoff

Edward C. May

Richard A. Mazak

Stephen G. Mazak Jr.

Richard E. Meinzen

August T. Mennicke

Arnold A. Messler

Kay Meyer

Charles S. Mueller

Elmer E. Mueller

Louise Mueller

N

Gary Nagy

Albert L. Neibacker

Rudolph F. Norden

O

Norbert C. Oesch

Armin C. Oldsen

P

Daniel E. Poellot

Arnim H. Polster

Carlos H. Puig

R

Dennis G. Rasper

Remus C. Rein

Oswald G. Riess

Gerhardt E. Ritz

Rudolph A. Ritz

Jack H. Ruff

S

Clemonce Sabourin

Theodore Schabacker

John Scharlemann

Herman C. Scherer

Henry R. Schiever

Vernon R. Schreiber

Kenneth Schueler

Dolores Schumann

William J. Shepman

Lois Sikorski

Andrew Simcak Jr.

Ronald C. Starenko

C. Leo Symmank

T

Melvin J. Tassler

V

Jaroslav J. Vajda

Leroy E. Vogel

W

Alvin E. Wagner

William Wagner

Martin Walker

Martin Walter

Herbert G. Walther

Edgar Walz

Alton F. Wedel

T. A. Weinhold

Ruth E. Willie

H. F. Wind

Z

Marcus T. Zill